The Eclipse of Keynesianism

The Eclipse of Keynesianism

The Political Economy of the Chicago Counter-Revolution

Robert Leeson
Associate Professor
Murdoch University
Murdoch
Australia

palgrave

First published 2000 by
PALGRAVE
Houndmills, Basingstoke, Hampshire RG21 6XS and
175 Fifth Avenue, New York, N. Y. 10010
Companies and representatives throughout the world

PALGRAVE is the new global academic imprint of St. Martin's Press LLC Scholarly and Reference Division and Palgrave Publishers Ltd (formerly Macmillan Press Ltd).

Outside North America
ISBN 0–333–73045–3

In North America
ISBN 0–312–23575–5

This book is printed on paper suitable for recycling and made from fully managed and sustained forest sources.

A catalogue record for this book is available from the British Library.

Library of Congress Cataloging-in-Publication Data
Leeson, Robert.
The eclipse of Keynesianism : the political economy of the Chicago counter-revolution / Robert Leeson.
p. cm.
Includes bibliographical references and index.
ISBN 0–312–23575–5
1. Chicago school of economics. 2. Keynesian economics. I. Title.
HB98.3 .L435 2000
330.15'6—dc21
00–031118

10 9 8 7 6 5 4 3 2 1
09 08 07 06 05 04 03 02 01 00

Printed and bound in Great Britain by
Antony Rowe Ltd, Chippenham, Wiltshire

Contents

Preface

The chapters of this book have been greatly improved by comments from economists associated with the University of Chicago, especially Milton Friedman, Deirdre McCloskey, Harry Block, Sherwin Rosen and Lester Telser. Harry Johnson and Don Patinkin also provided posthumous inspiration through their writings on Chicago. Many others provided assistance at various stages: Orley Ashenfelter, A. J. Brown, Steven Dowrick, Peter Howitt, Stephen Resnick, Robert Solow, Bradley Bateman, Robert Eisner, Hugo Keuzenkamp, Chris Archibald, Heinz Arndt, Richard Lipsey and Herb Thompson; plus participants at seminars at the Reserve Bank of Australia, the University of Western Ontario, Curtin University, the University of Christchurch, Lincoln University, the University of Waikato, Murdoch University, the University of Western Australia, the London School of Economics, Simon Fraser University, the 1995 conference of the Economic Society of Australia and the 1997 conference of the History of Economic Thought Society of Australia. I am grateful to Max Steuer for allowing me access to the M^2T seminar records. The usual disclaimers apply. Thanks to Anne Rafique for editorial assistance.

Chapter 3 has not been published previously. Shortened versions of Chapters 2, 5 and 6 have appeared before: Chapter 2 in *History of Political Economy*, Chapters 4 and 6 in *History of Economics Review*, and Chapter 5 in the *Cambridge Journal of Economics*.

1 Introduction

1.1 Economists and world history

This book examines the intellectual revolution that separates the last quarter of the twentieth century from the preceding four decades. It attempts to dissect and explain both the content and the reasons for the success of that revolution in a manner that should be accessible to all students of economics but also to that ubiquitous of all literary characters, the non-specialist, who is curious about how the economic, social and political world operates.

I will focus on two University of Chicago economists, Milton Friedman and George Stigler. Chicago is a remarkable city which grew from 30 000 inhabitants in 1850 to the world's sixth largest urban centre a mere forty years later. It symbolized the global ability of capitalism to generate markets from nowhere – to the dismay of Left revolutionaries who expected collapse and social revolution. These two Chicago economists were closely linked to the revival of the ideology of free-market libertarianism that shaped the last quarter of the twentieth century.

The 1970s was a period of crisis for capitalism and for the forces of the political Right. The price rises associated with the Organization of Petroleum Exporting Countries (OPEC) seemed to challenge the hegemony of the West; the instability of capitalist inflation contrasted markedly with the stability of prices in the communist world. In the United Kingdom, the 1973 National Union of Mineworker's strike led to the collapse of the Conservative government and its replacement by a government more sympathetic to trade union interests. In the United States, the Watergate scandal (1972–4) destroyed the Presidency of that old Cold Warrior, Richard M. Nixon. In 1975, the Americans scuttled from Vietnam, abandoning their South Vietnamese allies to their fate.

Elsewhere the same forces appeared to be present. In South America, Chile elected a Marxist President. Later, some Chicago economists played a controversial role in advising those who overthrew this democratically elected government in a military coup (Valdes, 1995; Friedman and Friedman 1998, ch. 24). In Africa in the mid-1970s, the collapse of the remnants of the Portuguese empire seemed to place further pressure on the remaining white regimes in Rhodesia and South Africa. The 1976 Soweto uprisings brought the South African apartheid regime face to face with both its past and its future.

With respect to intellectual forces, the Left Keynesian President-elect of the American Economic Association (AEA) declared that 'The early months of 1970 were just possibly decisive in the modern history of economics' (Galbraith, 1971: 73). John Kenneth Galbraith (1973: 11, 3, 1, 4) devoted his AEA Presidential Address to the call for 'the emancipation of economic belief... from the neoclassical belief in the market... I would judge as well as hope that the present attack [on neoclassical economics] will prove decisive.' President Nixon's 1971 New Economic Policy appeared to be a reversal of the domestic free-market policies that Chicago economists had placed so much faith in. Galbraith concluded that 'Mr. Nixon came to office with a firm commitment to neoclassical orthodoxy' but when facing re-election had found this faith to be 'a luxury he could no longer afford. He apostatized to wage and price control.'

Galbraith (who had once employed Nixon in the wartime Office of Price Administration) had acquired an aversion to an exclusively academic audience as a result of the professional response (or lack of it) to his *Theory of Price Control* (1952). Galbraith told the *New York Times* that it was the best book he had ever written: 'I made up my mind that I would never again place myself at the mercy of the technical economists who had the enormous power to ignore what I had written.' Henceforth they would '*have* [emphasis in original] to confront what I had written... by having the larger public say to them: "Where do you stand on Galbraith's idea of price control?"' (cited by Navasky, 1967: 3). Henceforth, Galbraith (1981: 174–5) decided, he would submit himself 'to a wider audience'.

Friedman and Stigler also courted both an academic and a wider audience. The 1980s were the Thatcher–Reagan years and the ongoing inability of governments to restrain wage inflation through various forms of incomes policies discredited Galbraithian-style theories of price control. Prices ceased to be a problem for governments to control in their pursuit of full employment. Instead they began to play the role allocated to them in Stigler's *The Theory of Price* (1946) and Friedman's *Price Theory* (1962). As communism collapsed and trade union power was undermined, the market was successfully portrayed as the superior social organizer. Policy-makers embraced the rhetoric of 'rolling back the frontiers of the state' and governments were portrayed as 'the problem not the solution'.

With respect to macroeconomic policy, Keynes led to Friedman via Phillips. The Keynesian revolution of the 1930s initially met with some resistance, but from the 1940s until the mid-1970s, most economists broadly accepted the Keynesian Neoclassical Synthesis as a framework for policy thinking. Rising inflation and unemployment discredited this framework and from the mid-1970s this consensus broke down. Joan Robinson (1962: 90–1), Galbraith's fellow Left Keynesian, felt confident about the irreversibility of certain desirable objectives:

> The objection to low unemployment has turned out to be relatively weak (at least in Great Britain); certainly any return to heavy unemployment would be violently resisted. Taking it by and large, Full Employment has become an orthodox objective of policy... a right wing slogan.

In the mid-1960s, the Right Keynesian Robert Solow (1965: 146) referred to Chicago as a mere centre of opposition. Yet shortly afterwards, the Right Keynesian Paul Samuelson (1972: 25) noted that 'the growing minority... [of] the Friedman camp... has established beachheads outside Cook County.' Within a very short time, Friedman's concept of the 'natural' rate of unemployment swept through the economics profession and the reduction of inflation took precedence over the maintenance of low levels of unemployment. The targeting of employment (or interest rates) was abandoned, replaced by faith in the ability of monetary targets to stabilize the economy. Keynesians were left to bemoan the fact that the 'insurgents' had 'sacked the Keynesian temple... as macroeconomics turned introspective and nihilistic' (Blinder, 1986: 209, 216).

Monetary targeting turned out to be an unsuccessful policy tool. It was replaced in the mid-1980s by inflation-targeting in the United States, the United Kingdom, Canada, New Zealand, Australia and elsewhere. Ironically, the inflationary turmoil of the 1960s and the disinflationary turmoil of the 1980s impacted more on the welfare state and the mixture of the mixed economy than it did on the relationship between aggregate demand and inflation in low or zero inflation regimes. After an inflationary interlude, the original low-inflation Phillips curve is alive and well and at the heart of contemporary policy choices.

These essays connect this episode of world history to the *internal* dynamics of the economics profession. A minority of economists seek to influence the direction of research and policy formulation; only a handful are truly successful. All economists are aware of Keynes's (1936a: 383) dictum about the power of ideas: 'Madmen in authority, who hear voices in the air, are distilling their frenzy from some academic scribbler of a few years back.' Friedman and Stigler sought and achieved an influence which only Keynes had previously achieved. Chicago's 'Mr Macro' (Friedman) and 'Mr Micro' (Stigler) became the most influential academic scribblers of their generation.

1.2 Macroeconometric and microeconometric races: the superiority of Chicago perceptions about the sociology of economic knowledge

Like Paul Samuelson (1998: 1378), Friedman and Stigler 'lived, breathed and slept economics' (Friedman and Friedman, 1998: 149). They were both extremely interested in the culture of the economics profession and in its dysfunctional aspects. Friedman often wondered why academic life 'converts so many promising intellectuals into second-rate, pedantic, unenterprising faculty' (Friedman and Friedman, 1998: 93). He 'infuriated' and horrified his opponents (Wallich, 1966: 25). He also sought agreement, sometimes in unconventional ways. Academic disputes are rarely resolved by a show of hands, but that is precisely what Friedman (1965: 91–3) proposed during a conference discussion about financial deregulation.

Friedman (1965: 12–13, 23) proposed a 'market' explanation for the 'extremely bad press' which the free market had tended to get. There was a noticeable contrast between 'the facts' relating to 'the performance of a free market society, and the attitudes of opinion makers, the intelligentsia and to a lesser extent the man in the street'. Since economists are trained to examine the workings of markets, it seems sensible to begin this examination by focusing on the competition for influence as a market exchange. Prior to the mid-1970s there was one dominant producer of economic knowledge: the Keynesian Neoclassical Synthesis whose headquarters were in Cambridge, Massachusetts (Harvard University and the Massachusetts Institute of Technology). In addition, there were also several minor producers. One group of these smaller producers (whose headquarters were at the University of Chicago) overcame the disadvantage of having only a limited market share and became a major supplier of economic knowledge. These essays attempt to explain how this change in the composition of the market occurred.

The dominant postwar suppliers of economic knowledge were confronted by a competitor who had adapted his product to suit the prevailing tastes (which had been fashioned by the Keynesian Neoclassical Synthesis). Prior to becoming a successful market competitor, Friedman was a brilliant irritant who had *opposed* the widespread and all-embracing use of formalist tools (that is, the Walrasian approach and macroeconometrics). But Friedman constructed his natural rate model using Walrasian language and monetarist policy propositions were supported by large volumes of macroeconometric evidence.

In the late 1950s, two econometric 'races' were proposed. The first was proposed by Friedman and was enthusiastically embraced by his Keynesian technocratic adversaries. This race purported to 'test' the Keynesian model against its monetarist rival. The second 'race' was proposed by Edward Chamberlin and Christopher Archibald, both profound critics of 'The Chicago School of Anti-Monopolistic Competition'. They proposed to 'test' the perfect competition model against its rival: Chamberlin's general microeconomic theory of monopolistic competition. Members of the Chicago School had faith in both perfect competition and in the quantity theory of money. But Friedman also understood that econometric disputation could only end inconclusively. When the Keynesian–monetarist 'race' ended inconclusively (as Friedman had predicted it would) this undermined the hegemony of the Keynesian model. The perfect-monopolistic competition 'race' never took place because Chicago economists refused to participate, and faith in perfect competition (or the belief that the perfectly competitive model provided a reasonable approximation to reality) prospered.

One general perception is that monetarists and Keynesians shared a common faith in the ability of econometrics to discriminate between alternative perspectives. This widely held view is based on a misunderstanding of Friedman's views of econometrics. Friedman expressed many reservations and doubts about econometrics. Econometric disputation was a technique that he adopted after failing to fully engage his Keynesian opponents in theoretical controversy.

Chapter 2 examines Friedman's use of econometrics in the context of a critique of econometrics that he shared with Keynes. This chapter also disputes the often-made assertion that Keynes was outdated by swimming against the econometric 'tide' that had been proposed in the 1930s by Jan Tinbergen. Keynes and Friedman were equally perceptive about the dubious nature of mechanical econometrics and equally doubtful that such practices could resolve economic disagreements. Later, contrary to common perceptions, Tinbergen came to accept much of Keynes's Critique and Keynes did not revise his objections to econometrics.

The high-inflation Phillips curve trade-off played an important role in undermining the credibility of Keynesian macroeconometrics. It is commonly believed that the weakness of the original Phillips curve lay in its neglect of (a) inflationary expectations (Friedman, 1966a, 1968a) and (b) rational expectations and the Lucas Critique (Lucas, 1976). The supposed neglect of inflationary expectations allowed the monetarist revolution to prosper; the neglect of the Lucas Critique created an intellectual space for New Classical economists. Chapter 2 also argues that Phillips was an insightful early critic of Phillips curve econometrics. In 1952 he provided Friedman with the adaptive inflationary expectations formula which was used to augment the original Phillips curve. Thus Keynes lead to Friedman via Phillips with a twist! In the 1960s, Phillips (prior to Lucas) also developed a critique of econometrics equally as potent as the critique named after Lucas (Court, 1999; Peter Phillips, 1999).

Friedman's methodology of positive economics focused attention on the *output* side of economic knowledge, suggesting that assumptions (the *input* side) were largely irrelevant. In contrast, Keynes at a macroeconomic level, and Joan Robinson and Edward Chamberlin at a microeconomic level, drew attention to the importance of assumptions and of reconstructing economics with supposedly more realistic assumptions. The macroeconometric disputation between Keynesians and monetarists was in a sense a logical extension of Friedman's methodology. But Friedman and Stigler refused the invitation to investigate the relative merits of perfect and monopolistic competition. This refusal is perfectly consistent with Stigler's model of the sociology of economic knowledge.

Chapter 3 describes Stigler's 'model' of the sociology of knowledge: the overwhelming hegemony of theory in economics; the crucial importance of internal developments as the primary force behind scientific change; his distinction between the elites and the masses in any discipline and the ability of the former to set the professional agenda; the usefulness of the technique of the huckster in popularizing economic ideas; and the unpredictable and therefore – to those in an hegemonic position – dangerous characteristics of the fox hunts of controversy. The sixth characteristic of Stigler's 'model' is a description of how to relegate to obscurity notions that might otherwise achieve prominence or even dominance. Stigler's model is used to explain why it was optimal for Chicago (as macroeconomic paradigmatic challenger) to initiate a statistical race over the comparative merits of the Keynesian and monetarist models, while declining to engage in a similar statistical race which would expose the dominant microeconomic model of perfect competition to competition from its paradigmatic challenger (monopolistic competition).

1.3 The natural rate of unemployment

The prevailing consensus about the natural-rate counter-revolution can be summarized as follows. Friedman, it is widely believed, used his famous methodology of positive economics to make a famous prediction: increasing inflation would be followed by increasing unemployment. In Friedman's framework, the macroeconomy could be characterized (in Phillips curve space) by the $ model (with inflation on the vertical axis and unemployment on the horizontal axis). The vertical spike of the $ model represented the natural rate of unemployment. If policy-makers attempted to keep unemployment below (to the left of) the natural rate of unemployment, inflation would increase as unemployment returned to 'natural' levels. The gravitational pull of the 'natural' rate of unemployment on the actual rate would ensure that any reduction in unemployment purchased by inflation would be purely temporary.

Likewise, if anti-inflation policies were required, policy-makers had only to temporarily push unemployment above (to the right of) the natural rate and this would control inflation. The gravitational pull of the 'natural' rate was symmetrical; any increase in unemployment above this unobservable natural level would be purely temporary, while the associated reduction in inflation would be permanent.

In the academic year 1964–5, Paul Samuelson considered but rejected the natural rate proposition (Akerlof, 1982: 337). Other Keynesians shared this judgement. After Friedman's AEA Presidential Address, James Tobin (1968: 50) noted that the natural rate proposition was 'an implication of simple rationality, absence of money illusion'. Solow (1968: 56) considered (and dismissed) what he called the idea of 'rational' expectations: 'It really doesn't matter from the practical point of view whether or not price expectations are ultimately rational. If the period of catch-up is very long, we still have the whole intervening period during which some sort of trade-off dilemma exists.' Harry Johnson (1969: ix) also dismissed the 'assumption of rational adjustment of expectations to experience...the empirical evidence is that lags in adjustment of expectations are sufficiently long for contemporary policy makers safely to disregard them.'

But Tobin (1968: 52), the Director of the Cowles Foundation, was also conscious of the intellectual appeal of econometric estimation (and the fickleness of some of the results from these exercises): 'I had intended to offer this morning the prediction that sooner or later an econometric study will surely enough produce the magic number one for the price coefficient of wage change. Mr Cagan says he's already got it, so he beat me to that.' It was this appeal to the 'tribe of econometricians' which Johnson (1975 [1971]: 96, 101) identified in his Richard T. Ely AEA Lecture as one of the reasons for the success of Friedman's counter-revolution.

Friedman dominated the methodology of economics prior to the monetarist counter-revolution. His methodology of positive economics instructs economists to judge the validity of economic theories not by the realism of their assumptions but by the accuracy of their predictions. According to Albert Rees (1970: 236–7, n.), Friedman 'many years ago' believed that a gentle inflation would reduce unemployment by allowing relative prices to fall in areas where unemployment might otherwise emerge (because relative prices were too high). But his famous 1967 AEA Presidential Address predicted stagflation (increasing inflation leading to increasing unemployment) at a time when some economists believed that inflation would reduce unemployment (the 'Keynesian' high-inflation Phillips curve trade-off). Subsequent events appeared to prove Friedman correct – and the Keynesians disastrously wrong.

But in the period in which inflation was clearly increasing, other economists were also predicting that unemployment was on the rise. Thus Friedman's insightful prediction was not unique to him – even ignoring Edmund Phelps's (1967, 1968) simultaneous prediction. What was unique was that Friedman marshalled his prediction as a counter-revolutionary challenge to the Keynesian hegemony. The other predictions of increasing inflation and unemployment were not part of a revolutionary agenda and therefore made little impression on the profession (Chapter 4).

Friedman (1992: 241) reflected that one should 'never underestimate the role of luck in the fate of individuals or nations.' Luck had an input into the timing of Friedman's AEA presidential address; his use of his own methodology to predict the breakdown of the Phillips curve trade-off was a pivotal moment in the fortunes of the Chicago counter-revolution. His high-profile AEA Presidential Address is clearly remembered;

his conference paper (1966a) and *Newsweek* column (1966b) in which the same prediction appears are now almost completely forgotten. Had Friedman's AEA presidential year occurred in 1974, he would have found another topical subject with which to illustrate his methodology and demonstrate the superior predictive power of Chicago economics. A likely subject would have been the use of competitive price theory to predict the demise of OPEC price-fixing: 'The world crude oil price cannot stay at $10 a barrel; it will drop dramatically within the next six or nine months . . .' (Friedman, 1974a: 12). Friedman's prediction was out – by eleven years. Had Friedman's economics been primarily associated with this predictive failure policy-makers might have looked elsewhere for guidance.

The potency of the Chicago message was greatly enhanced by the sense that they had located *permanent* economic forces (relating to unemployment and competitive pricing outcomes) from which the economy could only depart for *transitory* periods (government attempting to use aggregate demand to reduce unemployment below its 'natural' rate, and monopolistic forces attempting to achieve price outcomes above their 'natural' or competitive state). But the potency of the natural rate model is crucially dependent on the shape of the short-run Phillips curve. If the short-run Phillips curve is almost horizontal at higher levels of unemployment then policy-induced recessions (such as the one experienced by the British economy after 1979) cannot easily produce their desired result: low inflation and low unemployment. And yet as is pointed out in Chapter 5, Phillips's curve (that Friedman augmented with inflationary expectations) *did* become almost horizontal at higher levels of unemployment. Thus the apparently relentless increase in UK unemployment could have been predicted from the curves that Friedman used to popularize his counter-revolution. The existence of this 'expectations trap' renders the natural rate model invalid in the disinflationary zone.

Friedman (1965: 26) was a language revolutionary, who advocated 'a free market mechanism of persuasion. Let us look at the matter of language.' He believed that after the Chicago counter-revolution, 1950s-style Keynesianism was 'dead. The language remains, but the substance is gone' (Friedman and Friedman, 1998: 228). He offered a human capital augmenting research strategy (unlike Joan Robinson, a less successful intellectual revolutionary, who offered to destroy much of the received human capital of the economics profession). Inflation (and the high-inflation Phillips curve trade-off) was the major reason for the eclipse of Keynesianism. Chapter 6 examines the evolution of perceptions and language about inflation. The natural rate of unemployment is a Walrasian concept and Chapter 7 examines Friedman's use of Walrasian language in the context of his critique of that approach to economics.

Friedman reflected that 'economists like me... exert influence by keeping options available when something has to be done at a time of crisis' (Friedman and Friedman, 1998: 220). These essays examine the 'options' that were constructed by Friedman and Stigler with their masterful understanding of the structure of influence in the economics profession.

2

'The Ghosts I Called I Can't Get Rid of Now': the Keynes-Tinbergen-Friedman-Phillips Critique of Keynesian Macroeconometrics

2.1 Introduction

2.1.1

This chapter offers a fresh perspective on the much publicized dispute between those followers of Keynes who presented econometric evidence in favour of a Phillips curve trade-off, and those monetarists who presented counter econometric evidence. Contrary to common perceptions, the collapse of the Keynesian Phillips curve was a vindication of a common critique of macroeconometric practices, which was jointly authored by John Maynard Keynes, Jan Tinbergen, Milton Friedman and A. W. H. 'Bill' Phillips. This analysis is informed by the usual sources, plus two sources which had been thought to be no longer in existence (Phillips's private papers and the London School of Economics (LSE) Methodology, Measurement and Testing (M^2T) Staff Seminar records), plus two essays by Keynes (1938a, 1938b) which have been overlooked in this context.

Keynes's critique of econometrics can be disaggregated into three distinct categories, namely technical issues that could be overcome by further research; criticisms that were directed at macroeconometrics, but not necessarily at microeconometrics; plus concerns about the possibility that econometrics, in the wrong hands, would become a hazard for the economics profession. Econometricians have long been aware that Keynes's detailed technical criticisms were sometimes ill-founded

(Robert A. Gordon, 1949: 53, n. 4). Since this first category of Keynes' critique is not germane to the theme of this chapter, these can be safely relegated to a footnote.[1]

This framework is used to marshal evidence in favour of four propositions. The first (section 2.3) is that Tinbergen acknowledged the validity of the central thrust of Keynes's critique of the more mechanical aspects of the econometric practices that were developing in the late 1930s, practices that had been unwittingly stimulated by the *General Theory* (Stone, 1978: 62; Tinbergen, 1947). The second proposition (section 2.4) is that there is a considerable overlap between the views of Keynes and Friedman with respect to econometrics.

The third proposition (section 2.4) is that Friedman (who during the Second World War was Deputy Director of the Statistical Research Group, and who must be regarded as one of the most statistically literate economists of all time) was implicitly *predicting* that macroeconometric disputation could only end inconclusively. In the late 1950s, there was a changing of the Keynesian guard in Cambridge, Massachusetts, with Alvin Hansen, who was sceptical about econometrics, making way for younger Keynesians who apparently did not share these doubts. The year 1958 was pivotal in macroeconomic history: it was the year of Phillips's seminal empirical paper, and around this time, the Senator from Massachusetts began to mobilize his 'academic Kennedy gang' at Cambridge (Halberstam, 1972: 157; Leeson, 1997a, 1997b). It was also the year that H. S. Houthakker, on study leave at Harvard, chose to engage Friedman (1957) in an econometric dispute over the relative merits of rival consumption functions. This may also explain why the anti-Keynesian counter-revolution, when it came, was monetarist and not Austrian (section 2.4).

The fourth proposition (section 2.5) is that Phillips was an insightful early critic of Keynesian Phillips curve econometrics. This section is based, in part, on the recently discovered – and complete – seminar records of the LSE Staff Seminar on Methodology, Measurement and Testing (M^2T). This section, therefore, supplements Neil de Marchi's (1988) fascinating discussion, which was based on the best – but incomplete – records then available. Some concluding remarks are provided in section 2.6. A brief historical introduction is provided in section 2.2.

2.1.2

Econometrics has had some success stories; it has also had some less impressive episodes. More importantly, it has become an ambiguous but high-status language, engaging a large share of professional effort.

According to George Stigler (1962a: 1), the statistical evaluation of economic relationships is the only distinctive trait of modern economics; but in 1912, Fisher had been unable to find enough interested people (apart from W. C. Mitchell and a few others) to establish an Econometric Society. This Society was ultimately founded by only 16 people, at a meeting at the Statler Hotel, Cleveland, Ohio, in December 1930; the first European meeting of the Society, in Lausanne in 1931, attracted about twenty people; and the first edition of *Econometrica* had a circulation of less than 300 (Cowles, 1960: 173–4; Frisch, 1970: 152; Christ, 1952: 5; Bjerkholt, 1995: 755). But today, econometrics occupies a large proportion of the pages of the professional journals, and according to Darnell and Evans (1990: ix) some see econometrics as an 'umbrella discipline for economics'.

Some econometricians have made an impressive theoretical contribution to statistical analysis, but doubts remain about the value of the 'average economic regression'. In the pre-econometric age, the average academic economist could aspire to become an authority on some aspect of the economy; now, it seems, many economists find that professional advancement is more easily facilitated by applying (or misapplying) estimating techniques to data – the quality or relevance of which often remains unexamined – in spite of Keynes's warnings.

The econometric pioneers had great hopes that they were uncovering a 'rock' upon which to base reliable policy advice (Frisch, 1970). But later econometricians (Pagan, 1984: 103) have been scathing about the research strategy which underpinned the econometric models of the 1960s, which appeared to suggest that inflation would reduce unemployment. Econometricians (Laidler, 1985) have also been concerned that the unemployment cost of reducing inflation – the dominant policy derived from 'natural rate' econometric models from the 1970s onwards – was much greater than anticipated by those econometric models. An investigation into the origins of this unwarranted confidence in macroeconometric models is also, simultaneously, an investigation into the origins of these policy failures.

Despite Schumpeter's (1933: 5) protestations, many econometricians have neglected, if not 'belittle[d]', a superbly rich data source – the serial dependent history of their own subject. If the history of econometrics stood in equal status alongside other subdisciplines within economics, this might tend to alleviate some of the rather disturbing problems with regard to both graduate education and professional incentives: 'Something is terribly wrong in the economics profession and in the incentives that economists perceive . . . in economics normal science has run amok. The invisible hand of truth has lost its guiding influence' (Colander, 1989: 31, 34–5; Colander and Klamer, 1988).

2.2 Historical background

The econometrics movement was moulded, to a large extent, by the desire to understand and tame the interwar business cycle. In April 1928, Charles F. Roos, Ragnar Frisch and Irving Fisher met at Fisher's home in New Haven, to set in motion the ball that would lead to the Econometric Society. In 1931, Alfred Cowles discontinued his forecasting service, explaining to his clients that he was insufficiently informed about the nature of business and stock market fluctuations.[2] In October 1931, Roos – who initially thought that he had received a crank letter – met with Cowles and Fisher to discuss Cowles's offer to fund econometric research. Roos subsequently became Research Director of Roosevelt's National Recovery Administration, the first Director of Research at the Cowles Commission and, from 1937, the head of the Econometric Institute, a private forecasting agency (Christ, 1952: 3–17; Rima, 1988: 17; Cowles, 1960: 173–4). Roos's (1955: 394–5) monumental Survey Article on forecasting techniques expressed enormous confidence in econometric techniques; it also offered the prospect of rebutting Keynes's proposition that investment demand was beyond the reach of forecasters.

Keynesian and Marxian economics are modern versions of the 'endogenous instability of capitalism' thesis. In 1929, the Dutch Statistician's Office, under Tinbergen's editorship, began a statistical business cycle journal. The Great Depression gave an added dimension to these controversies. In the 1930s, many observers were concerned about the long-run viability of capitalism and of the apparently infeasible combination of political liberty and economic freedom (Desai, 1981: 41). Marschak initiated one of the earlier debates on the viability of socialism as an economic system, involving Pareto, Barone, von Mises, Schumpeter, von Hayek, Lange and Lerner. The 1940 Cowles Commission Report stated that unemployment was the primary economic problem to be tackled (Malinvaud, 1988: 191; Christ, 1952: 22). Many economists lost their faith in the ability of markets to solve the problem of unemployment, and many embraced the new faith of economic planning. Tinbergen (1984: 315), for example, retrained as an economist under the influence of the onset of world depression; he regarded his econometric work, and in particular his estimation of parameters, as providing the tools to effect socialist intervention in the economy in order to minimize cyclical fluctuations and poverty (Tinbergen, in Magnus and Morgan, 1987: 118–19; Knoester and Wellink, 1993: 19). The within-sample 'explanatory' power of Tinbergen's equations were high; generally his R^2 exceeded 0.98 (Epstein, 1987: 33, 48).

Lawrence Klein shared this approach to econometrics; later he would be persecuted because of his socialist convictions. Harold Hotelling also favoured market socialism (Arrow, 1990: 107). Oscar Lange was a 'proclaimed socialist', and later a member of the Polish Communist government (Friedman, 1974a: 15). Ragnar Frisch also had socialist leanings, according to Tinbergen (conversation with Arie Kapteyn, 15 November 1994; Blaug, 1985: 67). Frisch came to believe that uncovering the underlying structure of the economy – the structural parameters – would enable the business cycle to be tamed (Epstein, 1987: 41). Part of this optimism may reflect the initial training in physics which Tinbergen, Frisch, Koopmans and others had been exposed to (Kol and De Wolff, 1993: 29; Mirowski, 1989; Tinbergen, 1984: 315; Craver and Leijonhufvud, 1987: 175; but see Andvig, 1985).

These ideological undercurrents were present in many of the business cycle research institutes which were established all over Europe and the United States in the 1920s.[3] The New School for Social Research opened in 1919, attracting refugees from Europe, and from Columbia University, whose President, Nicholas Butler, had pledged the University to stand firm against the 'rule of the literary and academic Bolsheviki' (cited by Bender, 1987: 299). In Russia in 1917, there had been a political victory for those who believed in the endogenous instability of capitalism thesis. In 1920, the Konjunkture Institute of Moscow was founded, with Kondratieff as Director. The controversy over business cycles was more than idle speculation and involved political passions of 'venomous ferocity' (Schumpeter, 1954: 1158, n. 8). In 1928 the Konjunkture Institute was closed down and Kondratieff was sent to Siberia and subsequently shot, while his long wave theory of the business cycle was labelled 'wrong and reactionary' (Garvy, 1943: 204; Solzhenitsyn, 1973: 50; Nove, 1992; Morgan, 1990: 66–7).

Interest in the business cycle and its control were not, of course, an exclusively socialist preoccupation. In the nineteenth century, Marx used the business cycle as his fundamental unit of analysis; so too did W. S. Jevons (Schumpeter, 1954: 742; Morgan, 1990: 16). Marx built an endogenous instability of capitalism thesis; Jevons sought to locate the origins of commercial crises in *exogenous* forces, namely a 10.45 year sunspot cycle. As late as 1923, Henry Ludwell Moore outlined a similar causal sequence extending back to movements in the planet Venus

(Stigler, 1962a: 11). But Gottfried Haberler, whose League of Nations study *Prosperity and Depression* led directly to Tinbergen's econometric work, concluded that non-economic explanations of the origins of the business cycle were, by the interwar period, rare if not eccentric (1939: 9–10; but see Keynes, 1936a: 329–32).

After the war came the *methodenstreit* between the economic statisticians represented by Burns, Mitchell, Friedman and Vining at the NBER, and the econometricians, represented by Koopmans and the Cowles Commission. The context, and hence the emphatic nature of this *methodenstreit*, was the quite spectacular failure of Keynesian models in the immediate postwar period. After the US Full Employment Bill, the Cowles Commission Paper No. 23 stated that this *methodenstreit* was between 'the nonstatistical economist' and 'The Use[rs] of Econometric Models as a Guide to Economic Policy', concluding that 'the latter is better equipped' (Klein, 1947: 112). Paul Samuelson (1944a, 1944b, 1988: 63–4) predicted 'Unemployment Ahead'; and even though US unemployment in 1946 turned out to be 3 million, rather than the 8 million predicted in late 1945, the choice was now between tackling the forecasting problem 'with renewed vigour', or discarding econometrics and

> relax[ing] again into armchair comments ... the line of least resistance ... We cannot be very hopeful about solving our economic problems if we have to rely on such methods [of the pre-war guessers] in the future ... Econometric methods could not have been worse than any other methods that were used.
>
> (Klein, 1946: 302–6)

2.3 Tinbergen and Keynes

In the last decade, econometrics has begun to attract the attention of increasing numbers of historians of thought, much of it focused on the Keynes–Tinbergen exchange.[4] Most commentators have adopted one (or sometimes two) attitudes with respect to Keynes's critique. For some, it was a lamentable performance on Keynes's part (Klein, 1951: 450–1), traceable to his ill-health, technical rustiness and tactical predilections (Stone, 1978: 62–3). For some, Keynes simply misunderstood what Tinbergen was attempting to do (Klant, 1985), or 'he did not really have the necessary technical knowledge to understand what he was criticising' (Samuelson, 1946: 197, n. 11). For others, Keynes was, in a qualified way, more sympathetic to econometrics than had hitherto been supposed (Bateman, 1990). Keynes's reference to 'alchemy', it has been argued, might have been intended as a gesture of encouragement, suggesting that Tinbergen might ultimately succeed in creating the foundations of an econometric science (Rima, 1988: 16). Some have even speculated that had he lived longer, Keynes might have become a computer-based modeller at the centre of a 'high-tech "circus"' (Bodkin, Klein and Marwah, 1988: 9, n. 10, 10–11, n. 15). Alternatively, others have argued that Keynes's critique is still relevant to modern econometrics (Patinkin, 1976; Hendry, 1980). Indeed, the co-founder of the New Classical anti-Keynesian counter-revolution and the author of a devastating critique of econometric policy evaluation (constructed with Keynesian macroeconometrics in mind) recognized an irony: 'In referring to those who built in part on Tinbergen's work as "Keynesian" I am, then, contributing to the continuation of an historical injustice' (Lucas, 1977: 10, n. 5).

Too much of the history of macroeconomics has been bedevilled by attempts to label (and sometimes libel) the author of the macroeconomic Old Testament. Surprisingly, while there has been much discussion of the Keynes–Tinbergen debate, both at a general and at a specific level, there has previously been no attempt to dissect Keynes's critique into operational categories. By treating the Keynes critique *en bloc*, we are in danger of concluding that his suspicions about econometrics were 'invalid' (Malinvaud, 1991: 636), or 'venial and not to be remembered' (Stone, 1978: 88), or not worthy of mention (Stone, 1980: section III). A disaggregated approach allows much greater light to be shone on those aspects of Keynes's critique which have relevance to contemporary econometric practices. It also reveals that Tinbergen finally acknowledged the potency of *parts* of Keynes's critique, *as Keynes predicted he would* (1939: 568). The words from Goethe's *Zauberlehrling*, which forms part of the title of this chapter, were prophetically cited by Tinbergen on the occasion of his Nobel Lecture (Tinbergen, 1969: 43; for similar sentiments see Klein, 1971a: 416).[5]

Ragnar Frisch (1970: 164), Tinbergen's co-recipient of the first Nobel Prize in Economic Science, also bemoaned 'the cascade of papers of the playometric kind', and had long been sceptical about some of the directions of applied econometrics (Arrow, 1960: 183). Tinbergen (1967: 272) criticized economists for being averse to time-consuming factual and statistical research which was required for quality empirical research. Tinbergen (1956: 149–85) also developed parts of what became known as the Lucas Critique (Lucas, 1976: 20); and he assumed that 'expectations are "rational" i.e. are consistent with the economic relationships' ([1932] cited by Keuzenkamp, 1991: 1247). Half a century after the publication of his *Econometric Approach to Business Cycle Problems*, Magnus and Morgan (1987: 136) asked Tinbergen, 'How do you feel about the way econometrics has developed over the last twenty years or so? In 1952 you feared that techniques could take over from attention to human needs and problems in the field of economics. Do you feel this fear was justified?' Tinbergen replied: 'I'm afraid, yes.' Again, a vindication of *parts* of the Keynes Critique.

Keynes and Tinbergen are usually characterized as having incompatible views on econometrics. Yet, Tinbergen's Nobel Lecture can be viewed as the opening volley of the 'orgy of self-criticism' (Blaug, 1980: 253) which descended on the economics profession when the predictive power of many of the macroeconometric models of the period were found to be less than impressive (Leontief, 1971: 3; Worswick, 1972: 79; Phelps Brown, 1972: 6). Given that *some aspects* of Keynes's warnings still retain their validity (Samuelson, 1992: 243–4; Ormerod, 1994: 92–112), it is instructive to disaggregate his concerns about econometrics.

Keynes appreciated the qualities of 'a real trained statistician', and was 'in fundamental sympathy with the deep underlying conceptions of the statistical theory of the day'. The subject of his second known letter to a newspaper was the interpretation of statistics, and one of his earliest academic disputes was with Karl Pearson over the appropriate statistical methods of studying the effects of parental alcoholism on offspring, a dispute which illustrated 'the pitfalls of statistical inference' (Harrod, 1951: 154). His final posthumously published article was 'solely concerned with the available statistics'. One of the themes of his career was the analysis of 'the logical basis of statistical modes of argument' and the search for 'the principles of sound induction' which might constitute 'a good scientific argument...' Keynes had planned to specialize in logic and statistical theory, and *A Treatise on Probability* attempted to 'cover the whole field of empirical thinking...it would be difficult to find a parallel for a comprehensive attack of this kind since the days of Aristotle' (Harrod, 1951: 126, 133–4). The final section of his Fellowship Dissertation was entitled 'The Foundations of Statistical Inference', which concluded with an 'Outline of a Constructive Theory'. The union of descriptive and inferential statistics was

> the occasion of a great deal of confusion. The statistician who is mainly interested in the technical methods of his science is less concerned to discover the precise conditions in which a description can be legitimately extended by induction. He slips somewhat easily from one to the other, and having found a complete and satisfactory

> mode of description he may take less pains over the transitional argument... [but] he must pay attention to a new class of considerations and must display a different kind of capacity... He is faced, in fact, with the normal problems of inductive science... [involving material which] will be necessarily incapable of exact, numerical, or statistical treatment... Generally speaking, therefore, I think that the business of statistical technique ought to be strictly limited to preparing the numerical aspects of our material in an intelligent form, so as to be ready for the application of the usual inductive methods.

Most of the mathematical methods applied to statistical inference were invalid, and could 'only lead to error and to delusion' (Keynes's *Collected Works*, henceforth JMK, XV [1908]: 12; [1909]: 20–1; VIII [1921]: 359–60, 419, 427, 428, 468; XXVII [1946]: 428, 430)

Keynes informed the Macmillan Committee that although 'the empirical method is not by any means successful for the diagnosis [of the Depression] it is not by any means valueless for seeking the cure' (JMK, XX [1930]: 99). He concluded Volume II of his *Treatise on Money* (1930: 408) with a plea for greater quantitative knowledge: 'Statistics are of fundamental importance to suggest theories, to test them and make them convincing... [and] to eliminate impressionism.' He opened *The General Theory* with a call for a statistical examination of the relationship between changes in money wages and changes in real wages. It was on statistical grounds that he asserted that the wage units could 'only be reduced amidst the decay and dissolution of economic society' (1936a: 9–10, 40–1, 102–4, 340, n. 1). Keynes was particularly opposed to the statistical method underpinning the American Keynesian 'Phillips curve' trade-off (JMK, XXIII [1941]: 181–93). Chapter 6 of the unwritten *Footnotes to the General Theory* was entitled 'Statistical Notes' (JMK, XIV [1936]: 134). He told Austin Robinson (1972: 535) that 'all his best ideas came from messing around with figures and seeing what they must mean'. But throughout his career he opposed the use of mathematical methods in both statistics and economics. When it came to questions of inference, experimental methods were often to be preferred to statistical methods (JMK, XI [1911]: 216). Certain methods of statistical analysis led to invalid results. Investigations of samples, but not complete populations, were also suspect. For statistics to be decisive, they had to extend over a period long enough to eliminate other influences (1936a: 104; JMK, XIX.I [1923]: 122).

Keynes was suspicious of all numbers derived by formulae from non-experimental data, especially when the original data had been suppressed. To 'enable the reader to form some sort of independent judgement...the real character of the evidence' must be displayed; not just the products derived from applying 'mathematical machinery' (JMK, XI [1910]: 191). Graphs were highly suitable for 'publicity or propaganda purposes', as Florence Nightingale discovered; but Keynes warned of the

> horrid examples of the evils of the graphical method unsupported by tables of figures. Both for accurate understanding and particularly to facilitate the use of the same material by other people it is essential that graphs should not be published by themselves but only when supported by the tables which will lead up to them. It would be an exceedingly good rule to forbid in any scientific periodical the publication of graphs unsupported by tables.
>
> (JMK, XI [1938]: 234)

But he was unstinting in his support for the statistician Udny Yule in his quest for a lectureship in Cambridge (Skidelsky, 1983: 222). Appropriately, Yule (1926) went on to produce some classic work on 'nonsense correlations'.

In 1923, Keynes helped launch the regular London and Cambridge Economic Series barometric survey of business conditions, and he repeatedly campaigned for improved economic statistics, not to be used for regression analysis, but to offer intuitive insights into reality (Stone, 1978: 64–72; Skidelsky, 1992: 106, 414, 270; JMK, XXVII [1944]: 371). He was very supportive of James Meade, Richard Stone and the new Central Statistical Department, and he thought that it was 'most dangerous for too wide a gap to develop between inside and outside statistical information' (JMK, XXII [1941]: 329, 331). His first concern was whether the data were 'good enough to stand the strain which has been placed upon them'. The accuracy of statistics whose 'sole purpose is to satisfy the...troublesome and often trifling curiosity of the academic statistician' could not be relied upon (JMK, XI [1929]: 229; XV [1909]: 36; XVIII [1923]: 152; XXII [1939]: 82). 'The suspicion of quackery has not yet disappeared [from statistics]...There is still about it for scientists a smack of astrology, of alchemy' (JMK, VIII [1921]: 367). But he looked forward to a systematic theory of statistics and the continued quantification of economics: 'Whether the uniformity of economic settings is sufficient to enable the economist to make full use of this kind of work, time will show' (JMK, XI [1909]: 50–1, [1929]: 226). The 'excellently complete statistics now available in the United States' were available to illustrate aspects of the theory of the Trade Cycle (1936a: 332). If Tinbergen simply examined 'statistically particular cases, regarding them as particular cases, and no more . . . I am entirely in favour of him' (JMK, XIV [1938]: 302).

Keynes was a leading exponent of the 1930s revolt against non-quantitative economics:

> It was [Keynes's] natural inclination to approach any problem from the angle of measurement of the phenomena . . . But just as he was sceptical of ideas that could not be verified by measurement, so he was sceptical also of the adventures of the statisticians into the world of correlations built on insufficient logical foundations.
>
> (Robinson, 1947: 44; 1992: 211)

It was one of the principals of statistical method that 'elaborate calculations . . . confuse, though they might also impress, all readers outside a very restricted class'. It was

> the nature of valid argument which is in dispute . . . Professor Pearson may cover up by elaboration of method . . . [but] it is difficult to know how properly to characterise the work of a statistician who uses in controversy a table of this description with complete dogmatic assurance and without making plain to the reader the principles of its construction.
>
> (JMK, XXIII [1910]: 191–2, 199, 205)

With respect to Tinbergen, the problem of multicollinearity between variables exposed econometricians to 'the extraordinarily difficult and deceptive complications of "spurious" correlations'. Yule's discovery 'sprang a mine under the contraptions of optimistic statisticians . . . It becomes like those puzzles for children where you write down your age, multiply, add this and that, subtract something else, and eventually end up with the number of the Beast in Revelation' (JMK, XIV [1938]: 309–10; see also Tinbergen, 1992: 278). It was essential to investigate whether correlation coefficients were stable across subseries. Such was the excessive emphasis on 'the mathematical complications, that many statistical students hazily float between from defining the correlation coefficient as a statistical description to employing it as a measure of the probability of a statistical generalisation between quantitative variations' (JMK, VIII [1921]: 428, 464). The coefficients derived from the method of applying multiple correlations to

> unanalysed economic material, which we know to be non-homogenous through time...are not constant. There is no reason at all why they should not be different every year...How are these coefficients arrived at?...One gets the impression that it is a process of fitting a linear equation through trial and error.

Thus when Tinbergen and co-workers econometrically 'confirmed' Keynes's (JMK, II [1919]) intuition that the price elasticity of demand for a country's exports was −2, Keynes declined to interpret these econometric results as compelling: 'How nice for you to have found the correct figure!' he replied to Tinbergen (1979: 342).[6]

Tinbergen believed that he had tested for the constancy of his coefficients (JMK, XIV [1938]: 286–7, 292). Keynes, however, was absolutely correct. Pesaran and Smith (1985: 144) noted the complete absence of parameter stability when they re-estimated Tinbergen's investment equations: 'The estimated coefficients move all over the place.' Tinbergen (1969: 43) acknowledged that he and his fellow researchers found it safer 'to ask industrialists for their investment programs rather than rely on an econometric explanation', and the econometric modelling of investment remains a notoriously unsuccessful area of applied econometrics.

Keynes objected to econometrics for the same reason that he criticized the 'classical' economists:

> *Progress* in economics consists almost entirely in a progressive improvement in the choice of models. The grave fault of the later classical school, exemplified in Pigou, has been to overwork a too simple or out-of-date model...But it is the essence of a model that one does *not* fill in real values for the variable functions. To do so would make it useless as a model [emphases in text].

Economics was a method of thinking:

> The object of our analysis is, not to provide a machine, or method of blind manipulation, which will furnish an infallible answer, but to provide ourselves with an organised and orderly method of thinking out particular problems; and, after we have reached a provisional conclusion by isolating the complicating factors one by one, we then have to go back on ourselves and allow, as well as we can, for the probable interactions of the factors amongst themselves. This is the nature of economic thinking. Any other way of applying our

> formal principles of thought (without which, however, we shall be lost in the woods) will lead us into error.
>
> (1936a: 297; JMK, XIV [1938]: 296)

(For Friedman's approving echo of this Marshallian theme, see 1953: 7.)

Keynes was not 'content with the sort of broad general impression of how things worked that contents so many macroeconomists' (Robinson, 1972: 534). He warned his students that 'the stuff of economics was not sharp or precise, and it was too easy to distort it and create for it the impression of an exactitude that it really lacked, and by subjecting it to mathematical manipulation also to wind up with a seriously distorted picture of the economy' (Tarshis, 1977: 73). He was concerned about 'the appalling state of scholasticism into which the minds of so many economists have got which allows them to take leave of their intuitions altogether. Yet in writing economics one is not writing either a mathematical proof or a legal document' (JMK, XXIX [1935]: 150); 'The real tool is thought, and [equations] are not a substitute for it, but at most a guide or embodiment' (cited by Young, 1987: 13). Almost identical concerns were echoed a generation later by Frisch and Koopmans.[7]

Like Friedman (1967: 88; 1974), Keynes had a corresponding nosological concern about the economics profession. Keynes had 'a very poor opinion of Marschak', and described Colin Clark as 'almost the only economic statistician I have ever met who seems to me quite first class' (JMK, XXIX: 57, n. 11; O'Donnell, 1992: 16). He had long-held opinions concerning the fruitlessness of *certain* statistical rather than experimental methods of analysis, of the impossibility of reducing human conduct to a set of equations, and of using 'the collection of facts for the prediction of future frequencies and associations' (JMK, VIII [1921]: 368). There was 'great danger in quantitative forecasts which are based exclusively on statistics relating to conditions which are by no means parallel' (JMK, XXIII [1941]: 192).

He was concerned that the statisticians' occupational disease should not become the economists' occupation. As he wrote to Harrod (in reference to Tinbergen's work):

> I think it most important, for example, to investigate statistically the order of magnitude of the multiplier... [but] to convert a model into a quantitative formula is to destroy its usefulness as an instrument of thought... by filling in figures, which one can be quite sure will not apply next time, so far from increasing the value of his instrument, he has destroyed it.

Most of the claims derived from statistical inference, he argued, were inadmissible from the perspective of logic (of which economics was a branch), and were evidence of 'mathematical charlatanry' (cited by Skidelsky, 1983: 223). Keynes, like Harrod, held Tinbergen in the highest regard, yet Tinbergen's econometric work, he wrote in a note to Richard Kahn, was 'all hocus' and simply a 'mess of unintelligible figurings'. The influences on investment were variables, and, therefore, 'it is logically impossible to discover by Tinbergen's method the comparative dependence on profit lagged . . . I complain that this sort of logical point is not first discussed – or even mentioned. Until it is, the whole thing is charlatanism in spite of Tinbergen's admirable candour' (JMK, XIV [1938]: 301, 304, 289, 299, 332, 305).

In *The General Theory,* Keynes located one of the origins of macroeconomic instability in the 'animal spirits' of those undertaking investment, which depended upon 'the nerves and hysteria and even the digestion and reaction to the weather of those upon whose spontaneous activity it largely depends'. Crucial variables such as the rate of interest and the marginal efficiency of capital

> are particularly concerned with the indefinite character of actual expectations; they sum up the effect in men's market decisions of all sorts of vague doubts and fluctuating states of confidence and courage. They belong, that is to say, to a stage of our theory where we are no longer assuming a definite and calculable future . . . Our precision will be mock precision if we try to use such partly vague and non-quantitative concepts as the basis of a quantitative analysis.

Statistical comparison could be useful, 'depending on some broad element of judgement rather than strict calculation' (1936a: 161–2, 39–40; 1937: 151).

Multiple correlation analysis was 'too elaborate and adds little or nothing' ([1940], cited by Epstein, 1987: 143). This type of analysis requires that a *complete* set of relevant variables are included, and are accurately measurable (for Friedman's elaboration of this point, see 1953: 32, 49). There will be a 'serious misrepresentation of the causal process, if in fact some significant factors have been omitted.' As a piece of 'historical curve fitting and description . . . it is not a very lucid way of describing the past' (1939: 566; Carabelli, 1988: 291, n. 10). To derive inductive generalizations from statistical descriptions is a hazardous operation which requires that environmental conditions remain homogeneous and uniform in future time periods (JMK, VIII [1921]: 359–470).

The material to which economic models are applied is, 'in too many respects, not homogenous through time' (JMK, XIV [1938]: 296; for similar sentiments, see Alfred Marshall, approvingly cited by Friedman, 1953 [1949]: 90). This implies that econometrics is inappropriate in cases when 'political, social and physiological factors, including such things as government policy, the progress of invention, and the state of expectations may be significant. In particular, it is inapplicable to the problems of the Business Cycle' (1939: 561). In a letter to Gerald Shove, Keynes wrote that 'as soon as one is dealing with the influence of expectations and of transitory experience, one is, in the nature of things outside of the realm of the formally exact.' Keynes concluded that 'one feels a suspicion that the choice of factors is influenced (as is indeed only natural) by what statistics are available, and that many vital factors are ignored because they are statistically intractable or unprocurable.' On a visit to the United States, he cautioned younger economists such as Gilbert, Humphrey and Salant against neglecting important theoretical considerations 'in the interests of simplifying their statistical task' (JMK, XIV [1936]: 2; [1938]: 287; XXIII [1941]: 192).

Prophetically, as Friedman (1991: 36) pointed out, Keynes (1939: 568, 559) predicted that econometrics had acquired a momentum of its own that would tend to make its practitioners resistant to criticism. Tinbergen will probably

> engage another ten computers and drown his sorrows in arithmetic... The worst of him is that he is much more interested in getting on with the job than in spending time in deciding whether the job is worth getting on with. He so clearly prefers the mazes of arithmetic to the mazes of logic.

Keynes was clearly not opposed to statistical analysis, but 'he hated stupidity, not only with aesthetic but also with a moral hatred: stupidity prevented the accomplishment of what was best for the world' (Robinson, 1947: 29). He was primarily concerned that mechanical econometric practices might become a tangled web for the economics profession. He conducted a 'ferocious campaign to discredit the activities of Tinbergen and later Kalecki... Keynes' opposition to [multiple correlation analysis] was extraordinarily unyielding' (Epstein, 1987: 142–3). Skidelsky (1992: 618) reported that 'Keynes attacked Tinbergen's efforts with an astonishingly fierce barrage of arguments.' According to Pesaran and Smith (1985: 147) 'It was the unjustifiable inductive pretensions that provoked his venom.' Keynes also referred, perhaps mockingly, to 'nefarious econometrics' (Stone, 1978: 63), and in 1946 he told Jacob Viner (1964: 265) that he 'disowned any responsibility for their [his disciples] reliance on restricted and mechanical manipulations of a few statistical series, rather than making a broad survey of the significant factors and using judgement in assaying their importance and the nature of their impacts.'

W. C. Mitchell provided the momentum that led to the establishment of the Oxford Institute of Statistics (Young and Lee, 1993: 119–20; Harrod, 1949). Keynes was determined to establish a Cambridge department of what he called 'statistical realistic economics' in opposition to Tinbergen's macroeconometrics, and as a rival, perhaps, to the Oxford Institute of Statistics, which had appointed Marschak (who had fled both Lenin and Hitler) as Director, and where Klein would seek refuge during the McCarthyite period. Keynes favoured the use of balance sheets and survey data (which elicited preferences) in the investigation of quantitative policy issues (Epstein, 1987: 142–3). Richard Stone (1978: 83–7) became the first Director of the Cambridge Department of Applied Economics in April 1946, the month of Keynes's death. In one sense, Stone and his co-workers acknowledged Keynes's critique by focusing their research efforts on the econometric analysis of modern demand theory, which is widely regarded as an econometric success story, in contrast to the rather disappointing performance of the large macroeconometric models (Gilbert, 1991).

Finally, and perhaps most importantly for Keynes, was the question of the likelihood of self-deception, and of the integrity and biases of the econometrician – 'the spirit with which the subject is tackled', as Hendry (1980: 403) called it. Richard Feynman argued that the first principle of scientific integrity is that 'you must not fool yourself, and you are the easiest person to fool' (cited by Warsh, 1988: 251). For Keynes, 'the more complicated and technical the preliminary statistical investigations become, the more prone inquirers are to mistake the statistical description for an inductive generalisation.' In particular, *ad hoc* specifications of time-lags introduces the possibility that the econometrician will fidget 'about until he finds a time-lag which does not fit in too badly with the theory he is testing'. With respect to the assumption of linearity, Keynes warned that 'it would certainly seem that quite easy manipulation on these lines would make it possible to fit any explanation to any facts' (JMK, VIII [1921]: 361; 1939: 565, 563–4; 1940: 155; Klein, 1992: 184).

With respect to Tinbergen: 'There is no-one, therefore, so far as human qualities go, whom it would be safer to trust with black magic.

That there is anyone I would trust with it at the present stage or that this brand of statistical alchemy is ripe to become a branch of science, I am not yet persuaded.' It might be fruitful to use these methods to investigate more elementary cases, such as the estimation of the various influences on the net investment in railway rolling-stock (JMK, XIV [1940]: 320; [1938]: 287–9, 295, 317). Keynes (1938a) spoke highly of forecasts derived from statistical analysis – when applied to cases such as the international corn trade. But regression analysis could not legitimately be applied to macroeconomic problems such as the 'problem of imports as a whole' ([1939], cited by Carabelli, 1988: 291, n. 10).

2.4 Friedman and Keynes

2.4.1 Econometric disputation

Keynes (1936a: 33, vii–viii) and Friedman (1953: 30) are both associated with the idea that predictive failure is damaging to scientific status; both doubted the existence of 'conclusive' tests or evidence in economics. Both perceived themselves to be heirs to an 'oral tradition' in monetary theory (JMK, XI [1911]: 375; Friedman, 1956; Patinkin, 1969; Leeson, 1998; Leeson, 2000). But methodologically, *The General Theory* is a tract on the importance of examining the realism and relevance of assumptions (see, for example, 1936a: 276), and Milton Friedman (correspondence, 18 April 1995) has confirmed that his own methodology of positive economics was constructed in opposition to this tendency.

When it came to the 'scientific problems' associated with data analysis, for over half a century Friedman (1957: ix) has elaborated and echoed many of the themes discussed by Keynes. In his seven-page Centenary article for the *Economic Journal* (1991: 36–8), entitled appropriately 'Old Wine in New Bottles', Friedman humorously refers to some of his own regressions as a 'clear case of GIGO' (Garbage In, Garbage Out), but on a more serious note he concluded that the capacity to put data through the computer-based 'econometric wringer' has

> induced economists to carry reliance on mathematics and econometrics beyond the point of vanishing returns. I generate multiple regressions these days at a rate that I never would have contemplated three or four decades ago – and many more than I would have if I followed my own prescription for proper research procedures.

Friedman (1991: 36–8) also displayed an appreciation of the way in which 'the Keynesian revolution changed the language and tools with which economists analysed the aggregate economy'. He noted that the structure of professional incentives – 'the tendency to count rather than to evaluate publications' – had created an inbuilt bias toward generating low-quality econometric research, derived from data mining: 'There is wide agreement that GIGO . . . is a real problem.' His training as a statistician had made him acutely aware that all statisticians 'like to use our fancy techniques to see what the data show' (1963a: 8).

These themes occur throughout his career. His famous and influential methodology of positive economics (1953 [1947]: 301–19; 1953: 3–43) had been formulated in the context of some highly misleading Keynesian macroeconometric forecasts: 'Errors in forecasting may have nothing to do with the validity of many of the underlying theories . . . these [other] more accurate predictions do not prove that their methods are superior to those that failed' (Klein, 1946: 289). For Friedman, in contrast, the chief obstacle to the attainment of positive status was the difficulty of testing the validity of tentative hypotheses. Economic data were difficult to interpret: 'This hindered greatly the permanent weeding out of unsuccessful hypotheses. They are always cropping up again.' This led to an emphasis on the realism of assumptions,

> the battle cry of institutionalists and the closely related emphasis on extensive statistical studies of economic phenomena which constituted an easier test of hypotheses . . . Alfred Marshall's emphasis on the construction of an 'engine for the discovery of concrete truth' has tended to be submerged under the urge for descriptive realism.

Friedman approved of the Marshallian method used by Keynes to explore the theory of employment, but disapproved of the Walrasian method employed by some Keynesians (1952: 456–7; 1953 [1949]: 56–7, 92). However, from the mid-1930s, the formalist general equilibrium revolution began to supplant the Marshallian 'engineers'. Marshall's ambiguities, it was claimed, had 'paralysed the best brains in the Anglo Saxon branch of our profession for three decades' (Samuelson, 1967a: 109).

Lucas and Sargent (1978: 50) noted that the 'Keynesian revolution was, in the form in which it succeeded in the United States, a revolution in *method*' [emphasis in text]. Friedman (1953 [1944]: 277–300) led the 'Methodological Criticism' of Oscar Lange's 1944 Cowles Monograph, *Price Flexibility and Employment*. An economist, he argued, who is concerned about economic reality 'is not likely to stay within the bounds of a method of analysis that denies him the knowledge he seeks. He will escape the shackles of formalism, even if he has to resort to illogical devices and specious reasoning to do so.' For almost a decade, Frank Knight and Friedman led the 'fairly intense struggle' against the Cowles Commission at Chicago (Reder, 1982: 10). As part of his critique of the Cowles Commission approach to econometrics, Friedman (1951: 107) noted that 'we have fallen into the habit of not trying to test the validity of many hypotheses even when we can do so . . . After all most experiments are destined to be unsuccessful; the tragic thing is that in economics we so seldom find out that they are.'

Friedman took over much of the Keynes Critique and made it his own. Yet the evaluation of econometric evidence became the 'space-time' *arena* of the disputes between Keynesians and monetarists – who began to resemble electrons with opposite spin, in the same orbit. Paradigmatic challengers have to fight on grounds chosen by the dominant orthodoxy. Both sides confidently concluded that the evidence supported their a prioris, and was 'so strikingly one-sided' (Friedman, 1963a: 8; Stein, 1982: 209; Desai, 1981: 203). On the Keynesian side in particular, there was a belief that precision econometric modelling would eliminate the 'ambiguous use of language – [the] Marshallian legacy shamelessly indulged in by all sides' (Desai, 1981: 64). This episode of intellectual history revealed that econometrics was not powerful enough to unambiguously discriminate between alternative *Weltanschauungs*.

There is a paradox here. Keynesian macroeconometrics, at least initially, retained a faith in structural estimation as a tool for discriminating between the 'true' and the 'false' model, and also for effecting the type of government policies which would mitigate, if not eliminate, the business cycle. The losing side (in terms of policy-influence from the mid-1970s) suffered a double defeat. The winning side scored a double victory: monetary targeting (based, in part, on the results derived from monetarist macroeconometrics) temporarily replaced Phillips curve targeting; Friedman's (and Keynes's) suspicions about macroeconometrics also appeared to have been partly vindicated.

Harry Johnson, in his remarkable Richard T. Ely Lecture on 'The Keynesian Revolution and the Monetarist Counter–Revolution', wrote that one of the reasons for the success of the Keynesian revolution was that '*The General Theory* offered an important empirical relationship for the emerging tribe of econometricians to measure.' Likewise, monetarism advanced 'a new and important empirical relationship, suitable for determined estimation by the budding econometrician. That relationship was found in the demand function for money.' The methodology of positive economics 'offered liberation to the small-scale intellectual, since it freed his mind from dependence on the large-scale research teams and the large and expensive computer program.' The monetarist counter-revolution would 'peter out' because 'monetarism is seriously inadequate as an approach to monetary theory'; with its 'abnegation of responsibility for explaining the division of the effects of monetary changes between price and quantity movements... one should not be too fastidious in condemnation of the techniques of scholarly chicanery to promote a revolution or a counter-revolution in economic theory' (Johnson and Johnson, 1978 [1971]: 189, 196–8).

Milton Friedman (correspondence 18 April 1995) recalls that 'Harry Johnson was an extremely subtle and sophisticated person... Harry was originally a very strong Keynesian who was converted to monetarism. He remained something of a Keynesian whenever he was in Chicago and was a strong monetarist whenever he was in London.' Johnson was clearly fuelled by a variety of motives and inputs, and jealousy of his Chicago colleague may have been one of them. But Friedman's genius (like Keynes's) extends to an understanding of the sociology of knowledge in the economics profession (see, for example, 1955a: 902).

Keynes (1936a: 21, 81) highlighted the power of the 'optical illusion' of Say's Law. In his defence of Mitchell, Friedman (1950: 470, 467) drew the contrast between Mitchell's work and 'the shoddy work that passes for scientific'. He also bemoaned the ability of the Cowles Commission econometricians to successfully cultivate the 'illusion that Mitchell was antitheoretical'. He noted that 'worthless' Keynesian national income models, which misrepresented the underlying macroeconomic structure, could nevertheless become hegemonic on the back of a 'Statistical Illusion'–when accompanied by an analytical system which 'once mastered, appeared highly mechanical and capable of yielding far-reaching and important conclusions with a minimum of input' (Friedman and Becker, 1957: 68, 73; Friedman, 1970: 207, n. 6). His early sophisticated theoretical work on stabilization policy (1948a; 1953 [1951]: 117–32) had not noticeably undermined Keynesian confidence, nor had it stimulated much further research (see, for example, Neff, 1949a, b), despite his assertion that 'the question is empirical' (1949: 954). The Cowles–NBER methodological dispute had produced only 'desultory skirmishing' (1951: 114). His theoretical work left him feeling 'as if I were preaching in the wilderness and belaboring the obvious'. Even 'distressingly obvious' conclusions could be 'widely neglected' (1953 [1951]: 131; for almost identical words, see Keynes, 1936a: viii).

Likewise, his plea for a Marshallian redirection of economics – Walras's 'divorce of form from substance' had led to some 'nonsense' – failed to be persuasive (1955a: 980–9; for almost identical words, see Keynes, cited by Skidelsky, 1992: 615). Friedman (1955b: 402) found it 'fantastic' that his empirical estimates of the effect of unions on the wage structure should lead to only a rather unproductive theoretical rebuttal: 'I guess the farther grass looked greener to both of us.'

A Theory of the Consumption Function (1957) – which was labelled, in part, 'The Friedman Effect' – was perceived to have contributed towards putting 'trade cycle theory on what one might call "a fully expectational footing"' (Farrell, 1959: sections VII–VIII, 694). It also appears to occupy a transitional position with respect to Friedman's ability to engage his opponents in a statistical dispute. In his assault on one of Keynes's (1936a: 95) central propositions regarding the stability of the consumption function, Friedman (1957: 86, 231) argued that Keynesians such as Lawrence Klein had presented, as supporting evidence, regression results 'revealing a high degree of sophistication and ingenuity in statistical techniques and economic analysis', that were, nonetheless, 'almost worthless ... an illusion attributable to the method of analysis ... The consumption analyst, as it were, has been priding himself on his success in adding yet more epicycles.'

Friedman's (1957: ix) book is notable also for the 'almost complete absence of statistical tests of significance', but is widely regarded as 'one of the masterpieces of modern econometrics' (Blaug, 1985: 63). It also provoked an intense statistical exchange between Hendrik Houthakker (1958a, 1958b) and Robert Eisner (1958a) – who simultaneously (Eisner, 1958b) was defending Harrod-Domar-Hicks growth models against the 'Neo-Classical Resurgence', which was led by Tobin and Solow. Friedman (1958a: 991) thought he had been addressing the 'statistically sophisticated reader'. Houthakker, somewhat on the back foot, thought that 'Friedman had strained the statistical sophistication of his readers to the limit.' Part of the debate centred around 'alleged correlation[s]', and Houthakker (1958b: 991, 993) concluded by stating that 'the process of testing the hypothesis has only just begun'.

Houthakker's article was 'the first full frontal statistical assault on my work' (correspondence from Friedman, 18 April 1995). Friedman, and a growing body of associates and students, were venturing 'into almost virgin territory' which they expected would 'provoke controversy ... What the calculations of our critics do is to establish a presumption that further research along similar lines may be more rewarding than we thought was likely' (Friedman and Meiselman, 1965: 753, 784). What followed was the contest between the radio stations, FM versus AM (Ando and Modigliano). Friedman had found in econometric disputation the soft underbelly of the Keynesian system.

Schumpeter (1946: 196) wrote, in a now almost forgotten article on 'Keynes and Statistics', that 'Throwing discretion to the wind, they [the orthodox Keynesians] have attempted to rush trenches that are stronger than they looked to them. Econometricians behaved like the inexperienced armies of 1914–18, and with exactly analogous results... Keynes did not order these attacks.' It seems that those who neglect the study of history may be condemned to repeat it, the first time as tragedy, the second time as farce.

2.4.2 The Friedman critique of econometrics

Monetarism was projected, and interpreted, as a belief in the existence of a stable, empirically identifiable relationship between the rate of growth of the stock of money and the corresponding rate of inflation. However, although he is happy to describe himself as 'an empiricist', a perennial theme of Friedman's writings is a suspicion about the reliability of empirical results.[8] It was the 'impact of experience' of inflation which led to the 'rediscovery of money', not the 'serried masses of statistics massaged through modern computers'. What Koopmans in the 1940s called the 'Friedman critique', involved in part, an 'assault on structure', and in part was concerned to pour cold water on the postwar enthusiasm about the possibility of deriving causal relations from data. The 'exaggerated claims' of 'scientific magic' could not disguise the fact that 'every attempt... to forecast economic activity has to date met with failure.' In particular, it was 'a pure act of faith to assert that [Klein's] econometric model can predict the effect of policy changes, and there is no reason to share this faith until some evidence for it is presented' (Friedman, 1981: 30; 1975a, 176; 1948b, 140–1; 1951: 111). Robert Lucas (1976: 20) also found in Friedman's *A Theory of the Consumption Function* a forerunner of his critique of econometric policy evaluation.

A few citations from Friedman will illustrate this theme:

> Tinbergen's results are simple tautological reformulations of *selected* economic data... The methods used by Tinbergen do not and cannot provide an empirically tested explanation of business cycle movements. As W. C. Mitchell put it some years ago 'a competent statistician with sufficient clerical assistance and time at his command, can take almost any pair of time series for a given period and work them

into a form which will yield coefficients of correlation exceeding ±.9' [emphasis in text].

(1940: 659).

High *t* statistics and correlation coefficients are 'a test primarily of the skill and patience of the analyst' (1951: 108). Statistical evidence could be 'extremely misleading' (1962: 170), and was only available to confirm 'general reasoning' and to offer a guide to what is 'reasonable' (1953 [1951]: 231; 1953 [1947]: 312, n. 8); 'In view of the record of forecasters, it hardly needs to be argued that it would be better to shun forecasting and rely instead on as prompt an evaluation of the current situation as possible' (1948a: 253).

The opening words of *A Monetary History* were from Alfred Marshall:

> Experience in controversies such as these brings out the impossibility of learning anything from facts till they are examined and interpreted by reason; and teaches that the most reckless and treacherous of all theorists is he who professes to let facts and figures speak for themselves, who keeps in the background the part he has played, perhaps unconsciously, in selecting and grouping them, and in suggesting the argument *post hoc ergo propter hoc.*
>
> (1963)

> ... facts by themselves are silent ... The economist must be suspicious of any direct light that the past is said to throw on the problems of the present. He must stand fast by the more laborious plan of interrogating facts.
>
> (Marshall, cited by Friedman, 1953 [1949]: 90; 1950: 465; 1957, ix)

The interpretation of evidence 'cast up by experience, as opposed to controlled experiments, generally requires subtle analysis and involved chains of reasoning, which seldom carry real conviction' (1953: 10–11).

Friedman's (1957: 149–50; 1991: 36) emphasis on spurious correlation, and on the corresponding suspicion regarding statistics such as a high R^2, echoed Keynes's (1939: 561) sentiments and also foreshadowed later work by Tobin (1970), Granger and Newbold (1974) and Cooley and LeRoy (1981). It is consistent with Hendry's (1980) demonstration that cumulative rainfall outperforms the money stock in price equations, with R^2 approaching unity. Indeed, the problem of 'nonsense correlations' was commonly acknowledged in the interwar period (Yule, 1926), and Friedman was expressing a widely held view. The implication of Friedman's cynicism is that the 'shoot out at high noon' approach of the econometrics movement could only end inconclusively, at least at the level of conventional statistical criteria. (As it turned out this was highly accurate as a *prediction* of the forthcoming bouts between monetarists and Keynesians). The 'winner' would have to emerge on grounds other than those of conventional levels of statistical significance. Yet Friedman and Meiselman (1963: 166) were interpreted as having taken their stand in favour of the monetarist macroeconomic model on the grounds of superior econometric performance, as measured by the size of the correlation coefficient.[9] Rather late in the day, econometricians came to realize 'the futility of the R^2 game' (Poole and Kornblith, 1973: 916; Brainard and Cooper, 1975: 169–70; Samuelson, 1973: 389), that is the validity of parts of Friedman's critique of econometrics. A quarter of a century too late, Friedman's major empirical adversary recognized that with respect to the FM–AM dispute: 'I must acknowledge that the difference in parameters is partly the result of prior belief or ideology... There is obviously an ideological bias in assessing the value of parameters...we end up with somewhat different estimates of the same thing' (Modigliani, 1989: 578).

There were 'sharp differences of judgement' between members of the Cowles Commission (during its sojourn at Chicago) and economists at the University of Chicago (Hildreth, 1986: 5). In 1946–8, Friedman was a frequent participator at the Cowles Commission seminars. His relentless criticism prompted Koopmans to ask, 'But what if the investigator is honest?' (cited by Epstein, 1987: 107).[10] Friedman predicted that the Cowles Commission macroeconometric models would be revealed to be unsuccessful: 'The construction of a model for the economy as a whole is bound to be almost a complete groping in the dark. The probability that such a process will yield a meaningful result seems to be almost negligible.' Structural estimation was a 'blind alley for empirical research'; 'despairing of their abilities to reach quantitative answers by a direct analysis of these complex interrelationships, most investigators have sought refuge in empiricism and have based their estimations on historical relationships that have appeared fairly stable.' Like Keynes, he argued that prejudices or the 'psychological needs of particular investigators' would tend to predetermine the outcome: 'The background of the scientist is not irrelevant to the judgements they reach.' Friedman drew an analogy with Heisenberg's indeterminacy principle and 'the interaction between the observer and the process observed that is so prominent a feature of the social sciences...both have a counterpart in pure logic in Godel's theorem, asserting the impossibility of a comprehensive self-contained logic' (1943: 114; 1951: 113; 1953: 12, n. 11, 30, 5, n. 3).

In his contribution to *The Lives of the Laureates*, Friedman concluded that 'I've been very sceptical of the economic forecasts that people like myself and others make by using multiple regression analysis' (1988a: 88):

> I have long been sceptical of placing major emphasis on purely statistical tests, whether *t*-values, Durbin-Watson statistics, or any others. They are no doubt useful in guiding research, but they cannot be the major basis for judging the economic significance or reliability of the results and cannot be a substitute for a thorough examination of the quality of the data used.
>
> (1988b: 232, n. 11)

> Low standard errors of estimates, high *t*-values and the like are often attributes to the ingenuity and tenacity of the statistician rather than reliable evidence of the ability of the regression to predict data not used in constructing it ... In the course of decades [my] scepticism has been justified time and time again.
>
> (Friedman and Schwartz,, 1991: 49)

These judgements were not particularly original to Friedman; it would be equally appropriate to describe them as an elaboration of the Keynes Critique, or, indeed, as part of the Keynes-Tinbergen-Friedman-Phillips Critique.

2.4.3 The Keynes-Friedman Critique

Keynes noted that 'the inductive verification of the adherents of the [quantity] theory have been, I think, nearly as fallacious as those of its opponents'. Tinbergen's inclusion of a trend term was close to being 'a method for correcting imperfect results and obscuring the fact that the explanation given is the wrong one'. Superimposed on all of these problems is the 'frightful inadequacy of most of the statistics employed'. Keynes also highlighted what would later be called the model selection problem (JMK, XII [1912]: 765; 1939: 567; JMK, XIV [1938]: 287; 1940: 155–6). Statistical tests can neither prove a theory to be correct nor incorrect, since the latter requires that the proponents of the theory accept that all the auxiliary conditions of the test are neutral with respect to the refutation. The 'fiction' that econometricians can test the relationships provided by economic theory is retained only for the consumption of undergraduates (Pesaran and Smith, 1985: 145, 148, 139).

According to Roy Weintraub (1983: 18), in the 1930s there were two 'centres' of formalist work in the United States: the Cowles Commission and Paul Samuelson (later joined by Robert Solow). Samuelson (1976a: 25) observed that:

> By 1935 economics entered into a mathematical epoch. It became easier for a camel to pass through the eye of a needle than for a non-mathematical genius to enter into the pantheon of original theorist. A kind of Gresham's Law operated as those of us who benefited from it know only too well.

Keynes – with his 'tremendous capacity for mastery of detail' (Robinson, 1972: 534) – was concerned, in this context, that economists might 'lose sight of the complexities and interdependencies of the real world in a maze of pretentious and unhelpful symbols'. He cautioned against the 'pitfalls of a pseudo-mathematic method' (1936a: 298, 305, 275); he warned Sidney Alexander 'against the insidious disease of mathematics' (Samuelson, 1977: 73); and he wrote mockingly about 'those who feel a special confidence in a proposition which is expressed algebraically' (JMK, XI [1911]: 380–1). Samuelson (1946: 197) traced this animosity back to *A Treatise on Probability*. Economists were already too prone to 'specious precision' (Keynes, cited by Skidelsky, 1992: 540). Attempts to turn economics into a 'pseudo-natural science' would be counter-productive with respect to the training of economists: 'The pseudo-analogy with the physical sciences leads directly counter to the habit of much which is most important for an economist proper to acquire.' In his obituary of Marshall, Keynes (1924) emphasized that

> the master-economist must possess a rare *combination* of gifts. He must reach a high standard in several different directions and must combine talents not often found together. He must be a mathematician, historian, statesman, and philosopher – in some degree. He must understand symbols and speak in words.

W. S. Jevons brooded over his charts

> to discover their secrets. It is remarkable, looking back, how few followers and imitators he had in the black arts of inductive economics in the fifty years after 1862. But today he can certainly claim an

> unnumbered progeny, though the scientific flair which can safely read the shifting sands of economic statistics is no more common than it was.

This was the essence of Keynes's concern about the practices and habits likely to be acquired through the mechanical practice of econometrics: 'The question to be answered,

> however, is whether the complicated method ... employed [by Tinbergen] does not result in a false precision beyond what either the method or the statistics actually available can support. It may be that a more rough and ready method which preserves the original data in a more recognisable form may be safer.
>
> The truth is that sensible investigators only employ the correlation coefficient to test or confirm conclusions at which they have arrived on other grounds. But that does not validate the crude way in which the argument is sometimes presented, or prevent it from misleading the wary, – since not all investigators are sensible.
>
> (1924: 321; 1936b: 524; JMK, XIV [1938]: 296–7, 300; [1939]: 289; JMK, VIII [1921]: 466)

Thus, mechanical econometric procedures, Keynes thought, would 'displace insight and intuition and confine the scope of economics' (Pesaran and Smith, 1985: 146). Unlike intuition they could not offer a privileged description of economic reality (Keynes [1924], cited by Robinson, 1972: 536; Keynes [1942], cited by Dyson, 1979: 56–7).

Like Keynes, Friedman highlighted the objections to the Cowles Commission approach, based on 'the choice of "model" in their terminology ... the choice of a "structure" ... [and] the so-called "identification" problem'. Like Keynes (JMK, XIV [1938]: 287), he also discussed 'trial and error' specification searches and how they invalidate classical statistical inference procedures: 'Tinbergen's results cannot be judged by ordinary tests of statistical significance ... [his variables] have been selected after an extensive process of trial and error *because* [emphasis in text] they yield high coefficients of correlation.' Like Keynes, he objected to the use of trend terms, which were 'highly questionable on statistical grounds'. Like Keynes, he demonstrated that Tinbergen's coefficients were highly specific to the data that had been examined, and did not agree with other data. Like Keynes, he was alarmed by the 'excessively crude' data. Like Keynes, he questioned the validity of drawing meaningful interpretations from Tinbergen's results: 'The methods used by Tinbergen do not and cannot provide an empirically tested explanation of business cycle movements.' Like Keynes, he cautioned against economic theory becoming a species of 'disguised mathematics... a retreat into purely formal or tautological analysis' (1940: 659–60; 1953: 11–12, n. 11; 1953 [1949]: 77–8, n. 37; 1991).

2.4.4 The market for influence

The third perennial theme of Friedman's writing (in addition to confidence about monetarism and doubts about econometrics) is the Smithian case for competition as an irresistible force undermining the market power of producer groups (Friedman and Kuznets, 1945; Friedman, 1962b). Large-scale structural macroeconometric modelling was erecting (for non-Keynesians) a considerable barrier to entry into the policy marketplace (Walters, 1977: 834; Friedman, cited by Frazer, 1988: 707). Friedman had been preoccupied with monumental scholarly work, but from the mid-1950s, he began to address a wider audience (see, for example, Friedman, 1962b, his *Newsweek* column, his appearances before Congressional committees, plus his association with US Presidential candidate Barry Goldwater). As if to demonstrate the 'fertility of the market' and the 'generally unstable' and 'brief' (1962b: 158, 131) nature of these barriers to entry and other anti-competitive forces, he began to engage at this time in intense competition with Keynesian macroeconometrics:

> We were then trying to meet an argument on its own ground. I would never have been comfortable with the conclusions reached if the only basis for them had been the statistical correlations we were presenting. However, by 1963 the bulk of the *Monetary History* book had been written. I felt very confident in the evidence from history independently of the evidence from the statistical correlations, and hence regarded these as confirmatory rather than decisive evidence.
> (Correspondence from Friedman, 2 November 1993)

Friedman is widely regarded as the most persuasive debater in the economics profession (Blaug, 1985: 62; Stigler, cited by Rose Friedman, 1977: 26; Galbraith, 1987: 271). This stems, in part, from his conviction that 'You cannot be sure that you are right unless you understand the arguments against your views better than your opponents do' (1974: 16). His initial lack of influence has been attributed to 'his early habit of extreme aggressiveness in debate' (Breit and Ransom, 1971: 256, n. 57).

Indeed, in an article entitled 'Libertarians at Bay', Lincoln Gordon (1949: 976–8) from Harvard University argued that 'There has emerged in recent years a new fashion of egregious rudeness among self-styled libertarians . . . the Hayek-Mises-Jewkes-Graham manner . . . One can hardly escape the conclusion that Mr Graham's swimming suffers from a failure to understand which way is down.' But later, when the Keynesian tide turned, it was those who were losing policy-influence who displayed a 'bitterness beyond reason' (McCloskey, 1986: 184). A fair-minded observer noted that 'modern econometricians may well look askance at some of [Friedman's and Schwartz's] econometric methodology' (Goodhart, 1982: 1542). But the primary structural failure was not Friedman's lapse from best-practice structural estimation, but the failure of the econometrics fraternity to develop a suitably trained historical subdiscipline.

2.5 Phillips and Phillips curve econometrics: fresh textual evidence from 'The One and Only True and Complete Set of the Bones of The Saints'

Jacob Marschak had been Minister of Labour in the short-lived Menshevik government of the Terek Republic in the North Caucasus. He had an early encounter with perspicacious forecasts when a colleague warned him that this paedocracy (a government of children) would fall 'when the corn has grown high enough to conceal a man on horseback' (Koopmans, 1978: xii). He became Director (1943–8) of the Cowles Commission at Chicago, initially believing that structural estimation possessed a unique epistemological status: it was 'the Gospel . . . I hope we can become "social engineers"' (cited by Epstein, 1987: 69, 61, 67; Hildreth, 1986: 3–8; Malinvaud, 1988: 194; Klein, 1978: 326; Arrow, 1978). Frisch's description of the first European meeting of the Econometric Society at Lausanne in 1931 captured this heady enthusiasm.[11] Klein (1947: 111) believed that econometric models 'eventually should lead all investigators to the same conclusion'; Tinbergen believed that 'differences of opinion can, in principle, be localised' (1937: 73; Samuelson, 1992: 243).

At the risk of oversimplification we can describe the 'econometrics movement' as an attempt to locate the General Theory of Macroeconomic Structure, the quest for a 'single "final" equation' (Schumpeter, 1954: 1168, n. 20), or series of equations, with reliable estimated coefficients, a form of econometric fundamentalism. Combined with this pioneering confidence was a willingness to directly confront as many theoretical problems as their critics could muster, plus a deep understanding of the unsatisfactory nature of economic data. This sense of integrity gradually eroded such pioneering confidence, and contributed to the 'retreat from structure'. In many ways, it was Klein (1992: 184) who symbolized the ongoing faith in large-scale macroeconometric models, in opposition to the principle of parsimony.

The third 'wave' of macroeconometric enthusiasm – primarily associated with the construction of Keynesian Phillips curves – was the 'wave' most damaging to the prestige and scientific credibility of the economics profession. The opposition to the first 'wave' of macroeconometric enthusiasm (associated with Tinbergen's work in the 1930s) was led primarily by Keynes. The opposition to the second 'wave' (associated with the Cowles Commission) was led by Friedman.[12] This enthusiasm did not survive what Koopmans called the 'Friedman critique' (Epstein, 1987: 111). Disappointing empirical results led to the 'retreat from structure' after 1947.[13] Yet large-scale Keynesian macroeconometric models continued, often with *ad hoc* monetary sectors, and, following Klein and Goldberger (1955: 1), an ongoing 'constant adjustment'. Keynesian macroeconometricians abandoned their optimism concerning the revealing nature of structural estimation, and had come to rest, in part, on the *judgement* of the researcher (Tinbergen, 1969: 44; Zarnowitz, 1968: 427; Klein, 1971b: 48; Hildreth, 1986: 60; see Desai, 1981: 154 for the 'endogenise a bit more' approach to the pursuit of structure). The Keynesian Phillips curve macroeconometric models which collapsed in the 1970s were, together with their underlying method of research, effectively orphaned thrice: disowned by Keynes, abandoned by most of the Cowles Commission workers, and antithetical to both the spirit and the detail of Phillips's work.

Nevertheless, the third 'wave' of econometric optimism occurred simultaneously with the increased availability of computing power in the 1960s. Phillips was one of the most insightful critics of the Keynesian Phillips curve estimation industry. Like H. L. Moore (Stigler, 1962a), Phillips avoided controversy, but it is clear that in many important respects his work does not belong in the same category as most of the macroeconometric exercises of the 1960s. First, he pioneered the role of inflationary expectations in this type of macroeconomics. Secondly, many of these models did not adequately deal with money, but Phillips's model and his famous Machine were based on monetary dynamics. Thirdly, Phillips was opposed to the idea of trading off higher rates of inflation for supposed benefits with respect to unemployment. Fourthly, a decade before Clower and Leijonhufvud, Phillips was teaching Keynesian macroeconomics as a disequilibrium phenomenon (Lipsey, 1981: 547). Phillips's dynamic stabilization exercise was concerned to minimize the deviations of the business cycle 'pendulum', not to attempt to locate the macroeconomy at a point of other than 'rest'. Phillips provided the theoretical explanation behind Christopher Dow's (1967) subsequent empirical analysis of the destabilizing effects of fine tuning. His curve, however, came to be interpreted as a proposition that ongoing inflation would reduce the rate of unemployment, which Phillips had specifically cautioned against.

The complete, recently rediscovered seminar records of the LSE Staff Seminar on Methodology, Measurement and Testing (M^2T) capture the flavour of Phillips's influence. (The records of the M^2T Seminar series were titled by the words which head this section.) Richard Lipsey and his colleagues attempted to reconstruct economics as a series of empirically testable propositions. Arnold Harberger – who had been closely associated with the Cowles Commission during the 1950s (Hildreth, 1986: 64) and who shared Friedman's views of econometrics (correspondence from Friedman, 18 April 1995) – attempted to persuade the M^2T economists that their project was flawed because of the problem of the

> back door alibi ... Testing is subjective ... infinite number of possible H [hypotheses] to explain anything ... Trouble in econ[omics] – people will agree neither on which H are the most plausible nor on what experiment would be crucial ... Can't convince man who won't be convinced. Have to depend on what 'seems sensible' ... Scientist builds up picture of world. The more open to surprise the better. When surprised he amends picture. World complicated, need intuition.

Richard Lipsey explained that 'we want to be formal because we associate with people whose intuition we don't like and Harberger doesn't. Why does Harberger wince whenever Archibald says "rule"?' Harberger replied: 'Because these matters always subjective among the inquirers' (M^2T Seminar notes, February and March 1958).[14]

Phillips presented a paper on *The Problem of Refutation* on 27 April 1960 and 18 May 1960. He argued that static theory could not be tested from time-series data. Because of unstated maintained hypotheses, categorical statistical refutation was impossible. Autocorrelated time-series were treacherous data. 'Testing' was, in reality, little more than 'measurement plus' (M^2T Seminar notes). It seems that Phillips was influential in effecting the retreat from the 'Popperian notion of refutation' which Lipsey (1966: xx) drew attention to in the second edition of his *Introduction to Positive Economics*.

Rowley and Wilton (1973: 385, 387) re-estimated various Phillips curves using Generalized Least Squares, and concluded that the 'pseudo' *t*-values had been inflated by at least 100 per cent in most cases: 'One can only speculate whether the various authors would have advanced the Phillips curve model had they been faced with the GLS estimates rather than the OLS estimates.' Most of these models from the 1960s and early 1970s had been plagued by the unacknowledged problem of autocorrelation. Yet in the discussion following his paper on *The Problem of Refutation*, Phillips emphasized that with respect to data analysis he was only 'happy if not autocorrelated' (M^2T Seminar notes, May 1960). It is, therefore, appropriate to label these doubts about the macroeconometric practices that culminated in the Keynesian Phillips curve as the Keynes-Tinbergen-Friedman-Phillips Critique.[15]

2.6 Conclusion

The history of econometrics is worthy of more attention among practising econometricians than has hitherto been the case; it is a subject that should stand in equal status with other subdisciplines within econometrics. A disaggregated approach to Keynes's critique of econometrics reveals the nature of his objections to the underlying logic, and pretensions, of this relatively new approach to the analysis of economic data. His contemporaries were in no doubt as to the intensity of his hostility (Klein, 1951: 450–1). Keynes did not soften his position; in fact, Tinbergen came increasingly to recognize the validity of some of Keynes's criticisms.

There is a large degree of similarity between Keynes's position on econometrics and that of Friedman. The econometric disputes between Keynesians and monetarists which raged in (and perhaps disfigured) the profession were, from a methodological perspective, a sometimes ill-tempered conversation between Keynesians and the modern representative of Keynes. Keynes's opposition to macroeconometrics was based on the suspicion that results derived from this method of analysis would come (illegitimately) to be regarded as decisive evidence. This was also Friedman's suspicion. Likewise, Phillips deserves to be credited with a good deal of insight into the fundamental weaknesses of the Phillips curve estimation industry.

Gardiner Ackley (1961: 109) argued that historical misrepresentations (with respect to the myth of the 'Klassical' whipping boys) could be analytically fruitful. But analytically, Keynesian macroeconometrics left behind some 'jerry built structures' (Lucas, 1977) – most notably the trade-off interpretation of the Phillips curve – although Phillips (1968) developed parts of the critique which was subsequently named after Robert Lucas (Court, 1999; Peter Phillips, 1999). Friedman, Marschak and Tinbergen have also been credited with a similar approach to econometric policy evaluation (Lucas, 1976: 20; Pagan, 1987: 20). Thus, the collapse of the Keynesian Phillips curves in the 1970s was a vindication of both the Keynes-Tinbergen-Friedman-Phillips and the Friedman-Marschak-Tinbergen-Phillips critiques.

In his final posthumously published article, Keynes (1946: 177) bemoaned how much 'modernist stuff, gone wrong and turned sour and silly is circulating'. Many aspects of his critique of econometrics retain their validity with respect to contemporary practices.[16] Yet the tradition of 'fancier econometric footwork' (Lucas, 1976: 257) continues, often oblivious to some of the issues that alarmed Keynes, Friedman, Tinbergen, Phillips, et al.

Stigler (1963a: 63) suggested that 'methodological controversy has never had a marginal product (of scientific progress) above zero'; and this seems to capture Friedman's sentiments exactly. Friedman echoed Marshall's description of theory an 'a "language", designed to promote "systematic and organised methods of reasoning"'. Mitchell's style of research had fallen out of favour, in part, for reasons of 'language rather than substance ... and he uses no mathematics ... [but] his theoretical discussion can readily be translated into current jargon' (Friedman, 1953: 7; 1950: 489). Max Weber noted the tendency for intellectual opponents to avoid 'the other's terminology as though it were his toothbrush' (cited by Haberler, 1961: 40). Samuelson's formalist work, *Foundations of Economic Analysis* (1947), included on its title page the statement 'Mathematics is a Language.' Keynesian methods overran NBER statistical business cycle research, but Friedman's polemical genius led him to use Keynesian language (IS-LM, income-expenditure, money demand and econometrics) to effect a remarkable, if temporary, counter-revolution. Clearly, econometrics has a subterranean history which too many econometricians are unaware of.

I do not wish to be misunderstood. As David Hendry (1980: 395) put it, 'some editors can be persuaded to publish on the basis of econometric fools-gold: *caveat emptor*, but do not denigrate the whole project.' Econometric evidence has illuminated many debates and clarified some issues. It was, for example, careful empirical work which revealed that the consumption–income ratio appeared to be constant over long periods (Kuznets, 1942; Goldsmith, 1955), in contrast to the simple linear Keynesian consumption function (Keynes, 1936a: ch. 8; Davis, 1952). Yet the large macroeconometric forecasting models have not drastically improved in predictive accuracy in the last three decades (Hendry, 1980: 388; Leamer, 1983: 42; Pagan, 1987: 3–4; Epstein, 1987: 4; Rivlin, 1987: 2; Zarnowitz, 1992; Ormerod, 1994: 3). Neither can new classical macroeconometrics claim a greater degree of academic respectability than the Phillips curve equations which preoccupied applied econometricians in the 1960s. Monetary targeting, often based on applied econometric research, was also a disappointment. In addition, Friedman's forecasts of a surge in US inflation, beginning in mid-1984, and of a growth in real GNP of just 1 per cent for 1984: Q1, both proved to be inaccurate (Gordon, 1987: 441). He also made an unfortunate prediction that 'The world crude oil price cannot stay at $10 a barrel; it will drop dramatically within the next six or nine months...' (1974a: 12). Likewise, Granger-Sims style tests of exogeneity of the money supply have yielded mixed results (Cagan, 1989).

Macroeconometric modelling, however, remains a lucrative business (Tobin, 1977: 760; Galbraith, 1987: 261–2). Ragnar Frisch (1970: 152) spoke of the 'service to the econometrics fraternity by being critical and outspoken'. Clive Granger (1981: 124) has also appealed to model builders to pay more attention to econometric theory: 'One wonders what has been the purpose of the work of the majority of theoretical econometricians for the last twenty years, or of a third of the pages of *Econometrica.*' David Hendry (1980: 396) stated in his inaugural lecture that Keynes's critique should be 'compulsory reading' for econometricians. If applied econometricians paid as much attention to the history of their subject as they do to running regressions, this might improve the quality and reliability of the empirical side of our profession.

3
The Chicago Counter-Revolution and the Sociology of Economic Knowledge

3.1 Introduction[1]

3.1.1 Outline

George Stigler and Milton Friedman sought, and achieved, great influence both *internally* (within the economics profession) and *externally* (over a wider constituency).[2] The intellectual and policy transformations that occurred from the late 1960s were the combined product of internal forces (apparently impressive historical relationships between money and prices etc.) and external anxiety about perceived policy failures (high inflation and rising unemployment etc.). There is, of course, a link between the two (Keynes, 1936: 383–4). Stigler's *Theory of Price* was highly influential both within and outside the economics profession. When Stigler (1969a: 146) testified before the House of Representatives Select Committee on Small Business that his 'own goal is a competitive economy' (not a goal shared by Edward Chamberlin[3]), he was informed by the General Counsel that 'this subcommittee has a long record of being greatly infatuated with some of your ideas'; understanding his textbook had cost 'many hours of sleep' (Potvin, 1969: 150, 152).[4]

This chapter is concerned with the *internal* phenomenon. One model that can be invoked to explain this internal phenomenon is the classical process whereby evidence is patiently accumulated until the weight of the argument favours one side or another. Alternatively, Stigler's 'model' of the sociology of economic knowledge construction and destruction can be used to examine the internal opinion-changing process in the 'transition from the overwhelming defeat of Barry Goldwater in 1964 to the overwhelming victory of Ronald Reagan in 1980 – two men with essentially the same programme and the same message' (Friedman and Friedman, 1982: viii).

This essay takes the second route and constructs what Stigler (1982a: 92) called a 'science of science' explanation for the postwar Chicago academic and policy revolution.[5] It is inspired by Stigler's (1983a: 544) Nobel Lecture – 'learning more about how this search for new knowledge proceeds is itself a worthy search for new knowledge', – and by his reflection that 'it is true that in policy there is no tenable distinction between education and propaganda' (1967a: 285). Section 3.2 presents an overview of the 'sociological' perceptions of both Friedman and Stigler. Section 3.3 describes six aspects of Stigler's 'model' of the sociology of knowledge: the overwhelming hegemony of theory in economics (3.3.1); the crucial importance of internal developments as the primary force behind scientific change (3.3.2); his distinction between the elites and the masses in any discipline and the ability of the former to set the professional agenda (3.3.3); the usefulness of the technique of the huckster in popularizing economic ideas (3.3.4); and the unpredictable and therefore – to those in a hegemonic position – dangerous characteristics of the fox hunts of controversy (3.3.5). The sixth characteristic of Stigler's 'model' is a description of how to relegate to obscurity notions that might otherwise achieve prominence or even dominance (3.3.6).

The methodology of positive economics instructs researchers to tease out the *implications* of models and theories and to compare these implications with observed behaviour. Stigler's 'model' implies that paradigmatic challengers should unleash the unpredictable fox hunts of controversy, while those in hegemonic positions would be wiser to resist such challenges. Chicago *macro*economics was the paradigmatic challenger and Friedman successfully engaged his Keynesian opponents in a manner that could only undermine orthodoxy (Johnson, 1972). Chicago *micro*economics had powerful competitors originating from the two Cambridges, but 'the American Way... is to rely on competitive private enterprise' (Stigler, 1969b: 1) and Stigler and Friedman declined to provide combustible material which could fuel the monopolistic competition revolution. Section 3.4 outlines the emergence of what Chamberlin described as the 'Chicago School of Anti-Monopolistic Competition'. Section 3.5 describes Chamberlin's empirical challenge to Chicago (3.5.1); Stigler's views on the importance of testing economic theories and his encouragement of new and difficult research projects (3.5.2); and Stigler's and Friedman's exceptionally brief but firm refusal to engage either Chamberlin or Archibald in the kind of *micro*economic race that Chicago was successfully initiating at a *macro*economic level: 'The low point in the fortunes of imperfect competition' (Sutton, 1989: 226) (3.5.3). Concluding remarks are provided in section 3.6.6.

This chapter attempts to impose a framework on Stigler's thought that he would have recognized as a fair representation.[6] Two types of (diametrically opposed) readers may mistakenly conclude that I am inferring that Stigler and Friedman engaged in some sort of conspiracy (a view which Chamberlin came close to expressing[7]). The Chicago counter-revolution influenced the Thatcher–Reagan agenda (a topic that is outside the scope of this chapter) and its opponents feel they were manoeuvred from influence by devious means. Equally, some Chicago economists such as Harry Johnson (1971) and Don Patinkin (1969, 1972) have inferred that they detected some Chicago 'chicanery' in operation.[8] D. McCloskey (correspondence, 2 June 1997) also observed that 'I am one Chicago economist who can attest that George was little interested in scientific evidence, though he talked about it a lot – because he knew the culture honored it and he wanted to seem a scientist.'[9] But other Chicago economists have informed me that they regard Stigler as having been driven primarily by the weight of scientific evidence and only marginally by the sociological perceptions discussed in this chapter.[10] Indeed, one of 'Stigler's Laws' was paraphrased by Harry Johnson (1976: 19) as 'the more scientific it is, the less sociology helps to understand it.' But it is reasonable to infer that Stigler was motivated by a determination to further Chicago-style policies and perceptions (because he concluded that these perceptions were well supported by the evidence). This chapter is concerned to delineate the sociological influences that Stigler and Friedman brought to bear on their economics in general and the monopolistic competition revolution in particular. What follows is based on the assumption that Stigler's stated views on the sociology of economic knowledge are a reliable vehicle for such an analysis.

3.2 Stigler and Friedman

Stigler was a perceptive amateur sociologist of economic knowledge; he was awarded a Nobel Prize for his work on information theory and the functioning of markets, which he regarded as his most important contribution (1988b).[11] He also wrote about 'The Direction of Economic Research' and the market both *for* economists and *within* economics (1991, 1963b, 1967a, 1982a). Stigler thought that he had penetrated the veil of 'idealistic view[s]' which 'misdirects attention' but which are 'deeply imbedded' in professional economic thought. His 'model' of the sociology of economic knowledge was repeated in his Nobel Lecture (1983a: 536, 538, 542) and elsewhere; it consisted, among other things, of a human capital explanation of the reason why ideas in economics can be either fertile or sterile. His American Economic Association Presidential Address on 'The Economist and the State' began with a discussion of Smith's belief in the 'efficiency in the system of natural liberty' (1965a: 2), and contained several perceptive comments about the sociology of economic knowledge. These themes recurred throughout his career and informed his choice of research topics and (presumably) his method of popularizing the Chicago message. His perception was that there were basic similarities between 'Economic Competition and Political Competition' ; and that political decision-makers were endogenous participants in the political-economic process (1972a). Stigler (1987a: 52) 'frequently found great comfort' in reflecting on the confusion and misinformation that circulated among elites of which he disapproved.[12] He (1963c: 109) advocated competition between alternative perspectives on the grounds that it was unwise 'to give all our baskets to one egghead'. This chapter employs Stigler's analysis to explore the competition between the schools of economists that sought influence in the postwar period.

Milton Friedman never devoted as much ink as Stigler did to these sociological themes, but he was also a gifted amateur,[13] in addition to being a revolutionary historian (Friedman and Schwartz, 1963). He and Stigler were, intellectually and personally, very close: 'Mr. Micro and Mr. Macro at Chicago' (Becker, 1993: 762).[14] They were also both affiliated with the Mont Pelerin Society[15] and the Hoover Institution. Friedman (1986: 84) acknowledged his general intellectual debt to Stigler,[16] and it seems likely that he was influenced by Stigler in at least three crucial areas: his methodology of positive economics (section 3.5.2), running regression races between the quantity theory and the Keynesian consumption function (section 3.5.3) and the idea that misinformation in the labour market was responsible for deviations from the natural-rate of unemployment.[17] They were part of that extraordinary wave of Nobel Prize winning Chicago economists: Friedrich Hayek (1974), Friedman (1976), Theodore Schultz (1979), Stigler (1982), Merton Miller (1990), Ronald Coase (1991), Gary Becker (1992), Robert Fogel (1993), Robert Lucas (1995) and James Heckman (2000).

Stigler (1988a: 108–9) concluded that 'by 1980 there remained scarcely a trace of the two Harvard traditions of Chamberlin and Mason in the current work of economics', but monopolistic competition now appears to be fulfilling the promise that Harrod (1934: 470) discerned (it is currently central to new trade theory, game theoretic models and the New Keynesian revival). He had previously accepted, in part, the profession's 'hopelessly exaggerated opinion' concerning the importance of monopoly; but by the end of the 1950s he thought that 'the doctrine' of monopolistic competition was 'exhausted'. It is likely that Stigler contributed to this process: his 'negativism probably hindered further development...' (Rosen, 1993: 816).[18]

Hostility to various approaches to economics was not unique to Chicago and to Friedman and Stigler. Keynesians were hostile to the revival of the Quantity Theory, but they *failed* to undermine the revival. In contrast, the Chicago School were (at least for a while) *successfully* hostile to monopolistic competition, which according to Bishop (1964: 36) had become widely accepted and was opposed only by 'some determined pockets of resistance'. At an AEA symposium on Monopolistic Competition, the postwar Chicago tactics were perceived to have been counterproductive to the Chicago cause (Baumol, 1964: 44; Bain, 1964; Markham, 1964; Steiner, 1964). These or similar perceptions may have persuaded Friedman and Stigler to decline the invitation to be drawn into empirical testing. This chapter argues that the *tactics* of this hostility were consistent with Stigler's understanding of the sociology of economic knowledge [19]

Stigler argued that 'the chief work of economic theorists should for the present still be in the theory of perfect competition'; he was also concerned that formalist virtuosity and 'a mad scramble for originality [by] our younger theorists' had led to a 'poor use of the received doctrines'. He (1954a: 9; 1939: 481) wrote disparagingly of 'the tones of a stuffy formalist', and he sought to 'temper [the] over-enthusiastic devotees of the cult of correlations'. An 'indefinite period' (1955a: 300) could be devoted to the new analytical techniques associated with imperfect competition, which had become 'almost the dominant concern of economic theorists... a distracting fad'.[20] Monopolistic competition lent itself to one branch of the formalist revolution (mathematical investigations), and with the advance of computing power, Friedman successfully integrated the quantity theory into the other branch (econometrics). But monopolistic competition was denied the momentum that would have resulted from Stigler and Friedman accepting the challenge offered by Chamberlin and Archibald.

Stigler warned that 'intellectual and political influences are extraordinarily subtle and difficult to trace or measure'; 'all short answers are wrong'.[21] He (1988c: 9) concluded that Keynes sought to be, not a dentist, but 'a brain surgeon who operated on ideologies', and this analogy could be applied to Stigler and Friedman who sought to influence the process of knowledge construction and destruction. This chapter examines the Chicago counter-revolution as a product of their 'superior understanding' not so much of the behaviour of economic variables, but of the sociology of professional economic knowledge: 'Our ratio of objective scientific work to policy rationalization is high only in comparison to other social sciences'; 'We wish to be scientists... We wish also to be important... A curious tension' (Stigler 1975: 316–7; 1976a: 352–3). Friedman and Stigler spent time discussing the nature of influence and how opinions were to be changed (Stigler, 1980: 353; 1988c: 11; McCloskey, 1994: 341–2).[22] This chapter assumes that they behaved *as if* they were self-conscious counter-revolutionaries.

3.3 Stigler's 'model' of the sociology of economic knowledge

3.3.1 Theories are trumps

Stigler (1957b: 9; 1954b: 103) noted that economists have a tendency to 'float on the tide of theory'. He reflected that empirical generalizations 'fail to achieve the continuity and the widespread influence of the formal theories'.[23] He was also aware that for theorists, statistically derived relationships could be 'frankensteins over which he has little or no control'. Galbraith, for example, looked at the same empirical studies as himself but derived opposite inferences (Stigler, 1939: 470; 1949a: 96).

With respect to conclusions that contained policy implications, Stigler (1951: 127–8) sought to elevate received theory over empirical analysis.[24] The reason for this confidence in orthodoxy was that it was 'our *most tested* and reliable instrument for relating policies to effects [emphasis added]' (1964a: 421). Received theory, presumably, operated with a considerable advantage.[25] The idea that a new theory 'is presumed innocent until shown guilty... is the exact opposite of the presumption I would use' (1982b: 204; 1978: 191).

Not all theorists were to be trusted;[26] unorthodox approaches were sometimes denied the label 'theory'. Galbraith's notion of countervailing power was not a theory but a 'dogma' and rested on 'allegations' of economic life; in the 1930s it would 'have attracted no one'. Galbraith's policy implications should be 'left untouched' because to quarrel with those implications would imply 'that the theory had reached the stage of relevance to policy... Galbraith cannot persuade us that we should turn our economic problems over to Santa' (1954a: 9–10, 14). Likewise, monopolistic competition had 'failed to initiate a fundamentally new direction of economic theorising' (1988b: 93).

3.3.2 The crucial importance of internal developments

Stigler criticized the attempt to explain how economic ideas gained currency by reference to environmental factors, objecting to Wesley Mitchell's downgrading of 'intellectual stunt[s] [to] a secondary rather than a primary force'. Stigler concluded that the 'dominant influence upon the working range of economic theorists is the set of internal values and pressures of the discipline. The subjects for study are posed by the unfolding course of scientific developments' (1965b [1960]: 18, 22, 27–8; see also Sowell, 1987: 498). Friedman found Mitchell's course on the history of economic thought 'dull' and his view that 'theories had no life of their own' to be 'in sharp contrast to the history of thought as developed many years later by George Stigler'. Friedman shared Stigler's views about the importance of 'the internal logic of the subject... The contrast between Chicago and Columbia was sharp' (Friedman and Friedman, 1998: 44).

3.3.3 The elite and the masses

It was Stigler's ability to set the agenda (positively and negatively) which underpinned his influence among economists (McCann and Perlman, 1993: 997); he believed that any assessment of a scholar's achievements should include 'not only what he wrought but also what he prevented' (Stigler, 1990a: 12). Stigler (1969c: 227; 1951: 126; 1982a: 60) clearly distinguished between 'major scientific entrepreneurs' and the rest, some of whom could only employ 'an inferior mind', and some of whom were '*ersatz* economists'. They entered the market as demanders, not suppliers, of ideas, and conference participants reminded Stigler (1977: 441) of travelling salesman exchanging stale jokes. He believed that economists were analogous to the purchasers of second-hand automobiles and he wondered why some ideas 'wouldn't run far or carry many passengers' (1986 [1982]: 134–5; [1979]: 340). Part of the explanation involved a quality differential: 'which socialist propagandist has been as logically lucid as Friedman?'

Stigler (1978: 201) concluded in his study of 'The Literature of Economics' that two-thirds of the articles surveyed were virtually worthless.[27] There were commonly only about six really first-class scholars in any field (1963b: 37); a small minority in the profession had 'superb instincts' with regard to the pursuit of ideas. The 2 or 3 per cent of the profession who were 'active and ambitious' were also 'reform[ers] of economic science' (1988d: 95). Occasionally, 'economists-missionaries' successfully ventured into the territory of 'apprehensive and hostile natives' (1984: 304), but academic consensus (which could be unreliable) was achieved not by a professional 'plebiscite', but only by an elite group within the profession (1991: 44; 1985: 1). Science was *defined* as the consensus interpretations that emerged from this process.[28] In contrast, for the 'mass' of scholars in any discipline, risk aversion, and a desire to preserve already acquired human capital, created a bias in favour of scientific conservatism.

Given this structure of the sociology of economic knowledge, the 'most irresistible' of all the weapons of scholarship was 'infinite repetition', a 'form of the classical Chinese torture' (1965b: 4; 1984: 311; 1986 [1979]: 339). Stigler (1965b [1959]: 286) was impressed by the Fabian Society's 'effectiveness in shifting opinion. If enough able and determined men – and the number in the Fabian group was almost unbelievably small – denounce and denounce again a deficiency, that deficiency becomes grave.'

3.3.4 The technique of the huckster

Stigler displayed an understanding of 'the technique of the huckster' by which change is effected among economists. He believed that intellectuals suffered from 'romantic wishfulness' in their understanding about influence; a Darwinian 'survivor technique' was useful: 'if I wish to know whether a tiger or a panther is the stronger animal, I put them in the same cage and return after a few hours':

> Great economists are those who influence the profession as a whole, and this they can do if their doctrines do not involve too great a change from the views and the knowledge of the rank and file of the science. It is simply impossible for men to apprehend and to adopt wholly unfamiliar ideas... New ideas are even harder to sell than new products... One must put on the best face possible and much is possible. Wares must be shouted – the human mind is not a divining rod that quivers over truth. The techniques of persuasion also in the realm of ideas are generally repetition, inflated claims, and disproportionate emphases, and they have preceded and accompanied the adoption on a large scale of almost every new idea in economic theory... It is possible by mere skill of presentation to create a fad, but a deep and lasting impression on the science will be achieved

> only if the idea meets the more durable standards of the science. Among these standards is truth, but of course it is not the only one. (Stigler, 1975: 318–19; 1988b: 99, 108; 1968a: 72–4; 1955b: 294–6)[29]

The price mechanism operated here, as elsewhere: 'It is perfectly reasonable for individuals to purchase intellectual integrity as well as meat and wine – always provided that the price is not too high' (Stigler, 1988e: 8).

Stigler bemoaned the 'attitudes of professional economists . . . when economists agree that a movement is inevitable, it is not' (1950a: 30, 34). He argued that the knowledge production industry was a competitive industry in which 'confused' participants would 'watch their customers vanish, their best employees migrate, their assets dissipate'. A monopolist was 'overwhelmingly dominated by forces over which he has negligible control' (1963b: 42).

Stigler clearly had an ability to provoke his audience (Samuelson 1962: 9),[30] as illustrated by his Harvard lecture, 'The Politics of Political Economists', on the 'mysterious intellectual osmosis' that economists are subjected to. Radicals, he argued, tended to be anti-empirical, but scientifically trained economists tended to be politically conservative because of their exposure to price theory: 'We shall no doubt continue to bend before a strong [anti-conservative] wind, but I consider it a remarkable effect of our professional discipline that we shall not be contributing to the wind' (1959a: 528–5).[31]

Later, Stigler (1965b: 48–9) pondered about the role of 'fashion' in economics and the 'truly remarkable' process by which Keynesian economics diverted attention away from more traditional research agendas. He then echoed his Harvard sentiments: economics had become highly respectable but was 'lacking in promise in basic influence on policy in the future. I do not know whether it is an occasion for pride or for regret that the economist is using Marquis of Queensberry arguments in an arena where emotional brass knuckles continue in fashion.'

Stigler was impatient with alternative perspectives, and from the late 1970s he 'governed' the ethics of conversation at Chicago. Criticisms of his work, even those which appeared in major journals, often did not command his attention or respect,[32] and according to one of his Chicago colleagues, exchanges with Stigler were 'likely to be terminated by a positivist edict and a sneer' (McCloskey, 1994: 14).

3.3.5 The fox hunts of controversy

Stigler (1978: 200–1, 185) made numerous other perceptive comments about the nature of controversy in economics: 'If controversy is active almost every proposition seems open to debate, and the course of controversy shifts as rapidly as the situs of a fox hunt – indeed, a series of simultaneous and intersecting fox hunts.' The fundamentally pervasive concept of competition had long been treated with 'the kind of casualness with which one treats of the intuitively obvious'. But Frank Knight's *Risk, Uncertainty and Profit,* with its comprehensive and 'meticulous' discussion of perfect competition, was counterproductive for the Chicago School: it 'did most to drive home to economists generally the austere nature of the rigorously defined concept and so prepared the way for the widespread reaction against it in the 1930s.' Stigler (1956a: 270) reflected on Alfred Marshall's opposition to this ongoing attempt to attach 'more restrictive' conditions to the concept of competition. According to Stigler, Marshall's opposition was motivated by sociology of knowledge considerations: he sought to avoid introducing complications that might lessen the appeal of competition ('He wished to retain for competition its traditional claim as the great engine of progress...').

The 'more persuasive' defence of the concept of perfect competition is that it has 'defeated its newer rivals in the decisive area: the day-to-day work of the economic theorist' (1957b: 1, 11, 17). Price theory was scientifically more mature, and therefore stronger, than macroeconomics because of the homogeneity of doctoral citation practices – with the exception of the 'exclusive appeal of monopolistic competition to Harvard' (Stigler and Friedland, 1975: 503; 1979).

> Scientific literature is to a considerable degree controversial literature. New ideas are sold very much the way new automobiles are sold: by exaggerating their superiority over the older models... Scientific innovation proceeds more by disparagement of rivals than by excessive self-praise, perhaps because it appears more modest. The role of controversy is indeed to stimulate interest and animosity... The sterility of the early Walrasian system arose because it was ignored by most economists and adopted by a few but criticised by almost none. Milton Friedman's work was bound to be spread rapidly in the science and to achieve a wide scope and high rigour because of his wondrous gift of eliciting the probing attention of eminent contemporaries.
>
> (1969c: 222)

Friedman was 'a masterful peddler... intellectuals sell their wares to customers, and they – not the customers – do most of the adapting' (1975: 321, 315).[33]

3.3.6 Neglect – the highway to oblivion

Kelvin's dictum is inscribed on the front of the Chicago Social Science Research Building: 'When you cannot express it in numbers, your knowledge is of a meagre and unsatisfactory kind' (McCloskey, 1986: 7; Stigler, 1988c: 12). Knight (1960: 166, n.18) thought that this statement 'very largely means in practice, If you cannot measure, measure anyhow', and Viner rejoined that 'our knowledge after measurement would still be meagre and unsatisfactory' (cited by Stigler, 1982c: 23). Stigler (1992: 462) welcomed 'formidable' empirical challenges to economists: 'Ease of solution . . . is not the best guide in the selection of agenda for scientific research.'

Stigler (1959a: 529) and Friedman were prepared to find proxies for all sorts of variables, believing that empirical economics was the only way to obtain a reliable feel for the way an economic system functioned. The literature of the public utility specialists was defective because it had failed to measure the effects of regulation; but Stigler and Friedland (1962: 3, 11) were prepared to ask 'impertinent' empirical questions to remedy this defect. Stigler (1965d: 62–3, 68, 57) reflected on the 'truly remarkable . . . degree of indolence or lack of curiosity' which economists had exhibited by not empirically examining the regulatory experience. Economists had 'found imperfections, because this is an imperfect world', and they had advocated state intervention without investigating the consequences of intervention. Asking new empirical questions could lead to 'very striking' results. Economists had neglected the questions that Stigler had formulated: they had 'not studied the past'. This neglect had led to policy consequences that relied upon an exaggerated respect for the competence of the state and a diminished faith in market solutions.

But Stigler and Friedman declined to provide fuel for the locomotive of the monopolistic competition revolution of which they disapproved. This decision may have been influenced by Stigler's sociological perceptions:

> Once an idea is widely accepted, it is guaranteed a measure of immortality. Its decline in popularity is more often due to changing interests than to contrary evidence, no matter how powerful that evidence may be . . . Even to be demolished is better for one's self-esteem than to be ignored: It requires some ability to excite and especially to outrage one's fellow professionals . . . Neglect is the highway to oblivion.
>
> (Stigler, 1988a: 67, 75, 112, 157, 159, 97, 162, 166, 213, 216; Stigler and Kindahl, 1973: 721, n. 6)

Stigler's assault on the Giffen paradox was designed to push the discussion of it 'deeper into footnotes' (1947b: 156); to become boring was a preliminary to the dissipation of professional interest (1962b: 1).[34]

Stigler (1978: 200–1) also reflected that the textbooks of a discipline 'play a powerfully conservative role in the transmission of doctrine ... adverse empirical evidence is not a decisive factor... to understand the rate of decline of a theory.' In 1942, Stigler published half a textbook (*The Theory of Competitive Price*), and four years later he published the full version including material on monopolistic competition (*The Theory of Price*). This text was enormously influential; later imitators tended to be both sequence and content-takers. Just as the 'beginning student of physics does not demur at the absence of friction', so the student of economics is exposed first of all to perfect competition: 'competition is a better single assumption, even on the basis of realism, than monopoly' (Stigler, 1946: 23). According to Chamberlin (1946: 416), early reviewers objected that the 'natural and easy way' would have been to begin with the individual firm and monopolistic competition. Stigler was prompted to adopt this sequence because to reverse it would have meant 'not merely a reversal of order, but a revolution in the author's thinking'. From a pedagogical perspective, perfect competition and monopoly possess a simplicity and an accepted theoretical framework that cannot be found in the later chapters on oligopoly and monopolistic competition.

Stigler (1949a: 104) was alarmed about the nature of knowledge construction and destruction in economics: 'ours has become a flabby science'.[35] Means's theory of administered pricing had at first incited a lot of controversy and empirical analysis; later it displayed 'growing anaemia; it is fair to say that economists abandoned the close study of the subject, less because its lack of scientific import was established than because it became boring' (1968a [1962]: 235). The ideas of those who found a clash between traditional price theory and observed behaviour often had a 'Phoenix property', but 'it takes a locomotive of sorts to keep an idea moving in science': 'the reworking of predecessors' ideas will seldom lead to very fresh work, and after a while this source seems to become boring – at least these economists tend to leave economic theory after a while'; 'a concept without enemies... is also a concept without informed friends' (1982a: 52; 1951: 126).[36]

3.4 The emergence of the Chicago School of Anti-Monopolistic Competition

Paul Samuelson (1967: 108, n.5, 113, 116, 138), reflecting on 'Chamberlin's imperishable vision', predicted that:

> Reality will falsify *many* of the important qualitative and quantitative *predictions* of the competitive model . . . Chamberlin, Sraffa, Robinson and their contemporaries have led economists into a new land from which their critics will never evict us . . . Chicago economists can shout until they are blue in the face that there is no elegant alternative to the theory of perfect competition . . . it is significant that Marshall's remaining defenders among theorists tend to be those satisfied with perfect competition as an approximation to reality [emphases in text].

In contrast, Stigler (1955b: 301) described the 1930s as exhibiting 'an excess of originality'. His thesis supervisor, Frank Knight, stated that 'if there is anything I can't stand it's a Keynesian and a believer in monopolistic competition' (Samuelson, 1983: 7).[37] But Friedman and Stigler did not share Knight's fatalistic despair about the Chicago project for social and economic transformation;[38] neither did they share his lack of interest in empirical or policy-orientated economics or his belief in the inherent contradiction between thought and action (Stigler, 1982a: 167; Buchanan, 1991; Kern, 1987: 640; Patinkin, 1973: 796, 804–5). Both attended his seminars on the sociologist Max Weber; he was their dominant dinner-table subject of conversation (Wallis, 1993: 775). According to Shils, Knight 'offered a great deal to a sociologist' (1981: 181, 184; see also Schweitzer, 1975). This sociological perceptiveness involved doubt about the outcomes of rational debate: 'Frank Knight's First Law of Talk' was that 'cheaper talk drives out of circulation that which is less cheap' (Knight, cited by Patinkin, 1973: 807).

In the 1940s, what later became known as the Chicago School faced danger on two fronts. With the loss of Paul Douglas and Henry Schultz, and with Knight's diminished interest in economics, there was a shortage of intellectual leaders. There was also a struggle for academic dominance and institutional control at Chicago between the Friedman group and the Cowles Commission, a struggle that was resolved in 1955 with the departure of Cowles to Yale (Reder, 1982: 4; 1987: 415). 'The Chicago School of Anti-Monopolistic Competition' was first explicitly defined and described by Chamberlin (1957: 296); only then did economists begin to refer to Chicago as a School (Stigler, 1988a: 150).[39] The modern Chicago School began to take shape, culminating in the famous 1960 'Coase versus Pigou' evening at Aaron Director's house which was 'the most exciting intellectual event' of Stigler's life. The evening ended up with 'no votes for Pigou' and effectively partitioned economics into two epochs: A.C. and B.C. ('Before Coase'). According to Stigler (1983: 221; 1988a: 75, 148–69; 1992: 456; 1972b: 11) the previous epoch had confused 'all economists... from at least 1890 until 1961'.[40] The realization that Pigou had previously obtained such a 'hold', even in places like Chicago, generated both enthusiasm and sociological reflectiveness. It also laid out a detailed research agenda for the Chicago School and the *Journal of Law and Economics* (Coase, 1995: 242–4).[41] The potency of the Coase conversion evening may have been intensified for Stigler given the 'mistakenly' Pigovian role that Coase allocated to the second edition of his *Theory of Price* (1952).[42]

Knight had not provided a Chicago agenda of research (Stigler, 1973b: 520); only in the late 1950s was Friedman able to fully engage his Keynesian opponents. This was a fight – undertaken with strategic considerations in mind – against the 'conditioned reflex[es]' of 'entrenched Keynesianism' (Friedman, 1968: 5, n.2). In 1958, Friedman was joined at Chicago by Stigler, who, intellectually, became 'more vertically integrated' (Rosen, 1993: 814). Lester Telser concluded that 'perhaps what [Stigler] learnt from Friedman was focus'.[43] This enhanced focus and the connecting up of the various components of his expertise (microeconomics, controversy and sociology of economic knowledge) produced an extraordinarily creative phase, for which he would later be awarded a Nobel Prize (Stigler 1961b, 1962a). Harry Johnson's arrival in 1959 also strengthened the Chicago School, which was, according to Bhagwati (1977: 225–6), at the time

> very Friedmanesque... The seminars seemed to oscillate between proving that elasticities were large with markets therefore stable, and formulating competitive hypotheses for apparently imperfectly-competitive industries and coming up with high enough R^2s. Econometrics was the handmaiden of ideology: things looked imperfect to the naked eye, especially to that of Chamberlin and Joan Robinson, but they were 'really' not so and the world was 'as if' competitive... market imperfections were 'demonstrated' to be negligible and the imperfections rather of government intervention were the subject of active research.[44]

In terms of *micro*economic controversy, both Cambridges had powerful alternative theories to the Chicago belief that consumers direct the production process (Stigler, 1976a: 347). Chamberlin (1933) subtitled his book *A Reorientation of the Theory of Value*, and he devoted his career to the proposition that the firm is the essential structural unit of the economy (1957: 44). Joan Robinson (1933: v; 1934: 105) attempted to develop Sraffa's 'pregnant suggestion' that the whole theory of value should be reconstructed around the concept of monopoly, thus 'emancipating economic analysis from the tyranny of the assumption of perfect competition'. These were self-consciously revolutionary attempts to construct a general parameter theory (Schneider, 1967: 144), which could be combined with general equilibrium models (Chamberlin, 1957: 68; Jaffe, 1934: 27; Triffin, 1940). Together with Keynes's work, the monopolistic competition revolution captivated the economics profession both between the wars and in the immediate postwar period (Keynes, JMK, XXIX [1938]: 175–6; Nichol, 1934; Galbraith, 1948; Bain, 1948; Bishop, 1964). In the Preface to his seventh edition, Chamberlin (1956) noted that his bibliographic supplement had expanded by 806 titles in the eight years since the sixth edition. This was more than the entire period prior to 1948: 'important evidence' that monopolistic competition was acquiring the mantle of generality.

Traditional economic theory had created a presumption against social interference in the market place; but imperfect competition questioned the generally accepted conclusions of economic theory (Morrison, 1934: 30; Harrod 1934: 463; J. Robinson, 1952: 925–6). Although Chamberlin was personally quite conservative, monopolistic competition was associated with the weakening of competitive ideology, and its supporters tended to take their stand on a variety of positions that were antithetical to Chicago economics (Fellner, 1967: 12).[45] The immediate postwar period had witnessed 'frequent and heavy bombardment[s]' on monopolistic competition from Chicago (Markham, 1964: 53). These tactics were perceived to have been counter-productive to the Chicago cause: 'It must be emphasised here that even the writings of those who would minimise the contribution of monopolistic competition, by their very number and vociferousness combine to constitute an encomiast, as it were, praising by strong (and frequent) damns' (Baumol, 1964: 44).

Economic theory had long accepted the coexistence of perfect and imperfect competition, and Stigler (1948: 915) concluded that the latter was 'a minor variant' from competition. According to Arnold Harberger, the behaviour of the US manufacturing sector could be accurately analysed through the model of perfect competition; the per capita welfare losses associated with monopoly amounted to no more than $2 (1954; see also Friedman, 1965: 55). But Machlup (1939: 231, 236) concluded that the 'increased dose of realism that was won for economic theory' by monopolistic competition had led economists to *emphasize* product differentiation and the frequent occurrence of oligopoly. The new theories had 'clear practical value' for policy-makers.[46] These microeconomic disputes were ferociously debated: one of the discussants of the

Galbraith-Stigler AEA session on 'Fundamental Characteristics of the American Economy' concluded that the author of the notion of countervailing power was 'one of the most effective enemies of both capitalism and democracy' (McCord Wright, 1954: 30).

The cultures of Chicago and the two Cambridges appear to leave an indelible imprint on their respective students, and on the subject matter of their doctoral dissertations (*American Economic Review*, 1960: 864–91). Colander and Klamer's (1987) survey revealed that only 6 per cent of Chicago students thought that price rigidities were very important (compared to 38 per cent at Harvard), and 84 per cent of Chicago students (but only 7 per cent of MIT students) agreed that inflation was primarily a monetary phenomenon.[47] Stigler concluded that Friedman's 'persistent and skilful use of price theory in dealing with economic questions...was thoroughly drilled into graduate students' at Chicago (cited by Rose Friedman, 1977: 24). Stigler (1969c: 221) also complained of the 'block to proper reading' that MIT students exhibited towards Friedman's work, and a student trained using either the 1966 edition of Stigler's *The Theory of Price* or Friedman's *Price Theory* (1962) would remain unaware of the monopolistic competition revolution, with the exception of a footnote referring to Joan Robinson and the effect of price discrimination on output (Stigler, 1966: 214, n.12).[48] Friedman and Stigler concluded that monopolistic competition 'possesses none of the attributes that would make it a truly useful general theory...It is therefore incompetent to deal with a host of important problems.' Its contribution has been limited to 'enriching the vocabulary available for describing industrial experience' (Friedman, 1953: 38–9), of which 'something like 98 per cent of the general [industrial organization] literature is concerned, explicitly or implicitly with the question of monopoly' (Stigler, 1959a: 530). Monopolistic competition appears only in a single paragraph (plus the Appendix) in *The Organisation of Industry*, a paragraph which concludes that 'it has not been found useful in the analysis of concrete economic problems' (Stigler, 1968a: 13; in contrast, see Scherer, 1970).

Stigler's (1937: 707–8, 710, 713) second appearance in the professional literature, however, was an essay on 'A Generalization of the Theory of Imperfect Competition' in which he suggested a framework for research in the 'imperfections of competition in agriculture'. The essay examined the realism of the assumptions of perfect competition, concluding that one could 'add much realism' by eliminating some of these assumptions; the non-economic motives for land ownership by farmers 'seem exceptionally amenable to empirical investigation'.

3.5 Chamberlin and Archibald versus Chicago

3.5.1 Chamberlin's challenge

The Theory of Monopolistic Competition began as a doctoral dissertation (submitted in 1927) and went through eight editions (1933–62). According to Stigler (1988a: 96), Chamberlin (1899–1967) was 'possessed' by his theory.[49] Alfred Sherrard (1951: 126, 142) thought that Chamberlin's contribution had so far proven more 'illusory' than revolutionary:

> Another wing, or perhaps a porch, has been added to economic theory; but the structure retains its original form . . . But as deliberate product differentiation, advertising and salesmanship take the centre of the stage, economic theory in the traditional sense must depart. A revolution in analysis is called for – a new set of questions, a new philosophical foundation.

Wallis (1949: 559) suggested that monopolistic competition theories should be tested to see how well they could 'organise, predict or rationalise observed advertising behaviour'.

Chamberlin devoted less of his career to the empirical investigation of his favoured market structure than to his acute sense of product differentiation, insisting that every Harvard PhD candidate understood the precise differences between imperfect competition and monopolistic competition (Johnson and Johnson, 1978: 153; see, for example, Chamberlin, 1937).[50] But in *Towards a More General Theory of Value*, Chamberlin made a case for the revolutionary generality of his approach, citing Tinbergen's explanation for the unsatisfactory response of economists: 'There is a lag of measurement behind theory, which forces the users of applied economic theory to stick to the older and simpler theories' (Tinbergen, cited by Chamberlin, 1957: 9, n.10). The 'right wing orthodoxy' of the Chicago School who 'cling desperately to perfect competition' could offer only a 'jumble of reasons . . . a cloud of dust' to defend the status quo: 'mere tricks to bolster up what is at bottom an emotional position . . . surely better sticks than this could be found . . . people who live in *ad hoc* houses should be more indulgent' (1957: 13–15, 17, 26, 300, 305). Chamberlin sought to overcome this 'heavy' legacy by reformulating his theory to assist the process of measurement (1957: 24, 43, 70–91; 1957 [1948]: 226–49). He (1957: 305–6) concluded that his hypothesis had come into existence following the 'classical' scientific process outlined in 'The Methodology of Positive Economics'. He had edited the proceedings of an International Economic Association conference on *Monopoly and Competition* (1954b), contributing an essay on the difficulties of 'Measuring the Degree of Monopoly and Competition', which included a suggested classification of the concept of monopolistic competition (1954a: 265).

3.5.2 Stigler and the importance of testing theories

Stigler (1963c: 109) concluded that economics would have 'suffered grievously' had he been research 'dictator' in the 1940s.[51] Chamberlin (1957: 140, 299) also took an interest in this evolution of Stigler's position. As a graduate student at Chicago, Stigler organized Saturday morning seminars on monopolistic competition in the belief that Chamberlin's work would revolutionize economics (Wallis, 1993). About one-third of the first edition of Stigler's *The Theory of Price*[52] was devoted to a discussion of monopolistic competition (1946: v, 195–302, 312–14).[53] Referring to 'dissatisfaction with the neoclassical theory of competition', Stigler complained that economics was in an 'unsatisfactory state'. There were, he argued, two obstacles before perfect competition could render to monopolistic competition the mantle of generality. The first was variety, that is the infinite number of conceivable departures from perfect competition. But this was not insurmountable: 'It would usually be possible to establish sensible classifications which would reduce the problem to much more manageable proportions, and in fact this has been done in good part.' The second was 'ignorance... primarily an ignorance of relevant assumptions... the more urgent need is for factual knowledge. Until this knowledge becomes available – and this is a slow, accretionary process – the detailed content of the theory of imperfect competition will remain in large degree intuitive' (1946: 197–8, v). Stigler (1944: 81) objected to the 'formalism' associated with the theory: 'Real progress in the theory now requires a shift in emphasis from mathematical analysis... to detailed studies of individual market structures.'

Friedman dominated the thoughts and practices of the profession as a methodologist, several years before his thoughts on money attracted similar attention. For a decade he was closely involved with methodology, planning at one stage to write a book on the subject. In November 1947 he informed Stigler that 'I have gotten involved for various irrelevant reasons in a number of discussions of scientific methodology related to the kind of thing you are talking about'; this interest apparently waned after 1957 (Hammond, 1991b: 3, 34; Stigler, 1994). His methodology of positive economics was formulated as a 'reaction' to Robinson and Chamberlin, and a 'reply' to a series of empirical studies which questioned the relevance of orthodox price theory (Moss, 1984; Friedman, 1993: 770).[54] Keynesian economics and monopolistic competition share a common concern for the 'accuracy' of assumptions; the early drafts of his methodological essays reveal Friedman's interest in rebutting the assault on microeconomic orthodoxy.[55]

Stigler provided one of the first written expositions of this methodology of positive economics in a lecture at the LSE on 'Monopolistic Competition in Retrospect',[56] concluding that the dispute between monopolistic competition and the theory of competition was 'a question of fact, and must be resolved by empirical tests of the implications of the two theories (*a task the supporters of the theory of monopolistic competition have not yet undertaken*) [emphasis added]' (1949b: 22–5, 13, 45; 1949a: 102–4). Stigler (1955c: 13–14) stated that the dispute between full cost pricing and imperfect competition must 'first be settled . . . presumably by recourse to empirical tests'.

In the preface to the second edition of his textbook, Stigler (1952: v) sought to 'emphasize . . . how the theory is tested by evidence' and to 'incite the student to attempt to test parts of the theory for himself . . . I can assure him that some parts of the theory in this book are unquestionably wrong – and I should like to know which they are.' Stigler (1955a: 300) also stated that 'one can test empirically a crude theory as well as a refined one'. In a scathing article, entitled 'Alice in Fundland', Stigler (1967b: 12) ridiculed the 'Untrained Minds' of the Securities and Exchange Commission for lacking 'the humility to subject its policies to empirical test'. He commended the ongoing examination of 'untested hypotheses of which we have too many' (1959b: viii). Later, in his Nobel Lecture (1986 [1982]: 147), he reflected that such explorations were sometimes little more than tests of the 'intellectual fertility' of those doing the testing. In a lecture at Chicago, he also reflected on the difficulties of achieving 'objective discussion' about empirical work which stirred up strong emotional or moral implications, and he had been previously disappointed with the professional response to his tests of theories of which he disapproved (1984: 306). In 1947, he 'tested' Sweezy's demand theory,[57] but despite his adverse findings, for four decades the kinked demand curve continued to attract the attention of a large proportion of prominent economists (Stigler, 1978: 1982b).

Joan Robinson (1952: 925–6) reflected on the lineage of Galbraith's *American Capitalism: The Concept of Countervailing Power*: 'imperfect competition was essentially a debunking movement' which left the defenders of orthodoxy 'in an exposed position'. Her primary motive for writing about imperfect competition was to demonstrate that wages were not equal to the value of the marginal product of labour and that therefore labour was exploited under capitalism (Robinson, 1969: xii; Bishop, 1964: 37). She was also curious about how Galbraith's audience (different from her own) would respond. Galbraith (1954: 2) painted an unattractive picture of the 'men who resist any tampering with the rigidly idealised world of our ancestors . . . the self-designated protectors of our political morality'.[58] Galbraith emphasized the importance of accurate assumptions and offered the prospect of reformulating economics along unorthodox lines.[59]

Sympathetic reviewers found in Galbraith's book an invigorating questioning of 'classic premises'; he had 'certainly opened a door which will not be closed for a very long time' (Berle, 1953: 81, 84). The methodology of positive economics emphasized the output, not the input side of economic analysis, and in a famous attempt at door closing, Stigler (1954a: 12) 'tested' Galbraith's notion of countervailing power.[60] He concluded that the tests were 'not flattering to the dogma', but Galbraith's star continued to rise. Indeed, Galbraith was given an additional platform by the 1959 Kefauver Senate *Hearings on Administered Prices*,[61] and immediately prior to Archibald's challenge, Rudledge Vining, writing in the *American Economic Review*, reported the response that Joan Robinson was curious about: Galbraith's work had 'extraordinary public appeal'. Vining (a non-econometric economic statistician) described Galbraith's work as outlining an agenda for statisticians: 'a call to competent students and analysts to direct their attention to the essential descriptive and analytical tasks' (1959: 119).

Stigler (1949b: 23) noted that 'the discrepancies between pronouncements and practice are notorious in the field of methodology'. But with respect to the testing of hypotheses:

> We can be reasonably certain of what is right practice . . . Occasionally we lack the data necessary to carry out the tests but lack the slight imagination necessary to rework the theory so it bears on available information and the enormous energy necessary to ferret out the information . . . I do not wish to condone our impatience with laborious research, and I hope it will soon disappear.
>
> (1951: 126–7)

Stigler (1943: 532) welcomed Simon Kuznets's pioneering contribution to the 'new and . . . difficult' field of national income measurement.[62] He also attempted to test aspects of public choice theory related to size of legislatures, while admitting that his empirical analysis was 'long on problems and short on solutions' (Stigler, 1976b: 31).

Qualitative conclusions from the theory of consumer behaviour needed to be 'tested empirically'. Although the bridge between empirical demand curves and their theoretical counterparts would never be bridged, fruitful progress could still be made by statistically estimating those curves (1939: 472, 476, 481). During his stay at the NBER, Stigler completed three major empirical studies of *Domestic Servants in the United States* (1947c), *Trends in Output and Employment* (1947d) and *Employment and Compensation in Education* (1950b). His own extensive empirical work led him to believe that 'the classical theory of the market has direct applicability to empirical market determinations . . . the applications are manageable in both their data requirements and their methodology' (Stigler and Sherwin 1985: 584).

For Stigler (1949b: 54) the purpose of economics was to generate predictions: 'The sole test of a usefulness of an economic theory is the concordance between its predictions and the observable course of events.' He argued that there was never likely to be any evidence for the thesis that competition has steadily declined. It was therefore 'an obstacle to clear thinking on social policy' which needed to be abandoned.

Stigler and Friedland (1983: 258) concluded that the Berle and Means assault on the assumptions of traditional analysis received an 'astonishingly uncritical' reception, but traditional analysts continued to work in 'complete disregard of *The Modern Corporation*'. One explanation for the apparent absence of any discernible influence upon traditional economic theory may lie in the observation that 'the practice of testing economic theories was still extremely uncommon in the 1930s. Certainly no one dreamt of subjecting Chamberlin's *Monopolistic Competition* or Keynes's *Treatise* to a formal empirical test.' A series of tests had, however, been proposed by Chamberlin (1957), Archibald (1961) and Bishop (1964: 41–3). But the Chicago opponents of monopolistic competition declined to be drawn into the testing procedures.

3.5.3 Archibald's Challenge and Chicago's Response

The LSE Methodology, Measurement and Testing (M^2T) Staff Seminar Series not only 'tested' the Phillips curve, but sought to 'test' *all* economic theory. Invoking the names of both Popper and Friedman (they could have added Stigler), the M^2T prospectus (1957) stated that we agree with Friedman (although we doubt if he accepts the basic Popperian position that you advance knowledge through refutation, and must therefore *try* to refute) [emphasis in text], (see also Klappholz and Agassi, 1959: 67–8). Their faith in the potency of econometric estimation and the methodology of positive economics was matched only by Friedman's and Stigler's faith in the potency of perfect competition.

Popper did not participate in the M^2T meetings, but his student, Josef Agassi, did. Agassi (perceived by the M^2T group to be a 'proxy' for Popper's views) and Kurt Klappholtz castigated Friedman's dismissal of monopolistic competition; his criticisms rested mainly on 'impatient methodology and is conservative and discouraging rather than stimulating'. If the theory was untestable at that time then Friedman should assist in the process of making it testable (Klappholtz and Agassi, 1959: 66–9). Archibald (1959a: 61–2) doubted if the theory of the firm had ever been tested. Friedman, he argued, had not followed the guidelines of his own 'revolutionary' methodology:

> Is it not precisely those hypotheses which are wrapped in the cotton wool and authority of 'tradition and folklore' that most urgently require testing... [Friedman's] purport is to encourage complacency and to discourage that sceptical re-examination of the allegedly obvious that is the prerequisite of progress.

Five months of weekly M^2T meetings (February, March 1959, January, October, November 1961) were taken up on the theme of 'Testing Some Theories of the Firm'. The minutes record contributions from an impressive array of young economists, including Richard Lipsey and Kelvin Lancaster who had recently (1956) made a provocative contribution to welfare economics in the form of 'The General Theory of Second Best' which had severely weakened (if not completely undermined) the welfare presumption in favour of perfect competition (but see Friedman, 1965: 51).[63] Also present were Chris Archibald, Maurice Peston, Charles Holt, Bernard Corry, Lucian Foldes, Thomas Meyer, Josef Agassi, George Borts, Edward Mishan and Richard Quandt. Archibald (18, 22 February, 4 March 1959) was searching for generality: 'Our analysis applies to all cases.' He objected to the Hall and Hitch Oxford studies on the grounds that 'Their methodology is bad. They are not open to independent refutation'; and to Baumol's contribution to the theory of the firm on the grounds that 'His data is personal to him.' Agassi retorted: 'Then we can ignore his data.' Archibald (1960: 210, 213) dissected Jerome Stein's essay on 'The Predictive Accuracy of the Marginal Productivity Theory of Wages' and found it to 'lack discriminatory power'. There was, therefore, 'not much cause for congratulation or confidence' in the marginal productivity approach. Archibald then proposed a test of the marginal productivity approach that would be 'the same for perfect and imperfect competition'.

The M^2T economists were evangelical about reconstructing economic theory so as to make it *all* econometrically testable: 'There is a small supply of hypotheses and they are probably all wrong . . . The hypothesis must be improved to make sense of the data' (Archibald, 11 February, 4 March 1959). This process of creative theoretical destruction appears to have involved a deliberate attempt to be fair to those theories that appeared to have been refuted. Marginal productivity, for example, although apparently refuted, could be defended by alibis: 'It seems it might be worth trying to check these alibis' (Archibald, 1960: 213). Their evangelical zeal to generate testable implications was fuelled by Friedman's methodology of positive economics; they also sought to apply this method to areas in which Friedman had made seminal contributions.[64]

On 25 January 1961, the M^2T economists met to discuss Archibald's paper on 'Chamberlin versus Chicago'. Borts opened the discussion by asking: 'Archibald's objection is that the competitive model is false . . . What form will new general theory take?' Lipsey asked 'What set of observations would refute Chicago?'[65] Archibald (1961: 21, 2–5, 7) complained that there was a glaring inconsistency between the Chicago tendency to 'cling' to perfect competition and the '"new" or "Chicago" methodology'. When it came to monopolistic competition, the Chicago economists were engineers, not scientists, whose constructions had led them to neglect the 'enquiring, scientific question[s]'. Archibald outlined an *agenda* for a wide-reaching theoretical and empirical investigation: 'We require more facts, not for their own sake, but in order to put into the theory sufficient content for it to yield significant predictions . . . the new methodology provides a solution to our difficulties.' Archibald was *not an advocate* of the theory of monopolistic competition, which he found (at the stage it had then reached) to be disappointingly empty.[66]

Stigler (1962e: xvi) defined the 'fundamental characteristic' of scholarship as 'the discovery of relevant questions [rather] than the giving of conclusive answers', and Archibald was clearly attempting to *engage* the opponents of monopolistic competition by appealing to their own method of research: 'This justification should commend itself to Chicago methodologists.' Stigler (1983b: 416) wrote of Jevons being 'ridiculed into silence', and Archibald's 27-page essay elicited what must be among the shortest replies in the history of economic disputation:

'There is a real doubt that any communication between Archibald and me is possible' (Friedman, 1963: 66). Stigler (1946: v) had previously referred to the 'greater (or at least more explicit) empirical content ... [of] the theory of imperfect competition'. But now Stigler (1963a: 63) merely applauded Archibald's 'attack on Chamberlin', and ridiculed his discussion of Chicago as a 'detour... The methodological discussion is a detour on the detour.' In reply, Archibald (1963: 69) could only repeat his complaint about the methodological 'inconsistency in Friedman's and Stigler's dismissal of monopolistic competition on apparently *a priori* grounds'. They were, he stated, guilty of 'a shocking piece of obscurantism, and an indefensible attempt to close discussion'. This response echoed Chamberlin's (1957: 139) complaint about the 'set of preposterous misinterpretations so standardised that there could be no questioning the fact of their common intellectual origins'.

The Friedman-Stigler response could be interpreted in theological terms (as the invisible hand is sometimes interpreted): in the 'moral' struggle between the malevolent forces of monopoly and its nemesis, the virtuous forces of competition, there was no sympathy for the proposition that most, if not all, productive agents exhibited a cohabitating mixture of the two. Certainly, in reflecting on 'Perfect Competition: Historically Contemplated', Stigler (1957b) used theological language: 'The Critics of Private Enterprise' 'emphasised the evil tendencies which they believed flowed from [the] workings' of competition. In contrast, 'The vitality of the competitive concept in its normative role has been remarkable... That the concept of perfect competition has served these various needs as well as it has is providential.' The Stigler-Friedman methodology of positive economics was influenced by the Popperian demarcation line between science and non-science; they appeared to be relocating monopolistic competition on the non-science side of the demarcation line, while emphasising the 'providential' location of perfect competition on the science side. For Friedman (1953: 9), 'great confidence is attached to [a hypothesis] if it has survived many opportunities for contradiction'; perfect competition survived the opportunity for contradiction offered by Chamberlin and Archibald.

Stigler did not neglect monopolistic competition with his Chicago students at this time; he 'eviscerated' the concept and 'conduct[ed] a Demolition Derby... shattering theories with gusto'. This training led his students to find only 'meaninglessness' from advocates of alternative concepts (Sowell, 1993: 787).[67, 68] As *macro*economic paradigmatic challengers, Friedman and Stigler were only too willing to set up the 'fox hunts' of controversy. Indeed, according to Stigler (1962c: 1; 1965a: 16) the statistical evaluation of economic relationships was the only distinctive trait of modern economics; in his AEA Presidential Address he reiterated that the Keynesian revolution was one of several

> minor revisions compared to the vast implications of the growing insistence on quantification... comparable to the displacement of archers by canons... I am convinced that economics is finally at the threshold of its golden age – nay, we already have one foot through the door... the age of quantification is now full upon us.

Stigler (1982c: 13, 22–3) repeated this assessment at 'the high noon of capitalism... This is the age of quantification... An inconvenient *a priori* argument can always be eroded or blunted by challenging its exclusion or inclusion of some assumption, but economists find it difficult to resist well-established *empirical* [emphasis in text] findings.'

Stigler 'wore his passion for measurement on his sleeve' (Demsetz, 1993: 795);[69] he also noted the 'unfortunate paradox that the more meaningful a concept is for analytical purposes, the less useful it usually is for empirical investigations' (1939: 470). Stigler (1949a: 103) ran (possibly) the first Keynesian-Monetarist statistical race, finding for the latter a correlation coefficient of 0.904, and for the former 0.395. The testing procedure by which alternative ideas won or lost status involved 'trial by combat' – an art in which Stigler and Friedman were highly skilled, but their stated views on statistical trial by combat were rather different from those of their opponents (Stigler, 1988a: 116; 1988c: 12).[70]

3.6 Concluding remarks

The 1959 AEA conference programme had been drawn up by the AEA President (Arthur Burns) and Stigler. The conference opened with a joint session with the Econometric Society in which Samuelson and Solow (1960) outlined the empirical American Phillips curve trade-off that would unwittingly contribute to the Keynesian demise. The conference ended with a sociological paper from Stigler (1965b [1960]: 17) which sought to explain the 'areas of active work and the lines of attack' in the economics profession. The writing of history requires an organizing framework: these two implicit 'manifestos' illuminate much of the succeeding quarter of a century. This chapter has specifically examined the Chicago revolution in the light of one of these implicit 'manifestos'.

As Chicago revolutionaries, Stigler and Friedman complemented each other, and it is natural to seek a partial explanation for the success of the Chicago revolution in their combined talents (Friedman, 1993: 772; Sowell, 1993: 788). Friedman contributed to the attack on the 'accuracy of assumptions' method of the Keynesians and the advocates of monopolistic competition, and also to the direct assault on the Keynesian hegemony. Stigler brought to the partnership a masterful understanding of the nature of knowledge construction and destruction in the economics profession (an area in which Friedman was a highly perceptive amateur). This Chicago (but Fabian, that is gradualist) intellectual revolution was launched on a profession whose historical subdiscipline had been 'permanently declining in professional esteem', 'a nearly moribund subject in the United States' (Stigler, 1988a: 28; 1982a [1972]: 85).[71] For Stigler (1961b: 213) 'knowledge *is* power. And yet it occupies a slum dwelling in the town of economics' [emphasis in text]'.

In his definition of competition, Stigler (1968b: 181) thought that it would be shocking if competitors refused to compete.[72] But Friedman and Stigler declined to engage in the 'regression race' over monopolistic competition offered by Chamberlin and Archibald, although they had successfully engaged their macroeconomic opponents in such a race. Economists are *Free to Choose* their research priorities and the current revival of interest in theoretical models of monopolistic competition has yet to generate an impressive empirical counterpart. Besides, Chamberlin, Archibald et al. could conceivably have undertaken the 'race' themselves.[73] But Stigler (1971, 1974) contributed much to the analysis of asymmetric free or cheap rider situations where agents, in the absence of coercion, considered carefully who would appropriate the benefits before taking part in joint ventures.[74] Their response to Archibald and Chamberlin was the optimal allocation of Chicago energies, while constraining the vitality of monopolistic competition explanations. From the mid-1950s to the mid-1980s, testing monetarism and estimating money demand functions became major preoccupations for economists (Desai, 1981; Laidler, 1977; Stein, 1982); testing or investigating monopolistic competition never qualified for such attention during that period. Simultaneously, faith in competition rose, while faith in Keynesian economics fell.[75]

The defenders of microeconomic orthodoxy believed that the advocates of monopolistic competition had defined terms which 'evade the issue, introducing fuzziness and undefinable terms into the abstract model where they have no place, and serve only to make the theory analytically meaningless' (Friedman, 1953: 38). The defenders of Keynesian macroeconomic orthodoxy made similar accusations about the Chicago challengers. Stigler's understanding of the sociology of economic knowledge led him to predict that some commonly accepted theories would have a 'low vitality' (1949a: 104); a theory could 'limp along for a century, collecting large pieces of good reasoning, and small chunks of empirical evidence but never achieving scientific prosperity'; the academic poverty of a theory could be caused by its concepts having 'eluded confident measurement' (1968a: 71). Stigler and Friedman had reasons for not wishing to contribute to the process by which some theories (the ones they disapproved of) acquired confident measurement.

Stigler (1969c: 227) recognized that a fertile school requires an opposition with which to argue, and Stigler and Friedman were supremely skilful in both engaging in – and avoiding – ongoing controversy with their policy opponents: 'a scholar is an evangelist seeking to convert his learned brethren to the new enlightenment he is preaching' (Stigler, 1988a: 211). As macroeconomists they were reformers, or revolutionaries; as microeconomists they were conservatives: 'Unlike the reformers, who seek to convert, the conservatives seek to defeat... the successful conservative must also be an innovator' (Stigler, 1975: 320–1). As the paradigmatic challenger, Friedman brilliantly exploited the Keynesian faith in macroeconometric estimation, a faith he did not share. But monopolistic competition was an upstart that had failed to reconstruct microeconomics around the concept of monopoly. Competition was still 'the main dish' (Stigler, 1968a: 5), and microeconomic revolutionaries still had to overcome the 'heavy' legacy of pure competition (Chamberlin, 1957: 140). Stigler (1965d: 76) commented on the inherently asymmetric nature of this type of competition: 'If you support the majority view, a cliche is often enough to support the position. It is when you are with the minority that a real burden of evidence is put upon your arguments.' Despite its revolutionary potential, Stigler (1976a: 347; 1968a [1962]: 251) thought that monopolistic competition remained a species of 'Cambridge eccentricity', which involved 'irrelevant numbers' and 'dark suspicions'. Friedman and Stigler displayed tactical astuteness in declining the invitation to participate in the 'Chamberlin versus Chicago' competition.[76] The Chicago counter-revolution was, in part, the product of superior sociological perceptiveness.

Many Old Keynesians were taken aback by the success of the Chicago revolution of the 1960s and 1970s. Robert Solow (1965: 146) concluded:

> I think that most economists feel that short-run macroeconomic theory is pretty well in hand... The basic outlines of the dominant theory have not changed in years. All that is left is the trivial job of filling in the empty boxes, and that will not take more than fifty years of concentrated effort at a maximum.

The prospect of losing their hegemonic position was not, apparently, taken seriously: '*Après moi, la sociologie*' (Solow, 1967: 119). But a considerable volume of 'sociologie' of economic knowledge *preceded* the successful Chicago intellectual revolution, much of it authored by George Stigler.

One of Stigler's obituaries closed with Milton Friedman's assessment of the attitude of his friend and collaborator: 'Let the chips fall where they may, my task is to be objective, accurate and interesting' (cited by McCann and Perlman, 1993: 1012). But Stigler was also acutely interested in sociological questions (Rosenberg, 1993: 841).[77] Combined with this sociological perceptiveness was an almost 'irrational... sense of loyalty... Much of his work centred around saving the damsel in distress, neoclassicalism, from her attackers' (Friedland, 1993: 780; Demsetz, 1993: 794; Yordon, 1992: Freedman, 1995).[78] Chamberlin (1947: 416) complained that Stigler possessed a '"faithful until death" attitude towards perfect competition'. Stigler (1951: 126) acknowledged this tendency: 'The admonition to keep one's mind open and skeptical, for example, is fatal.'[79] In the 1950s, Stigler (1956a: 278–9) concluded that there was 'no prima facie contradiction of the classical view of the positive relationship between competition and progress or, indeed, as much support for the contrary view as the devil usually provides for clever heresies.' But by the late 1960s, confidence in the working of competition was 'at a low level... [and] the majority of economists have lost much of their faith'. According to Stigler (1967c: 356, 361) 'the only effective challenge to generous opportunism is a trenchant ideology, and that is precisely what we no longer have.'[80]

Stigler (1946: 3) opened the first edition of his *Theory of Price* textbook with the assessment that 'the important purpose of a scientific law is to permit prediction, and prediction is in turn sought because it permits control over phenomena.' Stigler and Friedman also sought influence and control over economists' research agenda. It is worth asking why they were (at least temporarily) successful in this regard. Beneath the veil of economics lie some fascinating processes of knowledge construction and destruction that follow laws and tendencies as examinable as the laws and tendencies of economic behaviour.

4
The Rise of the Natural-Rate of Unemployment Model

4.1 Introduction

With respect to political mythology, the Northern spring of 1968 is chiefly remembered (like its forerunner of 1848) as a 'springtime' of youthful and hirsute left-revolutionary fervour. This revolutionary wave could plausibly include a US President among its victims, broken by the weight of office.[1] In contrast to all this tragedy and melodrama, with respect to influence over economic policy and all that flows from that, the most revolutionary call to arms of that time was Milton Friedman's American Economic Association (AEA) Presidential Address. Neither youthful nor hirsute, he was an advocate of floating exchange rates, monetary targeting, low if not zero inflation, the abandonment of fine tuning, lower taxes and less regulated markets.

Within a decade or so all this became part of the fabric of economic policy, at least at the level of the rhetoric of commitment. By 1970, all countries seemed to be '"off the [Phillips] curve" in the same direction' (Solow, 1970: 95, 103); in 1971, the Bretton Woods system was effectively scuttled; from the mid-1970s Phillips curve targeting was replaced by monetary targeting; fine tuning was abandoned. Markets were increasingly deregulated, and no political party, it seemed, could win power unless committed to a reduction in taxes. Everywhere, it seemed, reducing inflation took priority over reducing unemployment, and the British Prime Minister announced the death of the Keynesian order to the 1976 Labour Party conference. In Tony Crosland's words 'the party is over', and 'the fiscal crisis of the state' had arrived (O'Connor, 1973; Stigler, 1988a: 10) The 'left wave' surged and broke, leaving the

Democratic Party and the British Labour Party out of office for much of the following two decades.[2]

There are many interesting aspects of this policy revolution, some relating to the process of knowledge destruction (McIvor, 1983). Milton Friedman formulated the Natural-Rate Expectations Augmented Phillips curve (the N-REAP model) at least as early as 1960, but his first written exposition came only in April 1966 (Leeson, 1997c). In the intervening period, Barry Goldwater (who had been advised by Friedman) had been defeated in the 1964 Presidential election; policy advice of the Keynesian variety was sought from Cambridge, Massachusetts; the times appeared to be unconducive to the Chicago cause. Friedman was clearly influenced by Goldwater's defeat. During his tenure as AEA President, Friedman (1967a: 87–8) reflected:

> The fact – or what I allege to be a fact – that differences about policy reflect mostly differences in predictions is concealed by the widespread tendency to attribute policy differences to differences in value judgements... I was particularly impressed by the seductiveness of this approach during the 1964 Presidential election campaign, when most of the intellectuals, of all people, largely cut off the possibility of rational discussion by refusing to recognize the possibility that Senator Goldwater might have much the same objectives as they and simply differ in his judgement about how to achieve them.

There are several other interesting aspects of this revolution. In *A Tract on Monetary Reform*, Keynes (JMK, IV [1923]: 27) argued that rises in money wages would be unstable if caused by 'some temporary and exhaustible influence connected with inflation'. It was also a commonplace of the somewhat marginalized economists of the Mont Pelerin Society that 'There is no need today to dwell on the problem of the falsification of economic calculation under inflationary conditions' (von Mises, 1974 [1951]: 127). But von Mises (1974 [1958]: 154, 159) specifically spelled out that 'inflation can cure unemployment only by curtailing the wage earner's *real* wages [emphasis in text]'; unemployment increased as inflationary expectations were revealed to be lower than actual inflation. An almost identical analysis of the way incorrect inflationary expectations can temporarily reduce unemployment can be found in the work of Hayek (1958; 1972 [1960]: 65–97) and Haberler (1958: 140). William Fellner (1959: 227, 235–6) and Raymond J. Saulnier (1963: 25–27), both highly influential economists, also worked out versions of the N-REAP model at this time.

These critiques made little impression at the time, and unlike Friedman's AEA address, are rarely remembered. Alvin Hansen (1964: 342–3, 288), the 'American Keynes', discussed and dismissed 'misguided expectations', preferring instead the 'objective causes of the cycle'. Paul Samuelson, Hansen's successor in the American Keynesian hierarchy, pondered before a blackboard in academic year 1964–5, and dismissed these early N-REAP models as being of doubtful validity (Akerlof, 1982: 337). In December, 1965, Samuelson acknowledged that targeting a point on a Phillips curve could shift the curve itself: 'One ought to admit that the overausterity of the Eisenhower Administration may have done something to give America a better Phillips curve' (cited by Haberler, 1966: 130). This chapter presents evidence which suggests that there were several economists who made statements which cannot be reconciled with the original Phillips curve trade-off. Inflation was clearly increasing; some economists also argued that unemployment was likely to increase. This implies stagflation, but before Friedman's AEA speech, this made little impression on professional opinion. This chapter, in part, therefore, analyses the pre-history of the belief that ongoing inflation would be accompanied by *increasing* rates of unemployment.

The conventional view of this episode is that Friedman patiently accumulated evidence relating money and prices, and (if we ignore Phelps) used this understanding to uniquely predict stagflation. This predictive success enhanced the reputation of both the quantity theory of money and Friedman's methodology of positive economics; it also elevated the N-REAP model to centre stage. Friedman (1968a: 8) constructed his N-REAP model in Walrasian terms, despite being a Marshallian sceptic about the practical significance of Walrasian economics. Using this Walrasian language, Friedman made a prediction (about stagflation) which would evict Keynesians from their position of policy influence (section 4.2). It was not a prediction that was unique to him, although his prediction was the most comprehensive. Section 4.3 describes the inflationary momentum of the 1960s (the prelude to the Natural-Rate revolution). The trade-off interpretation of the Phillips curve stated that this should be accompanied by a *reduction* in rates of unemployment. Section 4.4, in contrast, highlights the writings of those economists (mostly labour economists) who diagnosed that unemployment would *increase* during this period. Concluding remarks are provided in section 4.5.

4.2 Predictive success

The N-REAP model (the vehicle for Friedman's challenge) is an equilibrating story which can be described, in inflation-unemployment space, using the analogy of a $ (or an 'S' spiked by a vertical Natural-Rate of unemployment). The macrosystem is constrained to move along this 'S' shaped trajectory. Along the top half of the 'S', a Keynesian fall in the price of money can only be temporary – an inflationary boom can only dissipate itself, as Keynesian money turns 'dishonest'. Along the bottom half of the 'S', a monetarist rise in the price of money will dissipate itself by inducing self-destructing delusions about inflationary expectations (the short-run Phillips curve will shift inwards as unemployment increases). Monetarist money becomes 'honest' as the rate of inflation is forced down by the reduced rate of growth of the money supply. Monetary discipline, tied to accommodating wage behaviour, can be relied upon to produce permanent reductions in both inflation and unemployment.

Predictive success along the top half of the 'S' (representing macroeconomic 'bads') was regarded as sufficient evidence to formulate disinflationary policies on the expectation that the system could be moved along the bottom half of the 'S' (a temporary macroeconomic 'bad' plus a 'good', followed by two macroeconomic 'goods'). Friedman is one of the most brilliant economists of all time, but some of his predictions have been falsified. At the start of the Monetarist decade, Friedman (1974a: 12) predicted that 'the world crude oil price cannot stay at $10 a barrel; it will drop dramatically within the next six or nine months...' He also stated (1968a: 9) that the Natural-Rate of unemployment was held high by the strength of labour unions, but as trade union power waned during the 1980s, estimates of the Natural-Rate increased. And disinflation, at least in the UK, was far more costly than imagined (Laidler, 1985). The N-REAP model gave policy-makers confidence in monetary contractions as a vehicle for disinflation at a time when some form of disinflation was urgently required. But it has not, unambiguously, been *predictively* successful in the disinflationary period of its policy-influence – at least if one does not resort to epicycle explanations, such as a simultaneous increase in the Natural-Rate.[3]

There are no truly *general* theories in science; only *competing* explanations which, for a variety of reasons (not all to do with the 'classical' process), command varying degrees of respect among practitioners. The N-REAP model challenged its primary adversary, the trade-off interpretation of the Phillips curve, and is now challenged by models which invoke hysteresis, implicit contracts, insiders and outsiders, an expectations trap, efficiency wages, etc. Not all of these models deny that 'at any point in time' (to use Friedman's phrase) a Natural-Rate of unemployment might emerge from the Walrasian equations; but they tend to deny that the gravitational pull of any particular Natural-Rate is stronger that the gravitational pull of the *actual* rate of unemployment. The system is perceived as being path-dependent: the Natural-Rate is a weak, not a strong, attractor (Phelps, 1996). For Alfred Marshall (1920: 564), 'The most valuable of all capital is that invested in human beings', and unemployment above the Natural-Rate tends to reduce the stock of human capital (thus increasing the Natural-Rate), leaving a large pool of outsiders who have only a limited ability to affect the wages of insiders. Thus the idea of a unique and stable equilibrium configuration exerting an all-powerful influence on the actual course of unemployment has been challenged by the idea that the Natural-Rate limps behind, and tracks, the actual rate, with (in Keynes's phrase) 'not so lame a foot'.

One of the reasons for the success of the Monetarist challenge is Friedman's (1966a, 1966b, 1968a) prediction of (and an explanation for) stagflation (or positive co-movements of Phillips curve observations). Friedman made the 'prediction... *There will be an inflationary recession*' in his *Newsweek* column on 17 October 1966, and as even his critics put it, 'a prophet has only to be right once for his reputation to be secure forever' (Desai, 1981: 8); 'Basically, accelerationism was a pessimistic forecast rather than an explanation of experience; whatever else one thinks of the theory, the prophetic accuracy of its pessimism has to be admired... we are all accelerationists now' (Okun, 1975: 354).

Yet, the judgement that *both* inflation and unemployment would simultaneously increase was by no means a rare occurrence prior to the Keynesian discomfiture. Gottfried Haberler (1961: 10), for example, noted:

> We remain alert to the possibility that inflation may be combined with depression (or recession)... it is not at all unlikely that inflation will either eventually bring about deflation and depression or make it difficult to counteract a depression that has arisen independently. This is, in fact, one of the main economic dangers (apart from the social injustice that it engenders) of even a mild inflation.

The editorial in the (highly influential) *Journal of Commerce* for 13 February 1957 declared that 'creeping inflation will not lead to additional employment but will ultimately cause a decline in employment'.

In a letter to the editor, published in the same journal on 27 February 1957, Sumner Slichter of Harvard University – 'undoubtedly the best known economist of his day to the American community generally' (Dunlop, 1961: xxi) – interpreted this editorial as implying 'that the next decade or so will see, first, rather slowly rising, then rapidly rising prices, and finally, a big collapse and a severe depression'. Saulnier (1963: 26) also predicted that inflation would be followed by recession. Almost all economists were forecasting that inflation was on the increase; many economists also calculated that unemployment would *also increase*. Yet the trade-off interpretation of the Phillips curve appeared to imply that increases in inflation would be accompanied by reductions in rates of unemployment.

For Keynes, the long period was a 'subject for undergraduates' (Joan Robinson, 1962: 75; Eshag, 1963: 100, n. 118), and John Taylor (1979: 108), while accepting the vertical long-run Phillips curve, also noted that 'it has proven distressingly unspecific as a framework for the development of short-run dynamics'. Friedman concluded in his famous methodological essay:

> The weakest and least satisfactory part of current economic theory seems to me to be in the field of monetary dynamics, which is concerned with the process of adaptation of the economy as a whole to changes in conditions and so with short-period fluctuations in aggregate activity. In this field we do not even have a theory that can be appropriately called 'the' existing theory of monetary dynamics.
> (1953: 42; see also 1950: 467)

Friedman later referred to the short-run Phillips curve as the missing equation in the monetarist model (Laidler, 1981: 8). The N-REAP model subsequently became 'the' theory of monetary dynamics, because it was perceived to have predictively outperformed the (supposedly Keynesian) trade-off misinterpretation of Phillips's curve.

Thus, Friedman is credited with an achievement that normally guarantees immortality in the history of any science, that of using theory to predict what at the time was yet to be observed. In the nineteenth century, John Couch Adams and Leverrier deduced from general astronomical theory the existence and location of a hitherto unobserved planet. The planet was located at the time and place that Adams and Leverrier had predicted (Kline, 1990: 243). Uranus and Neptune were unknown to Newton, but were deduced by the application of his law of universal gravitation. Einstein became the most famous scientist of all time when his prediction about the effect of gravity on the frequency of light received empirical support from observations of a solar eclipse (Clark, 1984: 295). Likewise, Hubble's discovery that the universe is expanding had been independently predicted from the general theory of relativity by Alexander Friedman in 1922, and A.G. Lemaitre in 1927, several years before Hubble's discovery (Kilmister, 1971: 37, 97–8). By adding 'one wrinkle' to Phillips in the same way as Irving Fisher added 'only one wrinkle to Wicksell', Friedman (1968a: 8) predicted that the trade-off between inflation and unemployment always existed temporarily, but not permanently.

Robert J. Gordon (1978: xv) explained that he had found Milton Friedman's views 'outrageous' when he first joined the Chicago Money and Banking Workshop in 1968, but found them 'remarkably sensible' when he left in 1973. The first edition of Gordon's *Macroeconomics* was organized entirely around the N-REAP model, illustrating the extent to which even neo-Keynesians were retreating from previously held perspectives. Temporary recessions – which persisted only as long as expectations about inflation were inaccurate – would reduce inflation 'to any desired amount, to zero or even a negative number' (Gordon, 1978: 305). The N-REAP model became profoundly influential during the 1970s (Hargreaves Heap, 1980). In the 1960s, the Phillips curve came to be interpreted as a proposition that 'one can do business with the [inflation] dragon – buying some reduction in the degree of inflation by feeding him a certain number of jobs' (Lerner, 1967: 3). At the AEA Conference, in the year following Abba P. Lerner's Richard T. Ely Lecture, Friedman suggested that the inflation dragon would not digest the unemployed, but merely detain them away from the workplace, only as long as their delusions about inflationary expectations persisted. Unemployment came to be viewed by many economists as a variable that could not be directly targeted: it was 'a state of mind not a state statistic' (Cole et al., 1983: 93).

At the time of his AEA Presidential Address, Friedman was regarded as a brilliant phenomenon, but was also tainted with the failure of Barry Goldwater's 1964 US Presidential election challenge (Tobin, 1964). Many delegates to the 1967 AEA Conference believed that both Friedman and his prediction of stagflation would be shot down in flames (conversation with Ashenfelter, 2 October 1993; see also Hall and Taylor, 1986: 115). Yet stagflation appeared to discredit Keynesian economists, and for a decade from the mid-1970s policies derived from Friedman (at least rhetorically) were implemented in a variety of countries. He was credited, even by his opponents, with the introduction of inflationary expectations into the analysis of inflation and unemployment, and of using this approach to uniquely predict stagflation (Mankiw, 1990: 1647; Desai, 1981: 1–9). Inflation was clearly rising in the 1960s (section 4.3), and many other economists also calculated that unemployment was simultaneously increasing (section 4.4). But it was Friedman whose reputation was incalculably strengthened by this predictive success – which fitted in exactly with his method of positive economics.

4.3 Prelude to the natural-rate: the accelerating inflation of the 1960s

Arthur Okun (1972 [1969]: 150) described the war in Vietnam as 'the Danish Prince in the *Hamlet* of our economic history'. In the mid-1960s, the Johnson administration was increasingly losing control of both the economy and the war in Vietnam. The Chairman of the Council of Economic Advisers (CEA), Gardner Ackley, told a reporter from *The Wall Street Journal* (19 October 1966) that one could date the rapid rise in GNP to President Johnson's press conference (28 June 1965) announcing the dispatch of 50 000 American soldiers to Vietnam (Rosen, 1969: 84–5). During 1965 economists within the Johnson Administration became increasingly concerned that the 25 per cent increase in military expenditure might overwhelm the 'guideposts', and a special price-cost fighting apparatus was established (Cochrane, 1975). On 10 December 1965, the CEA urgently recommended a tax increase to finance the Vietnam war, although this recommendation was not included in the January 1966 *Economic Report of the President*, possibly because 1966 was an election year (Lekachman, 1973: 19). This was the year that the wage-price policy began to collapse (Cochrane, 1975: 263). According to Okun (1972 [1969]: 154) this was 'the first defeat of the new economics by the old politics' since 1962. In late 1966 the CEA again argued for a tax increase, and in January 1967 Johnson proposed an income tax surcharge, which was finally passed in July 1968. This belated tax increase

> ended the period of inappropriate budgetary stimulus, thirty-five months after it started, thirty months after it was first diagnosed by the President's economic advisers, and eleven months after the President urgently requested Congress to act. By [then] the boom and wage-price spiral had developed enormous momentum and they proved terribly difficult to stop... By the middle of 1968, inflation had become a raging disease.
>
> (Okun, 1972 [1969]: 163; see also Cochrane, 1975: 263)

Thus, even with inflation hovering around 5 per cent, *some* Keynesians perceived that it was acquiring a dangerous *momentum*.

The 1970 CEA Annual Report, signed by Paul McCracken, Hendrick Houthakker and Herbert Stein, declared that 'the current inflation was generated by the mounting budget deficits and rapid monetary expansion that began in 1965 with the escalation of the Vietnam War and the massive increase in federal spending for domestic programs' (cited by Okun, 1972: 180; de Marchi, 1975). The budget deficit for fiscal 1967 was $9.8 billion, and for 1968 $23 billion. The underestimate for defence outlays for fiscal 1967 was $10 billion (Tobin, 1988: 132). Walter Heller (1969: 36) acknowledged that the CEA and the Treasury were unaware of the Pentagon's expenditure plans for Vietnam, which were consistently underestimated. 'Covert operations' were also apparently required to finance the war. For Johnson, the price of honesty with respect to expenditures in Vietnam would have been the demise of his Great Society programme (Lekachman, 1973: 19). The war was clearly being financed in an inflationary manner, and the second half of 1965 saw the beginning of a dangerous inflationary boom (Okun, 1972 [1969]: 153; Cagan, 1979: 106).

The 1962 CEA Report (signed by Walter Heller, Kermit Gordon and James Tobin) had concluded that any expansion of demand above a 'full employment [figure of] 4.0 per cent [could] be met by only minor increases in employment and output, and by *major increases* [emphasis added] in prices and wages' (in Tobin and Weidenbaum, 1988: 46). Heller (1972 [1966]: 145) warned that at full employment 'the line between expansion and inflation becomes thinner'. Paul Samuelson (1953: 83) saw 4 per cent unemployment as a 'high employment ceiling'. The unemployment rate in both 1966 and 1967 was 3.8 per cent, and 3.5 per cent in 1968. Samuelson and Solow's (1960: 192) original US Phillips curve became very steep at low levels of unemployment. The same is true for Phillips's and Lipsey's original curves (Phillips, 1958: 285; 1959: figure 6; Lipsey, 1960: 4, 24). Regardless of whether or not a Phillips curve of any kind existed, inflation in the US had been increasing every year since 1962, rising from 1.1 per cent in that year to 4.0 per cent in 1968.

The non-financial business sector increased eightfold its volume of commercial paper issued between 1964–70. In 1967 and 1968 the average share price of a stock listed on the New York Stock Exchange increased by 40 per cent, well in excess of the earnings of listed companies (Burns, 1972: 225–6). On 21 July 1967 Ralph Saul, President of the American Stock Exchange, wrote to all 573 members warning that 'market conditions indicate a serious level of speculative activity'.[4] Pratson (1978: 98) stated that a group of money managers were warning of impending inflation in 1968.[5] Fiscal irresponsibility with respect to the Vietnam war (at least prior to the 1966 Congressional elections), was compensated for by a credit crunch. Following the election on 22 November the Open Market Committee of the Federal Reserve voted to 'uncrunch' the liquidity crisis, and in 1967 and 1968 the money stock was expanded faster than at any time since the Second World War (Cochrane, 1975: 266).

The US had formal wage and price 'guideposts' between 1962 and 1966. Solow (1966: 46) argued that these guideposts had left wage inflation 1.7 per cent lower, and wholesale price inflation 0.7 per cent lower than previous experience would have suggested. Heller declared them to have exercised a moderating influence in the 1961–5 period (1972: 149; Perry, 1967: 897–904). The Committee for Economic Development concurred,[6] as did the Chairman of the CEA,[7] and *Time* magazine.[8] In the UK, the Prices and Incomes Act was passed in August 1966. (A six-month freeze was proclaimed in October 1966, followed by six months of severe restraint.) However, the seamen's strike of May 1966, and the dock strike of 1967, were signs of impending wage inflation.[9] Indeed, sterling had been devalued from $2.80 to $2.40 in the month before Friedman's Presidential address. The Nixon administration had a fully fledged control programme between August 1971 and April 1974. In November 1972 a statutory 90–day freeze on pay, prices, rents and dividends was imposed, and this was later extended by a further 60 days. Solow (1966: 54, 47) argued that high employment and rising productivity 'depend for their success upon the containment of the inflationary forces which their pursuit may generate'. The guideposts, he argued, had facilitated structural change. The implication of Solow's analysis is that, in the absence of the guidelines, the inflationary forces unleashed would undermine high employment and rising productivity, in other words generate stagflation. Some Keynesians appeared to recognize that inflation was likely to be followed by stagflation, especially if the guideposts were abandoned.

Many economists were aware that inflation had acquired a powerful momentum and was likely to become a major political issue. In Phillips curve space this implies, at worst, a vertical co-movement of inflation-unemployment observations. Friedman's AEA Presidential Address implied a simultaneous increase in *both* inflation and unemployment. But stagflation is equally well explained by forces other than the gravitational pull of the Natural-Rate of unemployment (section 4.4).

4.4 Increasing unemployment

Friedman (1968a: 9) argued that legally enforced minimum wage rates, the strength of labour unions plus the Walsh Healey and Davis-Bacon Acts had all combined to increase unemployment. The authors of the trade-off interpretation of the Phillips curve agreed. Solow (1966: 51) argued that the Davis-Bacon Act was an impediment to the achievement of full employment and should be repealed. Samuelson (1967b: 56, 85, 64) stated that the location of Phillips curve observations was determined by, and was a problem for, anti-trust enforcement, labour legislation, excessively high minimum wage laws, manpower retraining, and labour market mobility programmes. A low unemployment rate may have been purchased at the cost of a higher future rate: the idea that there exists a trade-off between unemployment today, and unemployment tomorrow is 'true in part. I think that this effect is plausible from economic reasoning. I think that there is some experience in the statistics which suggests that this is in fact the case.'

Friedman (1977: 458) also argued that measured unemployment had increased because of the shifting structure of the labour force, reflecting an increase in the proportion of females, young people and part-time workers.[10] This had been a general trend of the postwar period. Between 1955 and 1975 the proportion of the US labour force accounted for by 16–24 year olds increased by over 50 per cent (Gordon, 1978: 251). The birth rate had increased substantially in the 1940s, and this led to a large increase in the number of new entrants into the US labour force – requiring an additional 1.5 million jobs per annum simply to avoid an increase in unemployment originating from these demographic factors (Cooper and Johnston, 1965). Even the 'aggregative'-dominated 1961 CEA concluded that approximately 22 per cent of the increase in measured unemployment could be attributed to changes in the age–sex composition of the labour force (Demsetz, 1961: 90, n. 7). Cooper and Johnston (1965: 129, 130) calculated that by 1970 there would be a 'dramatic' increase in the number of young workers. Part-time work was perceived to be particularly prevalent among these cohorts, many of whom would be seeking inexperienced entry-level occupations. The increased job mobility of these cohorts would tend to increase frictional and therefore aggregate measured unemployment. Lekachman (1966: 162) concluded that these circumstances could explain the very high levels of unemployment among the young. These high rates exerted an upward pressure on the aggregate unemployment rate. Both Lekachman and Demsetz (1961) concluded that a micro approach to these structural problems was needed rather than the use of aggregative techniques.

There had also been a considerable amount of discussion about increasing levels of structural unemployment in the US as a result of automation and technological advance. The 'majority' position was that the bulk of unemployment could be attributed to inadequate aggregate demand. The 'minority' position was that structural change would generate increasing joblessness, even in the context of general prosperity. The primary problem was not aggregate demand but structural barriers in the labour market.[11] The majority 'inadequate demand' position dominated the 1961 Joint Economic Committee (Knowles-Kalacheck) Report. Heller (CEA chairman) denied the significance of structural unemployment, and the 1961 CEA statement argued that the 'structuralist' argument was false (Tobin and Weidenbaum, 1988: 60):

> 'We' thought then, and Tobin and I think now that the arguments of the 'structuralists' were part muddled and part wrong...the real question was not the existence of structural unemployment which no one denied, but whether it had increased since 1955–6.
>
> (Correspondence from Solow, 11 August 1992)

Gilpatrick (1966: 12) argued that Heller's definition of inadequate demand appeared to suggest inadequacies even at cyclical peaks, and his test for structural unemployment was deemed to be inappropriate because he confined his examination to the 1957–60 period.[12] Demsetz also conducted statistical tests of the hypothesis that the number of hard-core unemployables was growing secularly and had come to account for a significant proportion of the unemployed. For none of the groups that Demsetz examined was this hypothesis rejected. He concluded that the hard-core unemployed appeared to be growing in importance; he predicted that structural unemployment would continue to become increasingly significant. The National Planning Association also calculated that structural unemployment had relentlessly increased (Demsetz, 1961: 81, 84, 87, 89, 90, 7).[13]

Gilpatrick (1966) argued that technological change had been rapid in the postwar period; there had been a change in the composition of final demand away from goods and towards services; distressed areas were identified as being caught in a vicious spiral. The permanent loss of jobs led to an outmigration of younger workers who typically had more transferable skills, thus reducing the attractiveness of these distressed areas to new enterprises. The four mechanisms of labour market adjustment – participation rates, job mobility, geographic mobility and educational attainment – were found to be inadequate to eliminate labour bottlenecks at both the top and the bottom of the skill hierarchy. The post-1956 period showed increasing signs of structural skill shortages, the pool of inappropriately trained youth had been growing dramatically and the percentage of black workers in low unemployment agriculture had severely declined. Low educational attainment led to a vicious spiral of poverty and a rise in black unemployment rates. Haber (1964: 11–14) calculated that 60 million workers in the US were in jobs that would cease to exist within 25 years, and that most were unprepared for this change.

Charles Killingsworth (1962) argued that over 9 per cent of those without an eighth-grade education were unemployed, whereas almost no college graduates were unemployed. In consequence, boosting aggregate demand may lead increasingly to a shortage of skilled labour, while leaving unskilled workers surplus to requirements (Garraty, 1978: 236–7). Structuralists argued that labour market imperfections required specific remedies. Gunnar Myrdal identified a 'manpower drag' which could be solved only by modernizing the labour market (Schlesinger, 1965: 497). Lekachman (1966: 162–3) concluded that structural unemployment was increasing alarmingly and that middle management in particular was faced with obsolescence. Stanley Lebergott (1964) noted that the long-term unemployed (more than 15 weeks) had tripled since 1957 (Garraty, 1978: 236–7, 244).

Friedman argued that the increased availability of unemployment assistance had tended to increase measured unemployment. Much of the stigma attached to claiming unemployment benefits had disappeared. Most economists would accept that unemployment compensation has the unintended side-effect of providing firms with an incentive to adjust to a temporary drop in demand by laying off workers. It also reduces the incentive for laid-off workers to search and increases the incentive to wait to be recalled to their old job. In addition, it increases the incentive for the non-laid-off unemployed to continue searching.[14] All of this tends to increase frictional unemployment which, together with structural unemployment, comprised the 'full' employment level of unemployment of the 1962 CEA Report.

Theobald (1968 [1964]: 62) argued that official US unemployment figures were biased downwards. If the statistics were to include discouraged workers, plus the 4 per cent of the labour force who wanted full-time employment but could find only part-time employment, plus the underemployed in the depressed agricultural, mining and industrial areas, then measured unemployment would be around 8 million instead of the 3.6 million in official statistics. The Secretary of Labor drew attention to the 350 000 males between 14 and 24 who had stopped looking for work (Theobald, 1968 [1964]: 62). The increased availability and generosity of unemployment assistance tended to increase the incentive to register for work and thus reduce the gap between measured unemployment and the true variable for which it is acting as a proxy.

Friedman's AEA address came shortly after two important pieces of legislation (1965–6) in the UK, the Redundancy Payments and National Insurance Acts. Both Acts had the effect of increasing measured unemployment by subsidising job search. British unemployment almost doubled between 1966 and 1967. The unemployment–vacancies curve shifted upwards from 1966; unemployment was higher for any given level of vacancies (Gujarati, 1972a). The net benefit earnings ratio for a family with two children rose from an average of 40 to 70 per cent between 1960 and 1967. The jump in 1966 is very prominent. Unemployment was calculated to be 200 000 higher as a result. The proportion of the labour force who had been unemployed for more than 26 weeks doubled between October 1966 and October 1967 (Brittan, 1975: 56, 65).

In addition to these supply side responses, these two Acts increased the quasi-fixed or overhead element of labour costs. The 3.0 per cent annual increase in GDP during 1967 and 1968 in the UK did not affect the unemployment rate, but the index of average of weekly hours worked per worker increased, as did the percentage of those working overtime. There appeared to have been a 'shake out' of previously hoarded labour (Taylor, 1972: 1360, 1354; see also Foster, 1973; Gujarati, 1972b and 1973).

Many economists noted that the business cycle had changed quite significantly in the postwar period, becoming shorter with average unemployment higher throughout. Lekachman, for example, noticed that the 1949–53 expansion resulted in a 2.7 per cent unemployment rate, the 1955–7 expansion culminated in a 4.2 per cent unemployment rate, and the 1958–60 expansion resulted in an unemployment rate of 5.2 per cent. Prophetically, Lekachman (1966: 189) suggested that the last recession (1958–60) had been accompanied by significant price inflation, generating a 'new paradox, simultaneous recession and price inflation'.[15]

4.6 Concluding remarks

The N-REAP counter-revolution was a genuine structural break in the history of economic research (Buchanan, 1987: 195–6; Lucas, 1994: 221;

Plosser, 1994: 280). In his Nobel Lecture, Friedman explained the success of the monetarist intellectual and policy revolution in terms of the classical process by which scientific theories are discarded: 'Brute experience proved far more potent than the strongest of political or ideological preferences... The natural rate hypothesis is by now widely accepted by economists' (1977: 470, 459; 1975a: 176). This 'classical' or 'idealist' internal assessment was accompanied by some external pressure: 'The resurgence of the quantity theory (renamed non-descriptively as "monetarism") and the rejection of simple Keynesianism have been a reaction to the emergence of inflation and stagflation' (Friedman and Schwartz, 1982: 70).

As a challenge to this widely accepted view this chapter has reconstructed some of the judgements made about the expected movements of inflation and unemployment in the period prior to the unambiguous collapse of the original Phillips curve trade-off. Inflation was commonly perceived as being on an upwards trajectory; many economists (without necessarily invoking the analysis of inflationary expectations) also calculated that unemployment would simultaneously increase. Much of the detailed analysis of labour market conditions in the inflationary environment of the 1960s calculated that increases in inflation would be associated with increasing rates of unemployment, although the Phillips curve trade-off was believed to be a hard empirical constant (having lasted over a hundred years). But these (mostly scattered) judgements were not packaged in such a way as to convince the economics profession of the un-wisdom of believing in the long-run inverse trade-off. Only Friedman, it seems, was able to accomplish that.

In so far as these intimations of stagflation were not scattered, they originated from the structuralist analysis of unemployment. The equilibrating power of the Natural-Rate of unemployment is not required to explain the stagflation which ended the Old Keynesian era. Friedman was one of several economists who perceived that *structural* unemployment had increased. Those who concluded that structural unemployment was increasing along with the inflation of the 1960s had their scientific competence questioned:

> Talk of 'structural unemployment' was loose in the land – indeed, very loose... Careful analysis of the statistical record within CEA convinced us that the structural-unemployment thesis was more fancy than fact... Employment decisions in 1965–66 rendered a clear cut verdict on the structural-unemployment thesis: the alleged

> hard core of unemployment lies not at 5 or 6 per cent, but even deeper than 4 per cent – how deep still remains to be ascertained.
>
> (Heller, 1966: 63–4)

> Never did so many write so much that is nonsense and inconclusive on this topic. The special American problems, that you [in Britain] seem not yet to have met, of whether there is a secular increase in 'structural unemployment', provided a marvellous example of what the new and brilliant Council of Economic Advisers (Heller, Tobin, Gordon, Solow and others) could contribute in their first months of office to this murky issue.
>
> (Samuelson, 1962a: 22)

For Samuelson (1967b: 54–5), the inverse trade-off was 'one of the most important concepts of our time. Any criticism of the guideposts which does not explicitly take into account the Phillips curve concept, I have to treat as having missed the fundamental point of all economic discussions.' Few, it seems (and this applies with particular force to the textbook writers, almost all of whom were copying Samuelson's best-selling formula) chose to be so treated in the 1960s.

The Chicago defenders of microeconomic orthodoxy believed that the advocates of monopolistic competition had defined terms which 'evade the issue, introducing fuzziness and undefinable terms into the abstract model where they have no place, and serve only to make the theory analytically meaningless' (Friedman, 1953: 38). George Stigler (1982d: 6) cautioned that no economist has 'any professional knowledge on which to base recommendations (concerning antitrust and monopolies) that should carry weight with a skeptical legislator'; he also defined the short run as 'at least a generation or two' (1982a: 32). Friedman (1968a: 11) initially estimated that full adjustment back to the Natural-Rate of unemployment would take 'a couple of decades'. Perhaps there is something inherently optimistic at the heart of successful revolutions, but Friedman's Natural-Rate (disinflation) prediction to the House of Commons Select Committee on Monetary Policy was less accurate than his Natural-Rate (inflationary) prediction to the AEA. Unlike the inflationary prediction that elevated the N-REAP model to centre stage, the disinflation prediction described the lower half of the 'S' – that is it described the *reduction* in unemployment that would (after a brief interval) follow from disinflation policies. From 'the best evidence', Friedman (1980: 61) predicted that '(a) only a modest reduction in output and employment will be a side effect of reducing inflation to single figures by 1982 and (b) the effect on investment and the potential for future growth will be highly favourable.' Unemployment was 'an unfortunate side effect of reducing inflation'; only rigidities stood in the way of a rapid return to the natural rate of unemployment: 'The mechanism causing the contraction in output is the slowing of nominal spending in response to the slowing of monetary growth and the inevitable lags in the absorption of slower spending by wages and prices.' Policies designed to produce 'high employment had led to high unemployment', but subsequent British unemployment experience was much worse than he predicted: 'a temporary retardation in economic growth' (Friedman, 1980: 61, 56). Harry Johnson's (1971) AEA prediction appears in retrospect to be more accurate:

> The most serious defects of the Monetarist counter-revolution from the academic point of view are, on the one hand, the abnegation of the restated quantity theory of money from the responsibility of providing a theory of the determination of prices and output [analysing the supply response of the economy to monetary impulses... whether monetary changes affected prices or quantities] and on the other hand, its continuing reliance on the methodology of positive economics... Personally, I expect [Monetarism] to peter out.

Stigler (1976a: 351) concluded that 'economists exert a minor and scarcely detectable influence on the societies in which they live', but faith in the Quantity Theory of Money gave President Reagan an unshakeable faith in the monetary method chosen to defeat inflation, even in the face of alarmingly high unemployment figures (conversation with Friedman, 7 August 1995). For Nigel Lawson (1992: 102), 'the most important point is that [the transitional cost in reducing inflation] is not a lasting cost'. Stigler (1973c) contributed to this confidence by finding that the volume of unemployment had no statistically significant effect on voting behaviour, but the rate of inflation was negatively related to the incumbent's share of votes. Stigler (1949b, 103) also ran (possibly) the first Keynesian–Monetarist statistical race, finding for the latter a correlation coefficient of 0.904, and for the former 0.395.

It was on empirical grounds that Friedman had taken his stand (1968b: 439; 1970: 234; 1974b: 61; Friedman and Meiselman 1965: 761). Yet, as A.J. Brown has pointed out, in the UK these positive co-movements were 'very visible from about 1966. Friedman's 1967 lecture had a powerful impact because be made a neat theoretical point which chimed in with what was being observed empirically' (correspondence from Brown, 1 June 1993; see also Cole et al., 1983: 88; Ball and Burns, 1977: 822). Some other economists also formed the judgement that both inflation and rates of unemployment would simultaneously increase, without invoking the idea of the gravitational pull of equilibrium. But Friedman offered the profession a model, or at least a tight macroeconomic narrative, with which to explain stagflation; the Phillips curve Keynesians did not, neither did the labour market analysts discussed in this chapter. Economists have a tendency to 'float on the tide of theory' (Stigler, 1957b: 9) and in Alvin Hansen's words, 'it takes a theory to kill a theory' (cited by Salant, 1977: 46). This explains, in part, the earlier success of the Keynesian revolution:

> [The] classical synthesis . . . for the first time, was confronted with a competing system – a well-reasoned body of thought containing among other things as many equations as unknowns. In short, like itself, a synthesis; and one which could swallow the classical system as a special case. A new *system*, that is what requires emphasis. Classical economics could withstand isolated criticism. Theories can always resist facts . . . Inevitably, at the earliest opportunity, the mind slips back into the old grooves of thought since analysis is utterly impossible without a frame of reference, a way of thinking about things, or in short a theory [emphasis in text].
>
> (Samuelson, 1964 [1946]: 318)

Policy influence subsequently came to Friedman partly as a result of the perception about predictive success discussed in this chapter. His influence can be attributed, in part, to his commitment to the vocation that Roy Harrod detected in Keynes, 'to intervene actively in shaping public opinion' (cited by Parsons, 1989: 52), in part to his 'Ruthless Concentration' (Solow, 1964a), and in part to the often unexamined dynamics of economic knowledge construction and destruction.

5

Does the Expectations Trap Render the Natural-Rate Model Invalid in the Disinflationary Zone?

This chapter raises some questions about the epistemological status of the theory underpinning the original Phillips curve formulation, and the correspondence between the empirical data and the textbook (theoretical) representations of the Natural-Rate Expectations Augmented Phillips (N-REAP) curve model. This is no antiquarian investigation, since these curves have dominated applied macroeconomics for over three decades.

Phillips presented the theory underpinning his dynamic stabilization exercise in his PhD (1953) and in a follow-up article in the *Economic Journal* (1954). But Richard Lipsey (1960) presented the first labour-market-based theoretical analysis of the Phillips curve. Unfortunately, it contained a theoretical inconsistency relating to the deflation region. In the inflationary zone (wage inflation in Lipsey's model), his curve described the data reasonably well, and visibly represented the theoretical underpinnings provided. But in the deflationary zone, Lipsey's theoretical curve became – like his empirical curve – a wage floor (or, more accurately, a wage change floor) shortly after crossing the horizontal axis. But his theoretical discussion implied a Phillips curve, in the deflationary region, with a slope of minus one – which was clearly an inadequate representation of the empirical data. Yet this internal inconsistency went unnoticed, until Lipsey (1978: 60) re-examined the issue for Phillips's posthumously published *Festschrift*. Thus, during its period of policy influence, the theoretical derivation of the Phillips curve contained a dormant but elementary error.

Phillips pioneered the introduction of adaptive inflationary expectations into this type of macroeconomics, but as is well known, when the trade-off interpretation of the Phillips curve unambiguously broke down, it was replaced, or augmented, by a family of short-run curves, along each of which inflationary expectations were held constant. This intellectual and policy revolution rapidly colonized the textbooks. Robert Gordon's intermediate macroeconomic textbook was the first of many to be organized around the N-REAP model. Under the heading 'Recession as a Cure for Inflation', Gordon (1978: 305) explained how policy-induced recessions can shift the short-run Phillips curve and 'reduce inflation by any desired amount, to zero or even to a negative number'. Gordon then presented a diagram (1978: fig. 11–1, 307) which has become a standard component of macroeconomics. Policy-induced unemployment creates a divergence between inflationary expectations (held constant along a short-run Phillips curve) and actual inflation. This shifts the short-run Phillips curve downwards, and unemployment returns to its 'natural' rate at a lower level of inflation. This is still the standard analysis presented in numerous textbooks.

Milton Friedman devoted substantial portions of his American Economic Association Presidential speech, his Nobel lecture, and his textbook on price theory to the N-REAP model. He expressed confidence in the curve as a short-run description of the macroeconomy during the previous century, where inflationary expectations had been constant, and equal to zero (1976: 221–2; 1977: 454). But in one crucial respect the diagram which Friedman presented (1976: fig. 12.3, p. 218, reproduced here as Figure 5.1) bears little resemblance to Phillips's scatter diagram.[1] Yet, it is Friedman's Phillips curve (not Phillips's or Lipsey's), which has dominated textbook representations of the short-run Phillips curve.

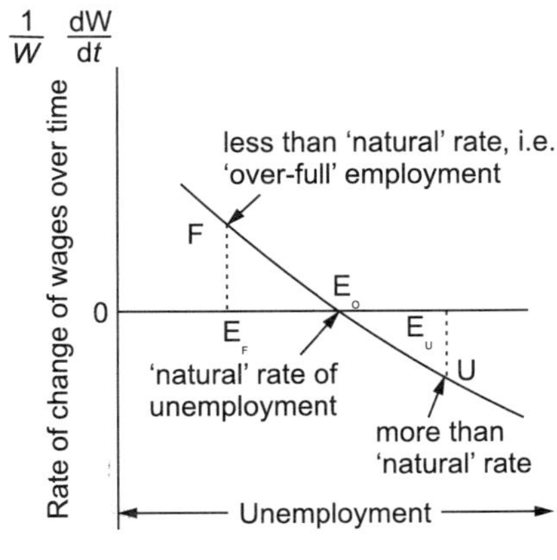

Figure 5.1 Friedman's portrayal of the Phillips curve.
Source: Friedman, 1976: 218.

Compare the slope of Friedman's short-run Phillips curve to the right of the 'natural' rate, with that of Phillips (Figure 5.2) and Lipsey (Figure 5.3). Phillips's curve becomes virtually a wage change floor at 5.5 per cent unemployment. A 5 per cent increase in unemployment, from 5.5 per cent to 10.5 per cent, produces approximately a 0.5 per cent reduction in the rate of change of money wage rates. Phillips (1958: 294) also found that in the six years following the policy-induced recession associated with the return to the gold standard, unemployment rose from 12.5 per cent in 1926, to 22.1 per cent in 1932, but wage inflation fell by only 0.6 per cent per annum. In Lipsey's post-1923 relationship, any increase in unemployment above approximately 4 per cent produces no apparent reduction in the rate of increase in money wage rates; there is a wage change floor at +1 per cent.[2] Since Friedman, like Phillips and Lipsey, did not see the translation from wages to prices as being troublesome,[3] this implies that any policy-induced unemployment above 4 per cent cannot reduce inflationary expectations, because these expectations are not being falsified.

Friedman's diagram (1976: fig. 12.7, p. 226, reproduced here as Figure 5.4) became the basis of the subsequently influential N-REAP model. Yet the shape of the (short-run) Phillips curve at higher levels of unemployment has shifted from its original slope of nearly zero (in Phillips's and Lipsey's expositions) to a slope which is clearly negative. The mechanism by which policy-induced recessions can produce beneficial results is

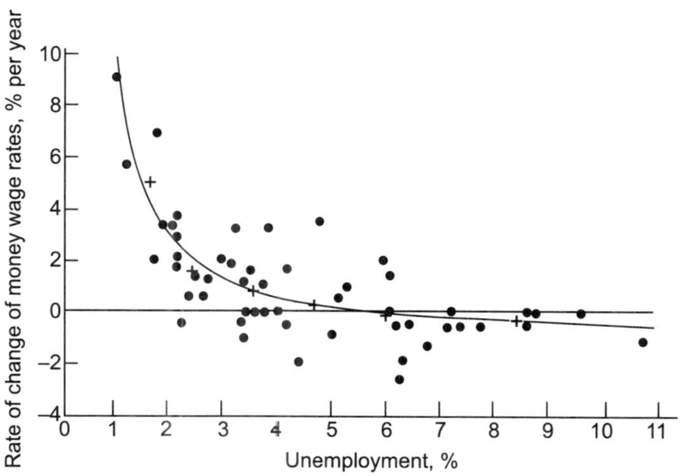

Figure 5.2 The Phillips curve.
Source: Phillips, 1958: 285.

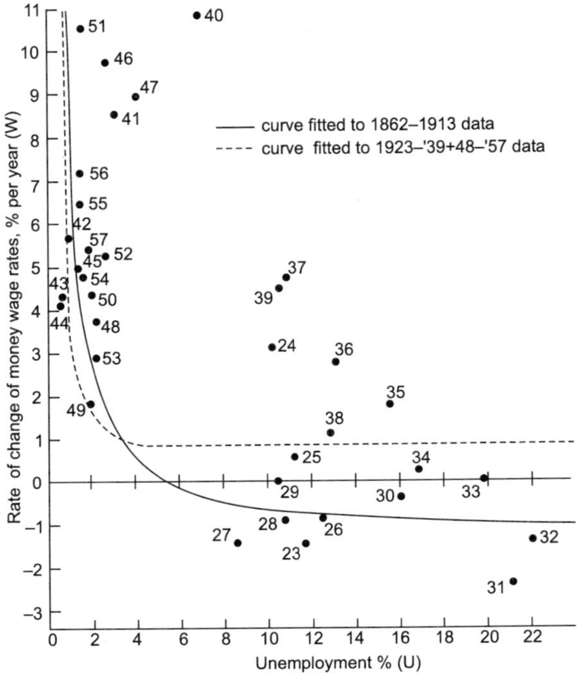

Figure 5.3 Lipsey's portrayal of the Phillips curve.
Source: Lipsey, 1960: 24.

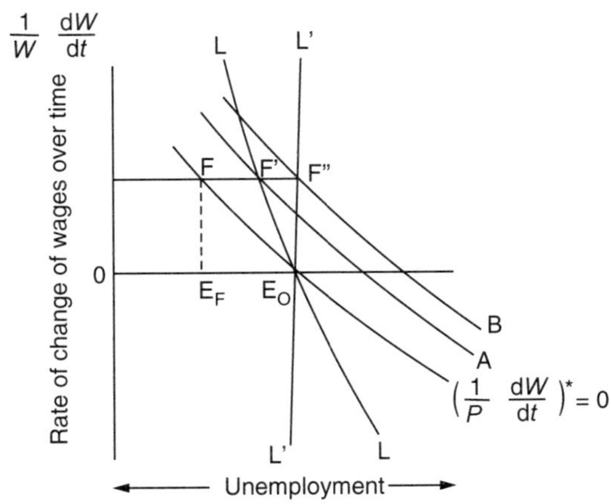

Figure 5.4 Basis of the N-REAP model.
Source: Friedman, 1976: 226.

crucially dependent on this slope being negative. Yet the empirical curves to which Friedman added inflationary expectations – 'only one wrinkle' (Friedman, 1968: 8) – contained evidence over a long period of data of an *expectations trap*[4] which would thwart the policy.

The expectations trap does not render the N-REAP model invalid in the inflationary zone (i.e. to the left in the 'natural' rate). Also, if the Phillips curve has a non-zero slope in the disinflationary zone, then *some* divergence between actual and expected inflation may be deemed to exist, thus facilitating the process – at least at the level of textbook theory – by which the N-REAP model may be said to plausibly represent the workings of an actual macroeconomy. The issue then reverts to a question of timing – how long would it take for inflationary expectations, and thereby measured inflation, and measured unemployment to fall? Friedman (1968: 11) calculated that full adjustment would take 'a couple of decades'.

But there appears to be no ambiguity with respect to that portion of a Phillips curve that has a slope of zero. The existence of a wage change floor implies that no matter how high unemployment reaches, expected inflation (and therefore actual inflation and measured unemployment) cannot fall. It is here – in the disinflationary region – that the expectations trap delivers a fatal blow to the N-REAP model.

Thus in 1978, Lipsey exposed a weakness in the inflation–unemployment thinking of the 1960s, but, simultaneously, textbooks began to elevate another misapprehension concerning the mechanism by which policy-induced recessions can, with patience, reduce both inflation and unemployment. Measured unemployment (U) was now, by definition, identically equal to the 'natural' rate of unemployment (U^N), plus any 'unnatural' increment (U^{UN}). This unnatural component of unemployment was, and is, perceived to be a function of a 'delusion' variable – the discrepancy between actual inflation (ΔP)and expected inflation (ΔP^e). Unemployment would return to its 'natural' level as soon as this delusion was overcome and wage contracts ceased to be based on unrealistic calculations of future inflation.

Formally, in the N-REAP model:

$$U = U^N + U^{UN}, \quad \text{and} \tag{5.1}$$

$$U^{UN} = f[\alpha(\Delta P^e - \Delta P)], \quad \text{where} \tag{5.2}$$

α = the speed of adjustment of incorrect inflationary expectations.

But as measured unemployment increases along a horizontal short-run Phillips curve, $\Delta P = \Delta P^e$, thereby frustrating the equilibrating mechanism of the N-REAP model in the disinflationary zone. The existence of an expectations trap, therefore, tends to indicate that the short-run Phillips curve does not offer a privileged description of an economy undergoing the process of a policy-induced recession.

The worst inflationary decade in world history began with what, in retrospect, we know to be an unwarranted confidence in the trade-off interpretation of the Phillips curve. This confidence might have been injured, if not punctured, had Lipsey – or someone else – noticed the inconsistency in the underlying theory that had been provided for it. The painful and uncertain episode of disinflation was accompanied by excessive confidence based, in part, on textbook representations of the N- REAP model. Yet, as Friedman (1953: 42) pointed out in his famous methodological essay, the short-run dynamics of disinflation were the 'weakest and least satisfactory part of current economic theory'.[5] His polemical genius helped to create both an environment and a political constituency in which disinflation could be undertaken. But if disinflation remains a twilight zone for economic theory – and also for econometric forecasting – then this, of course, remains one of the strongest motives for preventing the reignition of inflation.

6
Language and Inflation

6.1 Introduction

Macroeconomic controversy is largely a tale of three cities – Chicago and the two Cambridges – or more accurately a tale of the cultures and policy prescriptions associated with those cities. In the four decades between the *General Theory* and the monetarist counter-revolution, economists were 'normally' distributed around orthodoxy (the Keynesian Neoclassical Synthesis, the ISLM model, etc.) with the Chicago version of the Quantity Theory two standard deviations from the mean in the right tail, and the 'true believers' in Cambridge, England an equal distance from the mean in the left tail. The preferred method of orthodox research involved 'formalist' tools (a label that can be stretched to include econometrics and Walrasian equations). Penetrating the veil of macroeconomics reveals some successful language revolutions at work.[1]

At the front of the formalist 'manifesto' is the statement that 'Mathematics is a Language' (Samuelson, 1947, 1998), a sentiment echoed by Robert Solow (1954: 373–4): 'an immensely powerful and efficient device or vocabulary for thinking about certain kinds of problems'. Solow proposed a Darwinian survival procedure to supervise this language revolution: 'the profession (or Natural Selection or Supply and Demand) will judge'. The Chicago counter-revolutionaries also found a Darwinian 'survivor technique' useful: 'If I wish to know whether a tiger or a panther is the stronger animal, I put them in the same cage and return after a few hours' (Stigler, 1988b: 108). They were also conscious of the language dimension.[2] In his seminal essay on methodology, Friedman (1953: 7) wrote that economic theory is, in part, 'a language designed to promote systematic and organised methods of reasoning'.

Friedman cited the authority of Alfred Marshall to strengthen the argument. Friedman's essay was 'a marketing masterpiece' (Caldwell, 1982: 173) and was 'greeted with a sense of liberation' by empirical economists (Boylan and O'Gorman, 1995: 17); it provided legitimacy for the project of focusing on the output – not the input – side of economic knowledge, a highly fruitful vehicle for research.

The sociologist Max Weber noted the tendency for intellectual opponents to avoid 'the other's terminology as though it were his toothbrush' (cited by Haberler, 1961: 40); Friedman was introduced to Weber through Frank Knight's seminars (Shils, 1981: 181, 184). One of the reasons for Friedman's successful assault on orthodoxy was his determination to construct his arguments in the *language* of his opponents, although the word 'cause' did not figure in his studies of the relationship between money and prices: 'In my technical scientific writings I have to the best of my ability tried to avoid using the word', preferring instead to use what he called 'weasel words' such as 'substantial', 'rapid' and 'roughly corresponding' (Friedman, cited by Hammond, 1996: 3, 212). The contest between the radio stations, AM versus FM (Ando and Modigliani versus Friedman and Meiselman) involved torrents of econometric evidence which, if the R^2 was high enough, enabled both groups of partisans to claim that one variable *explained* another, thus settling macroeconomic controversy in 'a strikingly one-sided way' (Friedman, 1963a: 8; Desai, 1981: 203). Friedman's disinflation rhetoric gradually became convincing to policy-makers, in part because of his polemical ability to combine it with a somewhat mythical 'oral tradition'. His ex-Chicago colleague Don Patinkin (1972: 884; 1969) began a *Journal of Political Economy* essay on 'Friedman on the Quantity Theory and Keynesian Economics' with those famous words from Humpty Dumpty: 'When *I* use a word it means just what I choose it to mean – neither more nor less . . . The question is which is to be master – that's all.'

Friedman skilfully blended this oral tradition with orthodox and high-status language (income-expenditure, IS-LM, money demand, econometrics and Walrasian equations), despite being sceptical about the relationship between that language and the underlying structure of the economy. As a prelude, Friedman, with his 'Ruthless Concentration', influenced the 'talk' of economists before he influenced their language: 'Although only a small minority of the profession is persuaded by his opinions, around any academic lunch table on any given day, the talk is more likely to be about Milton Friedman than about any other economist' (Solow, 1964a: 710–11).[3]

Many Chicago economists objected to the words 'macroeconomics' and 'microeconomics', preferring instead the language of monetary and value theory (Stigler and Friedland, 1975: 478, n. 1). National Bureau of Economic Research methods had twice been the 'foil' for econometric revolutionaries, first the Cowles Commission, later Hendry's British econometrics (Hammond, 1996: 207; Hendry and Ericsson, 1991). Friedman had earlier been a persistent and observant critic of the Cowles Commission project during its stay at Chicago. The influence was two-way – the 'Friedman critique' contributed to the 'retreat from structure' at Cowles; in 'The Probability Approach to Econometrics', Haavelmo (1944: 43) argued that the question 'is not whether probabilities exist or not, but whether – if we proceed *as if* they existed – we are able to make statements about real phenomena that are correct for practical purposes [emphasis added]'. Friedman (1950: 489) defended the NBER-Mitchell research strategy by arguing that it was a matter of 'language rather than substance... [Mitchell's] theoretical discussion can readily be translated into current jargon.'

After 1956, Friedman led the revolt against Keynesian orthodoxy, organized around the twin themes of the *natural* – a highly persuasive word – rate of unemployment ground out by the Walrasian equations, and the *historic* – that is, highly persuasive – and exploitable relationship between money and prices. This money–prices nexus was a universal, inter-temporal, pan-cultural constant: a uniformity stronger than any other in the science of economics, possibly 'of the same order as many of the uniformities that form the basis of the physical sciences' (1969: 67).[4] Accused by Harry Johnson (1971) – whose alcohol consumption was legendary – of 'scholarly chicanery' in the process of promoting his counter-revolution, Friedman (1975c [1973]: 3) invested the natural rate of unemployment with the mantle of sobriety. Only a temporary alcohol-like euphoria could be purchased below the natural rate, followed inevitably by the unpleasant 'hangover' of disinflation, as unemployment had to be elevated above the natural rate to effect a 'drying out' cure.

According to Stigler (1988a: 33–4, 154), Friedman

> dominated the work in macroeconomics between 1960–1975... His attacks on the Keynesian system... were the centre of controversy among economists... he controlled the Cambridge universities and Yale. They were devoting much of their efforts to seeking to refute what he had recently written... he is quite talented in outraging his intellectual opponents, who have accordingly devoted much energy and knowledge to advertising his work.[5]

The word 'monetarism' became an evocative (almost Manichean) label: the British 'majority view bases itself on the axiom "monetarism" = Milton Friedman = "the Treasury View" = utter nonsense; in the same circles, incidentally, the corollary is "Keynesianism" = incomes policy' (Johnson, 1978: 126). Friedman (1968a: 15), a Marshallian, used the general equilibrium equations of the Walrasian system to argue that unemployment targeting is 'like a space vehicle that has taken a fix on the wrong star. No matter how sensitive and sophisticated its guiding apparatus the space vehicle will go astray.'

Partly because of Friedman's crusade, it is probably the case that more macroeconomic ink has been spilt over the origins of inflation than virtually any other topic. But one of the prime causes of inflation is reasonably straightforward – its toleration by politicians, policy-makers and advisers. For reasons that are perfectly understandable, a group of (mainly) Western Cambridge Keynesian economists became convinced that inflation could be tolerated because it was perceived to be associated with sustainably low rates of unemployment. Invoking the name and authority of Phillips (the designer and builder of possibly the first physical macroeconomic model), a brilliant collection of economists (including five future Nobel prize winners, Paul Samuelson, Robert Solow, James Tobin, Lawrence Klein and Franco Modigliani) constructed and popularized the Keynesian Phillips curve, which in many ways was a misinterpretation of the work of both Keynes and Phillips (Leeson, 1997c).

The two economists most closely associated with the 'precursor' to the Phillips curve trade-off were Alvin Hansen and Sumner Slichter (Leeson, 1997a, 1997b). Both were highly influential professors at Harvard; Hansen was the 'American Keynes' and the popularizer of the IS-LM model; Slichter's *Modern Economic Society* was the first-year textbook at both Harvard and Chicago (Samuelson, 1996: 147); he also achieved great influence through his journalism.[6] Both objected to the implications of the *word* 'inflation'.

In the same year as Phillips's famous curve, the Committee for Economic Development asked a variety of academic economists and industrialists to address the 'Most Important Problems' facing the United States. Hansen (1958: 110), Slichter (1958: 83) and Samuelson (1958a: 63) made almost identical predictions: inflation was unlikely to be a problem over the following two decades. In contrast, Friedman (1958c: 87) made a contrary prediction, and Hayek used his understanding of inflationary expectations to predict that 'those who believe that we have solved the problem of permanent full employment are in for a bad disillusionment' (1958: 53–4; see also Jacoby, 1958; Haberler, 1958).

The retired Chairman of Inland Steel described his own personal experiences of 'the whole mad process' of inflation: 'It is little wonder that professional economists are baffled by its impact ... the man who runs the factory knows the truth.' This became in part a linguistic argument: 'The outward manifestation of what is wrong with our economy is expressed by the word inflation' (Randall, 1958: 57–8).

In contrast, Samuelson (1958a: 63–4), in a subsection on 'The Irrelevance of Galloping Inflation', thought it 'almost a play on words' to discuss these types of inflation in the same breath as other types of inflation. Samuelson acknowledged 'natural rate' forces: 'After the inflation has been going on so long as to be obvious to everyone, many of its possibly beneficial effects – expansionary pressure on physical output and employment etc. – tend to disappear as people make adjustments to it'; he also highlighted what he regarded as the paradox of contemporary policy choice:

> To increase the now-negligible probability that American adults will within their lifetime experience hyper-inflation, you would have to preach extreme fiscal and economic orthodoxy – whose future consequences might then set the stage for a breakdown of American society and for an ensuing galloping inflation ... I fear inflation. And I fear the fear of inflation.

Two decades after the Hansen-Slichter-Samuelson prediction, another word, 'stagflation', was added to the language. It coincided with public perceptions about the competence of economists which were, to put it mildly, inflamed. This chapter provides an unusual perspective on this issue. It seeks to contribute to the project of unravelling the process by which this judgement became influential among economists and policy-makers, and to provide insights into the reasons for the demise of Old Keynesian economics. Section 6.2 offers a brief background discussion of the sociology of economic knowledge literature. Section 6.3 examines the rhetoric of inflation, and concluding remarks are provided in section 6.4.

6.2 The sociology of economic knowledge

All the Nobel Laureates mentioned above are, in one way or another, Charles River economists: Samuelson, Solow and Modigliani are at MIT; Klein's PhD, *The Keynesian Revolution*, was supervised by Samuelson; and Tobin was a student and staff member at Harvard. All were closely involved with the development of the Keynesian Neoclassical Synthesis and the trade-off interpretation of the Phillips curve. The Great Depression of the 1930s spawned a new subdiscipline, macroeconomics; the Great Inflation of the 1970s became the 'King Charles' head' of a professional civil war and ended the Old Keynesian era. It delivered policy influence to Friedman and his associates, virtually creating a new subdiscipline in economics – the sociology of scientific knowledge (Hands, 1994: 75; Boylan and O'Gorman, 1995: 9). Methodological disputes were not altogether uncommon before that time, but they were given a great boost by the disrepute into which economic forecasts (often derived from Phillips curves) had fallen.

Those who seek influence among economists have always, by necessity, developed a keen awareness of the nature of knowledge creation and dissemination. This was, I think, the reason Keynes opposed econometrics – he thought it would have a bad influence on the way economics was manufactured. Individual economists, most notably A. W. Coats (1993), have devoted substantial portions of their professional lives to these sociological themes, and it may be as a sociologist of economic knowledge that Harry Johnson is remembered long after his other contributions have ceased to arouse professional interest (see Johnson and Johnson, 1978).[7] But it apparently required the 'paradigmatic crisis' engendered by the inflation of the 1970s to stimulate the appearance of what can genuinely be called a subdiscipline within economics.

The 'rhetoric revolution' has been seminal (see, for example, Backhouse, 1994; Boylan and O'Gorman, 1995) and it is now academically respectable for economists to analyse economics as literature (Henderson, 1995). McCloskey's (1986: xi, 8–9, 4, 7, 18–19) work was inspired by the years (1968–80) he spent at Chicago (years which overlapped with the successful period of the monetarist counter-revolution), and by his despair over the 'unreasonable dogmatism of both sides of any debate involving Chicago'. Modernism and scientism were, in part, derived from the Chicago School, and the arguments of Friedman's methodology 'come readily to [the] lips' of American economists. But this modernist 'crusading faith' had 'hardened into ceremony', producing 'many crippled economists'. The 'official' formalist modernist methodology was oppressive; besides, the anti-Keynesian revolution was a 'nonmodernist victory for monetarism'.

Thomas Kuhn (1970 [1962]: xi) figures prominently in the early development of this literature, as does Western Cambridge: 'It was James B. Conant, then President of Harvard University, who first introduced me to the history of science and thus initiated the transformation in my conception of the nature of scientific advance.' In his *Guide to Keynes*, Alvin Hansen (1953: 6) cited from James B. Conant's (1947) *Understanding Science*: 'As Professor Conant has aptly put it: "It takes a new conceptual scheme to cause the abandonment of an old one". Men strive desperately "to modify an old idea to make it accord with new experiments". Facts alone will not destroy a theory.'[8] Conant (1970: 440–1) was also placed under pressure during the McCarthy period by those in the business community for whom Keynes's name was 'the proverbial red rag . . . to accuse a professor of being a Keynesian was almost equivalent to branding him a subversive agent'. The Cold War, and the Nixon–McCarthy threat were an important backdrop to the process by which economists began to see merits in ongoing inflation.

Hansen was a self-conscious revolutionary 'often called the American Keynes. But the title does not do him justice' (Samuelson, 1975a: 43). As Tobin (1976: 32) put it, 'no American economist was more important for the historic redirection of United States macroeconomic policy from 1935–1965 . . . the principal intellectual leader of the Keynesian conquest'. Tobin also noted that 'The channels of Hansen's influence were indirect.' So too did Samuelson (1975b): 'It is no exaggeration to say that his disciples dominated the World War II Washington ideology in economics. We live in the world Hansen helped create' – a world perceived in and through language.

6.3 Keynes and Western Cambridge

Keynes's influence rested, in part, on his highly persuasive literary ability: he complained that H. Stanley Jevons' use of words was 'hardly to be excused even by a prolonged residence in Australia' (JMK, XI [1910]: 508). He warned the Macmillan Committee that:

> It is very short-sighted to use words which are supposed to have an abusive flavour, like 'inflation', for something which is the remedy for deflation – you can only begin to use the word 'inflation' in an opprobrious sense when you have got back to equilibrium and are thinking of financing an artificial boom by giving businessmen abnormal profits at the expense of the consumers, and financing your boom out of those abnormal profits.
>
> (JMK, XX [1930]: 131; XXI [1937]: 404)

Keynes was the author of some of the most famous (and probably fictitious) words ever written about inflation: 'Lenin is said to have declared that the best way to destroy the capitalist system is to debauch the currency... Lenin was certainly right.' Inflation made the world 'so credulous of the unveracities of politicians... [it has] made us lose all sense of number and magnitude in matters of finance... the man in the street is now prepared to believe anything which is told him with some show of authority, and the larger the figure the more readily he swallows it' (JMK, IX [1919]: 57, 11; Fetter, 1977). In Chicago, this dubious attribution to Lenin was repeated, without acknowledgment to Keynes (Friedman, 1962b: 39). In Western Cambridge, similar apocryphal words were invoked by the doyen of Keynesianism to reduce the fear of inflation:

> An elder statesman once said, 'Inflation is worse than Stalin'. The neo-classical synthesis, which insists upon the potency of monetary and fiscal programs, suggests that any inflationary pressures resulting from our needed defence *can* be offset – if there is a will to do so [emphasis in text].
>
> (Samuelson, 1958b: 749)

It was this confidence in the easy reversibility of the high-inflation Phillips curve trade-off (and perhaps faith in the wisdom of the policy-makers) that undermined Old Keynesian economics.

The rhetorical debate about inflation was not new. The Treasury copy of Lloyd George's *We Can Conquer Unemployment* was defaced with the words, 'Extravagance, Inflation, Bankruptcy' (Clarke, 1988: frontispiece). Ralph Hawtrey is associated with the interwar Treasury View, against which Pigou, Keynes et al. campaigned. In his *Trade and Credit* Hawtrey (1928: 64) wrote that inflationism was 'a derogatory term thrown at a school of thought by their opponents, as the term Christian was by the people of Antioch at a new sect... The inflationist dog has been given a bad name.' Richard Kahn (1933: 170), in his American multiplier article on 'Public Works and Inflation', noted that 'as soon as recourse to the banking system is alluded to, the cry of "inflation" is raised and fears are expressed as to the "safety of the currency"; and the policy is probably doomed.' Abba P. Lerner (1958: 258) advised the Joint Economic Committee that the use of the 'condemnatory word inflation' could be extended to include 'Repressed inflation... a blacker name, and this seemed harmless even though it was something like calling an anti-Communist a certain kind of Communist.' Keynes (JMK, XXII [1939]: 77) noted that one of the first acts of the wartime Ministry of Information was to ban the word 'inflation' from the popular press, and at least one economist sought to ban the word from academic discourse: 'It seems wicked to use the word inflation ... to mean any rise in the price level ... It is respectfully suggested that economic scientists quietly or publicly drop the use of the word inflation' (Gifford, 1962: 65, 73).

Robert Solow also used rhetorical analogies to reduce the general sense of apprehension about inflation. The reduction of unemployment, Solow (1964b: 51) argued, needed 'a policy of determined expansion'. With respect to those who saw structural rather than demand deficient unemployment, Solow continued: 'Like any fireman, when you are trying to put out a fire, you are not much helped by people who go around claiming that it is not really a fire but only the end of the world.' Solow's (1970: 95) judgement was that 'the current inflation has been inflated as a social problem'. Paul Samuelson (1974 [1971]: 378, 380), a self-confessed 'Friedman watcher', informed the Joint Economic Committee that Friedman had failed to persuade the economics profession of the validity of his explanation of inflation: 'One man and an untruth constitutes a crank.' Mandatory controls, Samuelson argued, could 'help the inflation burn itself out'.

Later, as the Keynesian View was burning itself out in the conflagration of inflation, Solow (1975: 31, 56, 62, 66) reflected that

> inflation is a *substantial, sustained increase in the general level of prices* [emphasis in text]. The intrinsic vagueness of 'substantial' is harmless. One would not want to use a heavyweight word to describe a trivial rise in the price level; granted, it will never be perfectly clear where to draw the line, but neither can it be important *since only a word is at stake* [emphasis added].

The 'trade-off school' had a reply to the 'monetary school':

> Is there something qualitatively different about 'double digit' inflation? By any algebraic standards, of course, the difference between nine and 10 is no larger than the difference between eight and nine ... There is no abyss, just potholes ... Inflation is their [the mixed capitalist economies] way of adapting to change. The unusually rapid rise in prices during the past year and a half may simply reflect the fact that the world has been called upon to absorb some unusually large changes. In that case, it will burn itself out.

James Tobin (1966: viii) also analysed the *rhetoric* of the dispute over inflation:

> It is amazing how many reasons can be found to justify... waste: fears of inflation, balance-of-payments deficits, unbalanced budgets, excessive national debt, loss of confidence in the dollar, etc., etc. This catalogue of financial shibboleths and taboos scares the confused layman out of a commonsense, pragmatic approach to economic policy... Perhaps price stability, fixed exchange rates, balanced budgets, and the like can be justified as means to achieving and sustaining high employment, production, and consumption. Too often the means are accorded precedence over the end, and I am led to take up my pen to defend the basic objective of economic policy against it's spurious rivals.

In an article entitled 'Growth Through Taxation', Tobin (1966 [1960]: 87) advocated an unemployment target of no higher than 3 per cent.

In an obituary of his mentor, Alvin Hansen, Tobin (1976: 35) wrote that, 'Hansen must have found irony in the "new economics" label attached to the 1961–1965 revival of his central ideas, but he certainly rejoiced in the substance.' It is illuminating to follow this trail back. In 'The Generalised General Theory', John Hicks (1937: 159) concluded that 'one cannot escape the impression that there may be other conditions [apart from the Slump Economics with which Mr. Keynes is largely concerned] when expectations are tinder, when a slightly inflationary tendency lights them up very easily.' Alvin Hansen (1960: iv, 66, 25, 31, 23), the popularizer of the IS-LM analysis, argued, in his autumn 1959 Phillips Lectures, that the postwar average of unemployment of 5.1 per cent was 'intolerably high'. He warned against 'the bugaboo of inflation'. In earlier time periods

> the word 'inflation' was virtually unknown. Words, phrases, play a not inconsiderable role in popular psychology. You cannot frighten people out of their boots with the phrase 'high cost of living'... 'Inflation' implies that something is about to blow up. And in fact much of the current discussion partakes, I fear, of something unpleasantly akin to hysteria... We should stop trying to scare the wits out of people about the inflation issue. Fortunately the public puts little stock in this alarmist talk about the 'tinder of inflation lying all around us'. The inflation problem can be made and is being made into a powerful propaganda argument against increases in government expenditures...

Hansen (1960: 4) had seen a draft of the 'Samuelson-Solow schedule' prior to the 1959 American Economic Association meeting, and it was these two Cambridge economists – a generation younger than the septuagenarian Hansen – who launched the Phillips curve trade-off which appeared to imply that ongoing inflation could be tolerated. Hansen's Lectures were entitled *Economic Issues for the 1960s,* and by the end of that decade, inflation had become a central issue in the debates between Keynesians and Monetarists. But Alvin Hansen was quite legitimately analysing the use of language, or rhetoric, in a way that Donald McCloskey – a quarter of a century later – would recommend as an antidote to the sometimes 'Nasty Tone' of the (apparently) modernist Keynesian–Monetarist debate.

The year 1948, or thereabouts, was a watershed for perceptions about inflation, at least for a few highly-placed economists at Harvard and MIT. Before that time it was almost universally accepted that inflation was an unmitigated evil. As Raymond J. Saulnier (1963: 21–2, 27) – harking back to lost certainties – put it, 'there is no alternative to anti-inflationary policy. Anti-inflationism is the first imperative of economic policy. No other policy will work. No other policy is viable.' The reason that the 1946 Employment Act did not include price stability as a separate goal of economic policy was that it 'was too obvious to have commanded special attention'. The reason for this emphasis on anti-inflation was that as 'an inflationary psychology spreads and deepens ...employment declines; unemployment rises; incomes are reduced.' Saulnier was describing the prevailing consensus in the economics profession prior to the late 1940s, in addition to offering a Cassandra-like warning of what was in store only a few years after he wrote.

Other economists in the 1950s were, with the best of intentions, forming different judgements. It seems that these perceptions were incubated largely in Cambridge, USA. John Lewis (1959: 312, 172–3, 163), for example, who would later be a member of President Kennedy's Council of Economic Advisers (and who had been trained at Harvard) wrote that inflation

> is emphatically not the most critical national problem of our time ...There is no need at all, in short, to assume that...the problem [of inflation] is going to explode in our faces...the alarmist posture seems like the responsible, tough minded one. More and more, however, I am drawn to Professor Slichter's conclusion that we are conjuring up unnecessary nightmares when we take this line.

Richard Musgrave (1996: 194) was at Harvard between 1934 and 1981[9] but he learnt about inflation as a child after the First World War:

'It was so drastic that any later inflation seemed hardly worthy of the name.'

Keynes and almost all leading academic economists in the interwar period advocated *re*flation to mitigate the Great Depression; he was a consistent opponent of ongoing *in*flation. But Keynes perceived of what can be described as a positively sloped 'Phillips curve' as inflation took off (Leeson, 1999b). But the Keynesian Phillips curve trade-off implied otherwise. This enabled Friedman (1970: 209–10) to complain that Keynes paid only 'lip service' to the problems of inflation: 'At "full" employment, [Keynes] shifted to the quantity-theory model and asserted that all the adjustment would be in price – he designated this a situation of "true inflation". However, Keynes paid no more than lip service to this possibility, and his disciples have done the same ...' It was the *perception* that inflation had, for Keynesians, become merely a word to frighten the cautious, therefore requiring only 'lip service', which ended the Old Keynesian era.[10]

6.4 Concluding remarks

Those who advocated that there would be benefits associated with creeping inflation were self-conscious of the *rhetoric* conjured up by the image of inflation (although Samuelson, Solow, Tobin, Hansen, etc. were leaders of the modernist-formalist revolution – the dominance and pretensions of which would be a prime target for the leaders of the 'rhetoric revolution'). A parallel debate about language and inflation in the interwar period provides another link to Keynes and the formalist revolution:

> The quality common to the Mandarins was inflation ... it was this inflation which made an inevitable reaction against them ... The mass attack on the New Mandarins was launched in the late twenties. By that time these had squandered their cultural inheritance for their inflationary period coincided with the Boom and their adversaries came into their own with the Slump ... deflationary activities of the Cambridge critics ... had replaced the inflationism of Bloomsbury.
>
> (Connolly, 1983 [1938]: 55, 58, 73)

Inflation and language had become entwined in a *literary* dispute between the Cambridge deflationists (including F. R. Leavis) and the inflationary Mandarins of Bloomsbury.

Keynes was, of course, intimately connected with both Eastern Cambridge and Bloomsbury (Mini, 1991). One of his biographers wrote that Keynes

> was linked to modernism through his membership of Bloomsbury ... Bloomsbury's aesthetic theory – in so far as it was expressed in the writings of Roger Fry and Clive Bell – located beauty not in the subject matter or 'narrative' of a work of art, but in its formal structure, intuitively apprehended; the shift from flow of narrative to flow of thought is the distinctive mark of Virginia Woolf's novels. A parallel shift towards formalism, or model building, was taking place in economics.
>
> (Skidelsky, 1992: 407)

Keynes (1946: 177), like Friedman, was an opponent of the modernist-formalist revolution that was sweeping the newly formed subdiscipline of macroeconomics; in his final posthumously published article, he bemoaned how much 'modernist stuff, gone wrong and turned sour and silly is circulating'.

Keynes had 'an infectious semi-stammer' (Plumptre, 1947: 367) and his personal magnetism was based, in part, on his 'bewitching voice' (Hayek, 1972 [1966]: 99)[11] and on 'the incomparable sense of the fitness of words ... pure genius' (Robbins, cited by Harrod, 1951: 576). Those listening to his lectures were

> excited beyond belief. There were a couple of points that he made in the second year that stuck with me. I can still feel the funny prickling-in-the-back-of-your-neck feeling when he mentioned them ... I figured, after Keynes, why should I bother reading things which were clearly wrong. I *had* [emphasis in text] to read some of Pigou's *Theory of Employment* [*sic*] because I knew it would be asked about on the Tripos, but I couldn't get myself interested in it, except to find stupidities.
>
> (Tarshis, 1996: 60)

An unnamed senior opponent bemoaned that 'The worst of it is that Keynes' voice can persuade me of anything, however wrong-headed I believe it to be' (cited by Austin Robinson, 1947: 67; 1972: 546).

Keynes brought to the Wartime Treasury 'his gift for prose, surely among the highest ranges of our persuasive writing ... when we came back to the Treasury after Maynard's death, the drab corridors were grey and silent, the files were strangely heavy and lifeless' (Eady, 1951: 903, 920). In his study of *Intellectuals*, Paul Johnson (1989: 76) complained that historians paid insufficient attention to the persuasive power of an individual's humour; Keynes' 'flashes of humour' during his final years at the Treasury, 'were not merely irrepressible . . . You cannot go on disapproving of a man who has made you laugh' (Eady, 1951: 920). Similar humorous forces were also present in Friedman's and Stigler's Chicago.[12]

Elizabeth Johnson (1977: 95) was one of the editors of Keynes's *Collected Writings*. Her essay on 'Keynes as a literary craftsman' was written during the inflationary period when few industries were booming as much as the anti-Keynesian industry: 'So a con man typically snows his victims . . . was he [Keynes] a con man or do you prefer to look on him as a conjurer – a conjurer of words?' Her husband made similar accusations about his Chicago colleague, Milton Friedman (Johnson, 1971). But what Harry Johnson, Maynard Keynes and Milton Friedman all had in common was an extraordinary influence over their fellow economists, based, in part, on their insightful understanding of the sociology of economic knowledge construction, and in part, on the wizardry of their prose and persuasive style – a quality which too often goes without systematic investigation. The purpose of this chapter has been to contribute towards such an investigation.

7
Friedman and the Walrasian Equations of the Natural-Rate Counter-Revolution

7.1 Introduction

From the 1930s, economic controversy has been a tale of three cities (Chicago and the two Cambridges) and three General Theories. In the 1930s, there were, in addition to the General Theory of Employment (Keynesian Macroeconomics), two other revolutionary attempts to don the mantle of generality: the General Theory of Method (the formalist revolution, involving structural econometrics and Walrasian general equilibrium) and the General Theory of Value (organized around the concept of monopolistic, or imperfect, competition). The Keynesian and formalist general revolutions became symbiotic and dominated the postwar landscape of economists. In contrast, the monopolistic competition revolution did not readily lend itself to general equilibrium formalism and, so far, has yet to achieve its promise (Tinbergen, 1967: 268).

Edward Chamberlin (1957: 296) described the focus of opposition to the last of these three General Theories as 'The Chicago School of Anti-Monopolistic Competition'; only then did economists begin to refer to Chicago as a School (Stigler, 1988: 150).[1] Later, the term 'monetarism' was coined to describe the Chicago opposition to the Keynesian General Theory of Employment. For Chicago economists, the 1930s exhibited 'an excess of originality' (Stigler, 1955b: 301). The purpose of this chapter is to discuss Milton Friedman's opposition to the Walrasian component of the General Theory of Method.

Two of these revolutionary research agendas (Macroeconomics and Method) acquired postwar hegemonic ascendancy. But the two most influential revolutionary economists of the twentieth century were more united in their *opposition* to the General Theory of Method than is commonly supposed. J.M. Keynes and Milton Friedman had similar – and sceptical – views about econometrics. Keynes also informed Hicks that 'Walras' theory and all others along those lines are little better than nonsense' (cited by Skidelsky, 1992: 615). Keynes (1936a: 177) contrasted his own *General Theory* with a 'classical' caricature; Walras, he believed, was strictly in this classical tradition.

In apparent contrast, Friedman (1968a: 8) constructed his anti-Keynesian counter-revolution using Walrasian language:

> At any moment in time there is some level of employment which has the property that it is consistent with equilibrium in the structure of *real* wage rates . . . The 'natural-rate of unemployment', in other words, is the level that would be ground out by the Walrasian system of general equilibrium equations, provided that there is embedded in them the actual structural characteristics of the labor and commodity markets [emphasis in text].

Later, he augmented the quantity theory with the Walrasian equations of general equilibrium (1974b: 31–2). According to one of his most severe critics, 'Friedman, like all mainstream theorists, accepts the Walrasian system as the microfoundations of macroeconomic theory' (Davidson, 1989: 9).

But Friedman's research has always been in the Marshallian methodological tradition (Hammond, 1996) and Alfred Marshall was regarded as the 'patron saint of "positive economics"' (Clower, 1964: 367). Robert Clower (1965) and Axel Leijonhuvud (1967)[2] had recently questioned the legitimacy of the Walrasian Keynesianism of the Neoclassical Synthesis, and Clower (1964: 372) concluded that the Friedman and Schwartz research project was an assault on this neo-Walrasian orthodoxy: their conclusions were 'bound to be a bit upsetting to those whose vision of the working of the economic system is informed by neo-Walrasian theoretical conceptions, which is to say all but a small handful of contemporary economists.' Friedman (1974b: 159–60) was aware of this Walrasian dimension of the struggle for influence:

> Tobin's style goes further in Walras's direction than mine does . . . this difference in methodological style is an important reason why we seem to talk at cross purposes . . . Patinkin, even more than Tobin, is Walrasian, concerned with abstract completeness, rather than

> Marshallian, concerned with the construction of special tools for special problems.

Patinkin and Tobin (Friedman's Walrasian critics) objected to the *policy conclusions* of the (Walrasian) natural-rate model. The purpose of this chapter is to place Friedman's use of these equations in the context of his other statements about the limited role that should be allocated to Walrasian-style thinking.

Friedman's words were some of the most influential words ever spoken by a President of the American Economic Association (AEA); they launched the ongoing natural-rate research project around which modern macroeconomics has been organized for the last three decades. The natural-rate of unemployment is typically presented as a hard empirical constant, or as an empirically valid variable that changes only slowly. It is a relatively unobjectionable concept, in so far as it represents a speed limit, beyond which inflation will increase, and beyond which the associated gains with respect to unemployment will be temporary. But it also supposedly represents a gravitational force which ensures that *dis*inflation will have only temporary consequences: unemployment will, in time, return to its natural level (thought to be about 2 per cent in Britain in the mid-1970s, when the concept began to acquire overriding policy influence). The apparent paradox discussed in this chapter is that Friedman was – and continues to be – highly sceptical of such empirical measures. He also described as 'utterly unattainable' the accurate measurement of inflationary expectations (the equilibrating variable of the natural-rate model).

Friedman's (1968a: 14–15) AEA Presidential Address was a critique of '*employment as a criteria of policy* [emphasis in text]'. The apparent purpose of his counter-revolution was apparently not to launch a natural-rate estimating industry, but to suggest that using monetary policy to target unemployment was 'like a space vehicle that has taken a fix on the wrong star. No matter how sensitive and sophisticated its guiding apparatus, the space vehicle will go astray.' Thus, currently fashionable monetary policy rules (which suggest that interest rates should be fine-tuned to counteract deviations of current output or unemployment from numerically calculable natural levels) represent a reversal of Friedman's counter-revolution. They also represent (in Friedman's terms) the use of an abstract Walrasian concept in a practical area where only Marshallian tools are relevant.

To avoid ambiguity in the use of the terms 'Marshallian' and 'Walrasian', this chapter follows Friedman's (1974b: 143, 146, 159) use of these terms: the Walrasian approach is 'concerned with abstract completeness', in contrast to the Marshallian approach which is 'concerned with the construction of special tools for special problems'. Section 7.2 analyses Friedman's views on the Walrasian system. Friedman argued that it was unfortunate that Walrasian economics had overtaken Marshallian analysis. Formalism, Friedman argued, yielded few conclusions that were susceptible to empirical contradiction, and tended to rely on assertions about inflationary expectations that were empirically 'utterly unattainable' to measure. Walras's 'divorce of form from substance' had led to some 'nonsense'.

Section 7.3 places the Walrasian equations of the natural-rate counter-revolution in the context of Friedman's analysis of the limitations of Walrasian analysis. The implication of Friedman's analysis is that the vertical long-run Phillips curve is a 'language proposition' while the short-run Phillips curve is a 'substantive' proposition. The important question is empirical: some estimate can be made of a rate of unemployment to which the title 'natural' can be attached, but does this supposedly natural-rate exert any influence on the course of the actual rate? But this crucial empirical question is rarely addressed by those who estimate natural-rates. Friedman also stated that unemployment was a 'highly inefficient method' of adjustment – although increasing unemployment (to reduce inflationary expectations and shift the short-run Phillips curve downwards) is the adjustment mechanism of natural-rate models. Section 7.4 provides a brief outline of the process by which the natural-rate became influential in macroeconomics. Concluding remarks are provided in section 7.5.

7.2 Friedman on Walrasian economics

Friedman (1996a: 1989) describes himself as 'a long term Marshallian'; the label he put on his methodology is 'Marshallianism' (Hammond, 1996: 30). One of Friedman's (1940, 1941) earliest contributions to economic disputation was a critical review of Jan Tinbergen's macroeconometric project; this was followed almost immediately by a review of Robert Triffin's *Monopolistic Competition and General Equilibrium Theory.* Triffin (1941: 3) argued that the 'gravitational centre' of Marshallian economics was the industry: 'What we might well now do is to restate the whole problem in terms of the Walrasian, general equilibrium system of economic theory.' Friedman (1941: 390) replied that 'For these problems, we must continue to employ the Marshallian tools, until better ones are invented.'

Paul Samuelson (1983: 7) recalled that Frank Knight (the doyen of interwar Chicago) was fond of exclaiming that 'If there is anything I can't stand it's a Keynesian and a believer of monopolistic competition.' Friedman (the doyen of postwar Chicago) made his earliest contributions to the Chicago cause in opposition to two of the General Theories spawned by the 1930s (the Walrasian approach and monopolistic competition). As he explained to his students in the late 1940s, Marshall's *Principles* was 'still the best book available in economic theory. This is indeed a sad commentary on the economics of our time. Marshall's superiority is explained by his approach to economics as contrasted with the modern approach' (cited by Hammond, 1996: 31). Yet, it was Friedman's AEA Presidential use of Walrasian language which '*undermined... the whole intellectual basis of post war demand management by government* [emphasis in text]' (Laidler, 1975: 45). A Marshallian persuaded the economics profession that the 'gravitational centre' of the macroeconomy was the Walrasian natural-rate of unemployment.

Friedman (1953: 89–93) noted that 'by slow and gradual steps, the role assigned to economic theory has altered in the course of time until today we assign a substantially different role to theory than Marshall did. We curtsy to Marshall, but we walk with Walras.' According to Friedman, the important distinction between 'the conceptions of economic theory implicit in Marshall and Walras lie in the purpose for which the theory is constructed and used'. For Marshall, economic theory was 'an engine for the discovery of concrete truth'. In contrast, 'Abstractness, generality, and mathematical elegance have in some measure become ends in themselves, criteria by which to judge economic theory... much recent work on Keynes's theory of employment is Walrasian... so is current economic theory in general.' The fundamental distinction between Marshallian and Walrasian economics 'is treating economics as a serious subject versus treating it as a branch of mathematics, and treating it as a scientific subject as opposed to an aesthetic subject' (Friedman, conversation with Hammond, 1990: 168).

Much of the Walrasian formalist work took place at the Cowles Commission, during its sojourn at the University of Chicago. The Walras centennial programme in Chicago, hosted by the AEA, the Econometric Society and the American Statistical Association, stimulated a wide revival of interest in Walras; from the 1930s, general equilibrium was 'in the air' (Jaffe, 1935 Menger, 1973: 50–1, 57, n.24; Weintraub, 1983: 17, 19, 37). Between 1946 and 1948, Friedman was a frequent participant at Cowles Commission seminars. His relentless criticism of their econometric projects prompted Tjalling Koopmans to retort: 'But what if the investigator is honest?' (cited by Epstein, 1987: 107). Koopmans was reported to be relieved when he and the Cowles Commission left the University of Chicago, because his students and colleagues (such as Harry Markowitz and Gerard Debreu) had their work criticized as being mathematics rather than economics. According to Beckman (1991: 264–5, 253) the source of this antagonism was a Chicago economist whose 'star was just rising' and who later won a Nobel Prize. His identity can be determined by reference to the period (1944–55) Koopmans spent at Chicago.[3] Certainly, Markowitz (1992: 286) concluded his Nobel Lecture with the recollection that Friedman had attempted to persuade his dissertation committee not to award his PhD on the grounds that portfolio theory was not a legitimate part of economics.

Oscar Lange's 1944 Cowles monograph *Price Flexibility and Employment* challenged the Chicago view of general equilibrium theory (Reder, 1982: 5). Immediately, Friedman (1953 [1946]: 277–300) led the 'Methodological Criticism' on Lange's 'shackles of formalism . . . the analysis seems unreal and artificial . . . more nearly a rationalisation of policy conclusions previously reached than a basis for them . . . not a shred of evidence is offered for them.' Friedman criticized Lange's 'use of classifications that have no direct empirical counter-part . . . The resulting system of formal models has no solid basis in observed facts and yields few if any conclusions susceptible of empirical contradiction.' Friedman's reaction to Lange is interesting for its discussion of the complications associated with monetary changes, and the impossibility of incorporating an empirical counter-part to inflationary expectations:

> An example of a classification that has no direct empirical counterpart is Lange's classification of monetary changes . . . An explicit monetary policy aimed at achieving a neutral (or positive or negative) monetary effect would be exceedingly complicated, would involve action especially adapted to the particular disequilibrium to be corrected, and would involve knowledge about price expectations, that even in principle, let alone in practice, would be utterly unattainable.[4]

In Chicago in the 1950s, Friedman was 'excessively negative' about the 'sterile' and 'untestable' nature of general equilibrium analysis (Becker, 1991: 143). But the year after Friedman's methodological essay, Kenneth Arrow and Gerard Debreu (1954) demonstrated the existence of a general equilibrium solution (with perfect competition and forward markets in all goods and services); Walras increasingly came to be seen as the forefather of modern microeconomics (Debreu, 1984: 268; Schumpeter, 1954: 827).[5] William Jaffe's (1954) translation of Walras's *Elements of Pure Economics* was published for the AEA and the Royal Economic Society, and Friedman (1955), as one of the leading methodologists of his era, wrote a critique of 'Leon Walras and his Economic System' for the *American Economic Review*.

Friedman (1955a: 906–7) and Stigler (1949b: 38) noted that Marshall was Second Wrangler in mathematics, and that Walras, in contrast, had twice failed the entry examinations for the Ecole Polytechnique. Friedman (1955a: 904–9) argued that using 'very elementary mathematics indeed', Walras's work has led to a 'misconception' of economic theory. His general equilibrium system possessed 'an extraordinary aesthetic appeal as a beautifully articulated abstraction', but the failure to distinguish between the

> task Cournot outlined and the task accomplished by Walras . . . seems to me to be a primary source of methodological confusion in economics . . . [Walras's] problem is the problem of form not of content: of displaying an idealised picture of the economic system, not of constructing an engine for analysing concrete problems . . . [Cournot's] goal was an analysis that would, given the relevant statistical material, yield specific answers to specific empirical questions . . .

Walras's 'divorce of form from substance' had led to some 'nonsense'. The marginalist revolution assigned to *rareté* (marginal utility)

> an almost metaphysical role . . . 'it has no direct or measurable relation to space or time' [Walras, p.117] . . . He says nothing more on the subject and simply proceeds to take for granted that there is something called *rareté* which has numerical values that can be plotted . . . emphasis on pure form has an important role to play in providing a language, a classification scheme to use in organising materials – labels, as it were, for the compartments of our analytical filing box. This is Walras' great contribution.

One of Friedman's contributions has been to provide a classification scheme for all conceivable inflation-unemployment observations. Those who have followed him have 'taken for granted that there is something called the natural-rate of unemployment which has a numerical value that can be plotted'. Friedman's essay was written after a sabbatical at Cambridge where, in some powerful quarters, utility was regarded as a 'metaphysical concept of impregnable circularity', and where Friedman's methodology may have had an influence: 'The hallmark of a metaphysical proposition is that it is not capable of being tested' (Joan Robinson, 1962: 48, 8). The (rarely undertaken) test of the natural-rate model concerns its ability to *attract* the actual rate.

Prior to *Studies in the Quantity Theory of Money* (1956), Friedman's (1953: 7) major influence was as a methodologist: 'Viewed as a language, theory has no substantive content; it is a set of tautologies. Its function is to serve as a filing system for organising empirical material and facilitating our understanding of it.' It was 'factual evidence alone' which 'can show whether the categories of the "analytical filing system" have a meaningful empirical counterpart . . . the relevant question to be asked is usefulness and not rightness or wrongness.' Theory was perceived by Friedman (1976: 8) to be a series of substantial empirical propositions capable of being predictively tested:

> The definition of a *demand curve* is 'theory as language'. However, the statement that the demand curve slopes downward to the right is theory as a substantive empirical proposition. It has empirically observable consequences, whereas the definition of a *demand curve* does not. Theory as language coincides with Marshall's *engine of analysis*. The objective is to construct a language that will be most fruitful in both clarifying thought and facilitating the discovery of substantive propositions [emphases in text].

These demand curves are derived from a concept (utility) which may need no cardinal measure to assist the analysis. The value of the concept of the demand curve lies in its ability to organize 'knowledge and thinking about a problem' and to provide qualitative and 'quantitative estimates of the effects of various changes' (Friedman, 1976: 34). Friedman's framework suggests that the long-run Phillips curve is a language proposition, whereas the shape and gravitational characteristics of the short-run Phillips curves are substantial empirical propositions. In the disinflation zone, the natural-rate model adds value by providing quantitative estimates of the magnitude and duration of the unemployment required to reduce inflation to an acceptable level. But it is these substantial empirical propositions which are frequently less than adequately analysed by those who present estimates of the natural-rate of unemployment.

7.3 The Walrasian equations of the natural-rate counter-revolution

Keynes (1943: 185; JMK, XIII [1932]: 406; [1934]: 486–7) noted that 'the weapon of deliberately creating unemployment . . . to confine the tendency of wages to rise beyond the limits set by the volume of money . . . [is a] weapon the world after a good try, has decided to discard.' He constructed his policy revolution against the 'orthodox equilibrium theory' which saw strong 'natural forces' bringing output back to its optimal level.

But the Walrasian natural-rate model became the Marshallian 'special tool for the special problem' of formulating an appropriate policy response to the high inflation of the 1970s. The model assumes (usually without any supporting evidence) that there exists strong 'natural forces' pulling output and unemployment back to their natural levels. The natural-rate of unemployment is an *abstract* long-run concept, but the path towards it (if it exists and if it provides a magnetized trail for the actual rate of unemployment) is dependent upon the *actual* short-run characteristics of the economy in response to 'unnatural' levels of unemployment. Friedman (1974b: 150) specified:

> The long-run equilibrium in which, as I put it, 'all anticipations are realised' and that is determined by 'the earlier quantity theory plus the Walrasian equations of general equilibrium' is not a state that is assumed ever to be attained in practice. It is a logical construct that defines the norm or trend from which the actual world is always deviating but to which it is returning or about which it tends to fluctuate.

The correctness of the hypothesis 'is a question of fact to be determined by the consistency of the hypothesis with experience'.

The natural-rate model is a hypothesis to be tested (if it is capable of being falsified); it is not a species of revealed truth. As noted above, Koopmans referred to the 'Friedman critique' of econometrics; Don Patinkin (another Cowles economist) described the 'Friedman question' as 'under what circumstances would you abandon your pet theory?' (cited by Leeson, 1998: 443–4). Friedman (1974b: 1) claimed that the quantity theory framework 'has probably been "tested: with quantitative data more extensively than any other set of propositions in formal economics – unless it be the negatively sloped demand curve.' The negatively sloped demand curve coincides 'with Marshall's *engine of analysis*', but Friedman's (1968a: 9) quantity theory contains the proposition that the 'natural' rate of unemployment analytically separates 'real forces from monetary forces'. Estimates of the Walrasian natural-rate of unemployment which emerge from these 'real forces' are rarely subjected to 'Friedman's question'.

'At any moment in time', *if* the grinding of the Walrasian equations were possible, then a natural-rate of unemployment might emerge from those structural equations. But the implication of Friedman's view is that the crucial question is empirical: is the actual rate of unemployment gravitating towards or fluctuating around some estimate of equilibrium unemployment? Before the natural-rate concept is invested with any validity it must first pass the empirical test: is the actual rate returning to the natural-rate? There was no evidence to suggest that there were strong gravitational forces at work in the British economy which were returning the actual rate to the natural-rate. The British evidence suggests that the natural-rate is an untestable and unfalsifiable concept – an estimate of some abstract measure of unemployment that is graced with the unjustified title of 'natural'.

The natural-rate model *implies* (usually without any supporting evidence) that it is possible to provide policy-makers with accurate econometric estimates of the magnitude of the natural-rate of unemployment, and that this natural-rate exerts a reliably strong gravitational pull on the actual rate. Measured unemployment (U) differs from its natural level (U^N), only because of expectationary disequilibrium (i.e. inflationary expectations, ΔP^e, are not equal to actual inflation ΔP). Thus, any 'unnatural' (U^{UN}) divergence of U from U^N is a function of the speed of adjustment (α) of incorrect inflationary expectations.
The natural-rate model can be expressed as:

$$U = U^N + U^{UN} \tag{7.1}$$

$$U^{UN} = f[\alpha(\Delta P^e - \Delta P)] \tag{7.2}$$

While U^N can be reduced by microeconomic manipulation (improving labour market flexibility etc.), macroeconomic policy can affect disinflation only by increasing U above U^N; the speed of reduction of and therefore U^{UN} depends on α – the delusion variable. 'Unnatural' rates of unemployment are therefore attributed to this 'delusion' and will reduce to zero as inflationary expectations cease to be inaccurate. Equally, macroeconomic policy cannot sustainably reduce U below U^N, without incurring the cost of accelerating inflation. But at the core of this model lie two variables (P^e and U^N) which, Friedman has argued, are either impossible or extremely difficult to accurately measure.

Friedman's framework implies that the vertical long-run Phillips curve is a language proposition; the shape of the short-run Phillips curve and the gravitational pull of the natural-rate (and hence the speed of adjustment) are substantive propositions. The shape of the short-run Phillips curve in the natural-rate model (the crucial mechanism for the disinflation adjustment mechanism) is noticeably different from the shape of Phillips's (1958) and Lipsey's (1960) curves as unemployment reaches four or five per cent. The data (in contrast to the natural-rate model) suggests the existence of an important degree of downwards wage inflexibility – there appears to be an expectations trap preventing inflationary expectations from falling. As a substantive empirical proposition, the natural-rate of unemployment appears to be model specific, and not a general property of the macroeconomy.

Friedman (1953: 165) cautioned that 'wage rates tend to be among the less flexible prices', and thus unemployment was 'a highly inefficient method' of adjustment, because the 'adjustment will not have been completed until the deflation has run its sorry course'.[6] Later, Friedman (1977: 454; 1976: 215) thought that he saw in Phillips's work evidence of 'deflation' and 'falling wages' at higher levels of unemployment. Phillips (1958: 283), in contrast, found that in his 'highly non-linear' relationship, 'wage rates fall only very slowly'. In Phillips's data there were eight examples in the post-1904 period of falling wages (with unemployment ranging from 10 to 22 per cent); high levels of unemployment were more commonly associated with positive rates of wage inflation. With this degree of downwards wage stickiness, the natural-rate model suggests that 'unnatural' levels of unemployment would persist for lengthy periods.

7.4 The Walrasian colonization of the profession

Although Keynes was sceptical about the Walrasian approach, Hicks's *Value and Capital* (1939) was self-consciously in the Walrasian tradition, as was Samuelson's *Foundations of Economic Analysis* (1947).[7] These two books, together with *The General Theory*, were the foundations of professional training in the postwar period, and Keynesian macroeconomics came to be perceived as 'a short cut "general equilibrium" theory'. Since then, Walras and Marshall 'have been contesting for the souls of economists' (Tobin, 1987: 118; 1972: 104–5; Hicks, 1934: 347; Dreze, 1991: 7–8).

In his AEA Presidential Address, Friedman (1968a: 10) concluded that the monetary authorities 'cannot know what the "natural" rate is. Unfortunately, we have as yet devised no method to estimate accurately and readily the natural-rate of either interest or employment.' Three decades later, this empirical measurement exercise was still out of reach:

> As the coiner of the term, I am disturbed at its widespread misuse and misunderstanding. The natural-rate is not a fixed number. It is not 6% or 5%, or some other magic number... The natural-rate is a concept that does have an empirical counterpart – but that counterpart is not easy to measure and will depend on particular circumstances of time and place.
>
> (Friedman, 1996b)

But Friedman's Address was followed by numerous attempts to quantify this supposedly natural-rate of unemployment. Social Science Research Council funding for the Manchester Inflation Workshop began in July 1971; David Laidler (1975: 45), in presenting the 'implications of [Friedman's] ideas for our understanding of the British economy', reported that the 'preliminary results of work in progress at Manchester University' suggested that the natural-rate of unemployment was 'perhaps a little less than 2% in Britain, although such an estimate is necessarily subject to a wide margin of error... we shall nevertheless probably see an average of a million unemployed for five years or more if we are to get the inflation rate down below, say, five per cent by 1980.' Laidler's judgement was that this was 'too much unemployment for too long' and he argued that widespread indexation might reduce the unemployment cost of disinflation.

Laidler (1976: 71) concluded that 'we therefore have no way of putting the expectations augmented Phillips curve to the test in a way which will generate results that command widespread assent', although he hoped that reliable price expectations data might subsequently be generated from survey data. Laidler (1975: 42) also discussed the possibility that the natural-rate 'hypothesis' might be false. But in his Nobel Lecture, Friedman (1977: 459) declared that 'The natural-rate hypothesis is by now widely accepted by economists'; the economy would return, after disinflation, to the natural-rate. The policy choice was therefore a question of timing:

> When reporters and others ask how much unemployment it would cost to reduce unemployment, I say to them, when did you last beat

> your wife? How much unemployment will it cost *not* to beat inflation? ... *if you continue to let inflation accelerate you are going to have higher unemployment either way.* So you only have a choice between which way you want the unemployment to come. Do you want it to come while you are getting sicker or do you want it to come while you are getting better? [emphases in text]
>
> (Friedman, 1975b: 32)

But this 1975 account is not a completely accurate representation of the vertical long-run Phillips curve model (neither does it fully describe the positively sloped long-run Phillips curve that Friedman later described in his Nobel Lecture). The higher unemployment that follows a policy-induced increase in inflation is the product of centripetal force: the benign 'return' to the natural-rate (which acts as a gravitational brake, halting the rise in unemployment beyond the natural-rate). But the higher unemployment that follows from policy-induced *dis*inflation is the result of centrifugal force: unemployment increases beyond the natural-rate until the centripetal force of error correction (with respect to incorrect inflationary expectations) pulls the system back to centre at the natural-rate of unemployment. The first scenario is a constrained rise in unemployment; the natural-rate model tells us nothing, *ex ante*, about the level and duration of unemployment associated with the second scenario.

Ex post, the margin of error was revealed to be much wider than expected: none of us expected the deep and prolonged depression that ensued... the experience has been chastening (Laidler, 1985). Patrick Minford (1994: 230) recalled that:

> At the beginning of the 1980s, I was helping to push the incoming Tories towards the idea of a medium term financial strategy to control inflation and I tended to think of the natural-rate of unemployment as something that would not be too outrageous a number. I don't think it ever crossed my mind that it was anything like three million.

Measured unemployment increased from 2.1 per cent in 1973 to 13 per cent in 1985 (3.2 million) and remained over 2 million until January 1985 (Kavanagh, 1990: 231–2).

It is often said that economists, like photographers, fall in love with their models; certainly Minford appears to be prepared to acknowledge a personal forecasting failure in preference to the idea that he was led into error by the natural-rate framework. According to Friedman's (1968a: 9) exposition, the natural-rate of unemployment should have *fallen* as a result of the labour market reform and diminution of trade union power of the Thatcher years. Any framework that can lead such an economist to 'go astray' by 'taking a fix on the wrong model' must be regarded as suspect: either the natural-rate inexplicably increased over sixfold in less than a decade, or the model is an unreliable guide to policy.

There is another alternative. The gravitational pull of the natural-rate may be so weak that 'full adjustment to the new rate of inflation takes about as long for employment as for interest rates, say, a couple of decades' – which was exactly Friedman's (1968a: 11) AEA Presidential prediction. But in contrast to this pessimistic scenario, Patrick Minford informed the 1980 House of Commons Select Committee that (on New Classical assumptions), 'the disturbance to output and employment from reduction in the money supply and P[ublic] S[ector]B[orrowing] R[equirement] would be minimal' (cited by Jay, 1986: 208). Likewise, before the same Committee, Friedman (1980: 61, 56) predicted that from 'the best evidence... (a) only a modest reduction in output and employment will be a side effect of reducing inflation to single figures by 1982 [... a temporary retardation in economic growth] and (b) the effect on investment and the potential for future growth will be highly favourable.' Unemployment was 'an unfortunate side effect of reducing inflation'; only rigidities stood in the way of a rapid return to the natural-rate of unemployment: 'The mechanism causing the contraction in output is the slowing of nominal spending in response to the slowing of monetary growth and the inevitable lags in the absorption of slower spending by wages and prices.'

Nearly all the discussion of the natural-rate model provided by Friedman relates to the behaviour of the economy on the expansionary side of the natural-rate, where increases in unemployment are constrained by powerful centripetal forces. The closest reference to policy-induced *dis*inflation in his Presidential Address (1968a: 10) is the reference to monetary authorities choosing a target rate of unemployment above the natural-rate: 'They will be led to produce a deflation and an accelerating deflation at that.' In 'Wage Determination and Unemployment' there are ten examples of unanticipated changes in aggregate demand, but the first nine all relate to unanticipated *increases* in nominal aggregate demand (1976: 216, 222, 224, 226, 227, 230, 232, 233, 234). Friedman concluded that the natural-rate model was validated by experience: any resemblance between the model and 'what has been happening in Britain is not coincidental: what British governments have tried to do is to keep unemployment below the natural-rate, and to do so they have had to accelerate inflation – from 3.9 percent in 1964 to 16 percent in 1974.'

Few economists would object to this explanation; Phillips (1962: 1–2), for example, noted that unacceptably high British inflation had been caused by the government maintaining employment at an 'extremely high level'. But this reveals nothing about the existence (or non-existence) of a natural-rate of unemployment. Neither does it provide any information about the behaviour of an economy undergoing *dis*inflation. Of Friedman's ten examples, only the last discusses the main monetarist policy proposition, an unanticipated *decline* in aggregate demand:

> Conversely let there be an unanticipated decline in aggregate demand, so that employers are willing to hire fewer workers at each real wage rate as perceived by them. Workers searching for jobs will find fewer offers that, on the basis of their unchanged anticipations, are attractive enough to compensate them for giving up the search. The average time between jobs will lengthen, and so will recorded unemployment. As the less attractive employment situation becomes more widely known, job-seekers will revise their anticipation about opportunities, become less choosy, and recorded unemployment will decline towards its natural level.
>
> (1976: 235)

It is not clear why unemployed job-seekers should take two decades to become 'less choosy', but this is the substantial empirical proposition of the natural-rate model. Perhaps this individualistic explanation of the cause of unemployment appealed to Mrs Thatcher (1995: 126, 95, 417) who echoed both the sentiments and the language of Friedman's (1968a: 14–15) Presidential analogy of steering by the stars:

> Alan [Walters'] view was that . . . the monetary base was the best, indeed the only reliable star to steer by . . . True, inflation had moved up from the low point it had reached after the [1983] election, and unemployment, always a lagging indicator remained stubbornly high . . . [but we] knew how to control the money supply through interest rates and did so.

During the course of the 1979–83 Parliament, unemployment rose from 5.4 per cent to 12.7 per cent and industrial output fell by over 11 per cent (Kavanagh, 1990: 231). In 1980, Nigel Lawson informed the press that the 'medium-term financial strategy is essentially a monetary – or if you like monetarist – strategy' (cited by Congdon, 1989: 231). But when asked in January 1985 by Peter Jay 'with all-time record unemployment figures this week, have [we] yet reached that natural-rate', Mrs Thatcher replied: 'It's not a doctrine to which I've subscribed. It's one which I think came in with Milton Friedman. I used to look at it, I used to look at it and not adopt it' (cited by Smith, 1987: 122). Shortly afterwards, the *Financial Times* ran a lead article under the headline 'Monetarism Dead – Official'. But some economists continue to estimate the natural-rate of unemployment that supposedly results from unemployed workers loosing their delusions and choosiness. Friedman (1976: 221) described as 'somewhat ludicrous the confident statements that many economists had made about 'trade offs' based on empirically fitted Phillips curves'. A similar (or harsher) judgement could be made about statements concerning the unemployment costs of disinflation based on the natural-rate model.

The leading Keynesian formalist described the 'virus' quality of Keynes's *General Theory* (Samuelson, 1964: 315) but the 1976 edition of his textbook accorded only a footnote to the natural-rate model (Samuelson, 1976b: 835, n.8). Shortly afterwards, however, that model conquered the profession, in part for reasons that Friedman found less than satisfactory about Walras: it was 'an elegant and concise representation of the inflationary process for the long-run' (Taylor, 1979: 108; Blinder, 1979: 19–20). Robert J. Gordon (1978), and Rudiger Dornbusch and Stanley Fischer (1978), incorporated the natural-rate model as the organizing concept of macroeconomics into the first editions of their intermediate textbooks. But the relevant substantive empirical questions are rarely asked by those who present estimates of supposedly natural-rates of unemployment. The various editions of Gordon's textbook, for example, present scientific estimates of the natural-rate of unemployment in the United States from 1890 to the present day, with no examination of the 'substantive' empirical question (including 'Friedman's question').

Keynes had somewhat of a Cassandra complex and during the Monetarist decade many Keynesians shared this fate. Followers of the formalist and Keynesian revolutions displayed little immunity as the Old Keynesian era ended. For Keynes, the long run was a 'subject for undergraduates' (Joan Robinson, 1962: 75; Eshag, 1963: 100, n.118), and Robert Solow (1987: 183) complained that the way macroeconomists used the natural-rate of unemployment was an 'intellectual scandal'. But during the current period of Keynesian revival, the procedure of comparing 'magic' estimates of the natural-rate of unemployment with the actual rate of unemployment to describe a monetary policy rule still retains an 'amaz[ing]...status' (Rogerson, 1996: 86). Ironically, these anti-formalist objections echo Keynes's (1939: 559) complaint about Tinbergen: 'The worst of him is that he is much more interested in getting on with the job than in deciding whether the job is worth getting on with.'

There are no truly general theories in science, only competing explanations which, for a variety of reasons (not all to do with the 'classical' process), command varying degrees of respect among practitioners. The natural-rate model challenged its primary adversary, the high-inflation trade-off interpretation of the Phillips curve, and is now challenged by models which invoke hysteresis, implicit contracts, insiders and outsiders, an expectations trap, efficiency wages, etc. Not all of these models deny that 'at any point in time' (to use Friedman's phrase) a natural-rate of unemployment might emerge from the Walrasian equations, but they tend to deny that the gravitational pull of any particular natural-rate is stronger than the gravitational pull of the *actual* rate of unemployment (Phelps, 1996).[8] The positive co-movements of inflation–unemployment observations in the 1960s *appeared* to be a vindication of the power of the equilibrating forces of the natural-rate model; and this led to a widely held conviction that these equilibrating forces could be relied upon (in the disinflation zone) as unemployment increased in the 1970s and 1980s. But the forces set up by both inflation and policy-induced recession seem to resemble unpredictable chain reactions rather than the attractive equilibrating forces of the natural-rate model – causing some Monetarists to question the validity of their earlier policy optimism.

For Alfred Marshall (1920: 564), 'The most valuable of all capital is that invested in human beings', and increasing unemployment above the natural-rate tends to reduce the stock of human capital (thus increasing the natural-rate), leaving a large pool of outsiders who have only a limited ability to affect the wages of insiders. Thus the idea of a unique and stable equilibrium configuration exerting an all-powerful influence on the actual course of unemployment has been challenged by the idea that the natural-rate limps behind, and tracks, the actual rate, with (in Keynes's phrase) 'not so lame a foot' (JMK, XXII [1940]: 120–1).

7.5 Concluding remarks

In Stigler's (1983c: 210) judgement, had Friedman been a Walrasian, not a Marshallian, much of the Chicago research programme would, he judged, have been thwarted.[9] But as Harry Johnson (1971) pointed out, the natural-rate model is silent about the short run (the speed and effectiveness of unemployment-induced disinflation):

> The most serious defects of the Monetarist counter-revolution from the academic point of view are, on the one hand, the abnegation of the restated quantity theory of money from the responsibility of providing a theory of the determination of prices and output [analysing the supply response of the economy to monetary impulses... whether monetary changes affected prices or quantities] and on the other hand, its continuing reliance on the methodology of positive economics... Personally, I expect [Monetarism] to peter out

After Friedman's AEA Address, Johnson (a Chicago colleague) and Patinkin (an ex-Chicago colleague) became two of Friedman's most bitter adversaries. Patinkin (1969: 1974) focused on the supposedly bogus role of an interwar Chicago oral quantity theory tradition, while Johnson (1970: 85–86, 107, 48) suggested that Friedman had constructed his counter-revolution by imitating the tactics of the Keynesian revolution:

> My personal hypothesis is that, as a result of his studies of the Marshallian demand curve and his year as a visitor at Cambridge, Friedman became enamoured of the "Cambridge oral tradition" as a concept permitting the attribution to an institution of a wisdom exceeding that displayed in its published works, and unconsciously stole a leaf from Cambridge's book for the benefit of his own institution.

With respect to Friedman, Johnson (1971) concluded that 'one should not be too fastidious in condemnation of the techniques of scholarly chicanery to promote a revolution or counter-revolution in economic theory.'

The truth-content of Friedman's 'oral tradition' continues to generate passionate scholarly interest, often involving speculation about what Johnson described as the 'motivational construction' behind Friedman's monetarist counter-revolution (Parkin, 1986; Patinkin, 1986; Steindl, 1990; Tavlas, 1998a and b; Laidler, 1993, 1998a and b; Leeson 1998). It certainly appears that Friedman and Stigler brought a considerable degree of sociological perceptiveness to their assault on (and defence of) various aspects of economic orthodoxy. Friedman enhanced his policy-revolution by embracing the *language* of his opponents (IS-LM, econometrics, income-expenditure, money demand), a language that he was often sceptical about. As a *language revolution*, the natural-rate model is comparable, in terms of influence, to the Keynesian revolution that it sought to overthrow.

Friedman's macroeconomics was a continuation of the business cycle research associated with Arthur Burns and W. C. Mitchell that was undertaken at the National Bureau of Economic Research. Koopmans (1947) savaged the Burns-Mitchell research methods as 'measurement without theory'.[10] In reply, Friedman (1950: 489) noted (in defence of Mitchell, his mentor) that the failure to use high-status modern language could destroy almost completely the influence of an economist. Friedman reflected that Mitchell's lack of a 'more direct, obvious and far-reaching influence' (in a profession increasingly dominated by Walrasians and Keynesians) could be explained by his 'own attitude towards his empirical work as expressed in his research program . . . the elaborately casual language in which it is presented, and the extent to which its abstract elements are concealed . . . He uses none of the jargon we have grown so fond of.'

Did Friedman construct the natural-rate model so as to maximize its appeal to an audience that was captivated by high-status Walrasian language? Or are those who estimate natural-rate models 'Bastard Monetarists'? It is unlikely that there will ever be a consensus about such motivational questions. Certainly, Friedman's (1968b: 5, n.2) engagement with the economics profession was undertaken with strategic considerations in mind – against the 'conditioned reflex[es]' of 'entrenched Keynesianism'. Equally, the natural-rate model appears to be a carefully constructed Chicago candidate, designed to challenge macroeconomic orthodoxy. There are similarities, even of language, between Walras's marginalist revolt against the widely accepted labour theory of value, and Friedman's natural-rate revolt against the Keynesian hegemony: 'Any value in exchange, once established, partakes of the character of a natural phenomenon, natural in its origins, natural in its manifestations and natural in essence' (Walras, 1954: 69). In constructing his counter-revolution, Friedman (1974a), a self-confessed 'collector of schools', was behaving *as if* he were a self-conscious revolutionary, aware of these historical precedents. In preparing his review of Walras, Friedman (1955: 907, n.7) had access to a (then) unpublished doctoral dissertation on *The Rise of the Marginal Utility School, 1870–89*, by a Chicago student, Richard Howey. According to Howey (1989: xxiii, 38), Walras 'had a plan for scientific revolution . . . Later he sensed correctly that if he was to "assume" measurability, the less said about it the better'.

Friedman (1953: 7) described theory as a 'filing system', and the great contribution of the natural-rate concept is in providing a 'filing system' for *all* conceivable inflation–unemployment observations, even if the natural-rate model remains unfalsifiable and untestable. Indeed, many macroeconomists *assume* measurability, or rather assume that estimates of the natural-rate (however derived) exert some gravitational pull on the actual rate.

Monetary targeting may have petered out – but the Monetarist natural-rate model remains at the core of applied macroeconomics. This was, in part, because a Marshallian had placed a Walrasian concept at the core of an increasingly Walrasian discipline, despite his belief that Walrasian analysis has 'value for a very different purpose. It is an extremely useful abstract conception to bring out the logic of the interrelation of the price system; [but] it cannot be used to analyse a concrete problem' (Friedman, 1976: 26).[11] No doubt, fancier econometric footwork will continue to produce estimates of the natural-rate of unemployment. But these estimates will serve to mislead policy-makers until the 'concrete problem' of the gravitational pull on the actual rate is successfully addressed.

Notes

2 'The Ghosts I Called I Can't Get Rid of Now': the Keynes-Tinbergen-Friedman-Phillips Critique of Keynesian Macroeconometrics

1. The question of how variables were measured, and in what units, left open the possibility of 'devastating inconsistencies'. Secondly, the assumption of linearity with respect to *all* economic forces was, he thought, 'ridiculous'. Thirdly, the arbitrary choice of the first and last year of a series for which a time trend is calculated 'looks to be a disastrous procedure' (Keynes, 1939: 563–6; 1940: 155; see also Klein, 1992: 184)
2. A similar fate befell the Harvard Economic Society, whose econometric forecasts misread the downturn in 1929 (Galbraith, 1987: 262).
3. Interwar business cycle research was dominated by the empirical projects of W. C. Mitchell and Warren M. Persons (Morgan, 1990: 40). During his period at the New School (1919–22), Mitchell organized the NBER, which devoted its resources to the statistical investigation of the business cycle (Dorfman, 1949: 456). Mitchell distrusted correlation techniques, and was concerned that invalid causal implications could be derived from them. He was alarmed by the possibility that professional ethical standards could become corrupted in this enlarged world of business cycle statistics, forecasts and funding: '-[Economists] do not always decline the over-flattering invitation with the firmness which befits a scientific conscience' (cited by Dorfman, 1959: 210). In its first research project, the NBER became engaged in an early econometric dispute about the validity of Pareto's 'law' of income distribution (Dorfman, 1959: 204–5), and it was as Secretary to the NBER Conference on Research in Income and Wealth (1937–40) that Milton Friedman became more of an economist than a statistician.
4. Most students who have passed through the various econometrics courses offered by our profession would be forgiven for thinking that this subject lacked a systematically analysed history: 'It is a minor scandal that there is no comprehensive history of either the rise of econometrics or the mathematization of economics' (Weintraub, 1985: 140). In recent years we have benefited from some excellent research into the history of econometrics from Darnell (1984), Christ (1985), Epstein (1987), Morgan (1990), Darnell and Evans (1990), Keuzenkamp (1991), Dharmapala (1993) and others, plus the contributors to the special issue of *Oxford Economic Papers* (1989), edited by de Marchi and Gilbert.
5. Tinbergen (1969: 43) wrote: 'Returning to models, I am sometimes wondering whether, upon looking at some recent work by planners, I should not repeat the famous words by Goethe's Zauberlehrling... "The ghosts I called I can't get rid of now". Sometimes indeed some of our followers *overdo* model building' [emphasis in original].

6. Tinbergen (1979: 342–3) knew what Keynes meant: 'Sometimes, indeed, intuition constitutes a basis for new scientific results. It should be the intuition of a genius, however. For simpler souls, intuition may be less reliable.'
7. Frisch (1970: 165) quoted approvingly Norbert Weiner's remark about the economists' habit of 'dressing up their rather imprecise ideas in the language of the infinitesimal calculus', which was analogous to the vague feelings that 'these magic rites and vestments will at once put them abreast of modern culture and technique'. Frisch concluded that 'I am sorry to say that some econometricians have often been liable to forget these basic principles in practice and, therefore, have not been critical enough when they apply their techniques and mathematical analyses. This remark is particular important when it is a question of drawing conclusions about *the economic policy to be followed in a concrete situation'* [emphasis in text]. Koopmans (1949: 70) stated that 'the econometric approach is not a substitute for theory, but one of the servants of theory', but later (1957: 170, 198) reflected:

   > In principle, tools have a servant's status . . . if we look with a historian's interest at the development of a science, however, we find that tools also have a life of their own. They may even come to dominate an entire period or school of thought . . . Our servants may thus become our guides, for better or for worse . . . It should be kept in mind that the sharpness and power of these remarkable tools of inductive reasoning are bought by willingness to adopt a specification of the universe in a form suitable for mathematical analysis.

8. Friedman knows more about the use and abuse of statistics than most economists: he studied at Columbia University under the mathematical statistician Harold Hotelling (1933–4); he was a statistical assistant to Henry Schultz at Chicago (1934–5); he worked with economic measurement and data analysis at the NBER (1937–40); he was Statistical Director of the Wisconsin Income Study (1940–1). Friedman's early career either combined, or alternated between, mathematical statistics and economics. For most of the war years, at least, he was exclusively concerned with mathematical statistics (Rose Friedman, 1976: 22; Friedman, 1988a: 83–6; Wallis, 1980: 322).
9. Critics argued that they did not test the restrictions imposed, and they were accused of a misspecification, which influenced the outcome of the race, and were 'setting up two strawmen and crowning one of them' (Desai, 1981: 112, 104–6; Ando and Modigliani, 1965; de Prano and Mayer, 1965; Hester, 1964).
10. Koopmans' rejoinder (1947) indicated that the pioneer econometricians did not regard the Keynes-Friedman critique as fatal to their project. This brilliant group of scholars (including nine future Nobel Laureates, Simon, Debreu, Becker, Arrow, Tobin, Koopmans, Modigliani, Markowitz and Klein) proceeded to lay the theoretical foundations of econometrics. Eleven of the 33 research associates (1939–55) were elected to membership of the National Academy of Sciences, and 22 became presidents of major professional associations (Hildreth, 1986: 111; Klein, 1978: 326). Frisch and Tinbergen shared the first Nobel Prize in Economics. This econometric work was in stark contrast to the 'statistical economics' of Burns and Mitchell at the NBER,

who, Koopmans believed, studied business cycles 'as if they were the eruptions of a mysterious volcano' (cited by Epstein, 1987: 64).

11. 'We the Lausanne people, were indeed so enthusiastic all of us about the new venture and eager to give and take, that we had hardly time to eat when we sat together at lunch or at dinner with our notes floating around on the table to the despair of the waiters' (Frisch, 1970: 152). It was what Martin Beckman called 'the heroic age of econometrics' (cited by Craver and Leijonhufvud, 1987: 181).
12. In the postwar period the 'economics miracle' really took off: it was as if economics became the 'language' of government, and there was a great demand for those who spoke the language (Stein, 1986). Samuelson described the period from 1932 to 1975 for economists as 'the great wave of a Kondratieff expansion [for economists]. The New Deal and Welfare State created a vast new market for economists in government... Then came the post-war boom in education' (1988: 60–1; Desai, 1981: 55; Pesaran and Smith, 1985: 148). The 1940s and 1950s were the decades of enthusiasm and optimism for government planning, and this created a massive demand for advice from economists, often of a technical nature. The entire economies of Japan and West Germany were available for experimentation. The price mechanism had, it was believed, failed in the 1930s and had subsequently played little role in allocating resources during the war (at least at the governmental level). Foreign aid and the Marshall Plan would, it was believed, restructure the non-communist world. A new subdiscipline, development economics, emerged, much influenced by the structuralist approach to planning (Little, 1982: 76–85; Meier and Seers, 1984). The emerging welfare state required a broad tax base to fund it, and taxes came to be perceived primarily as a technical tool to be manipulated by policy makers in order to contain inflation. A flavour of the confidence of the time can be sampled by reference to the papers by Marschak, Klein and Edward Teller, and Marschak and Klein (the latter delivered to the Econometrics Society meeting in 1946), which advocated an expenditure of 20 billion dollars per year over 15 years to relocate all inhabitants of cities with over 50 000 inhabitants to ribbon cities or underground cities in order to minimise the effects of an atomic assault on the US (Epstein, 1987: 81, 95, n. 8).
13. The pioneering optimism of this second wave was almost immediately confronted with scepticism. The Institute for Mathematical Statistics meeting in Ithaca, New York, in August 1946 concluded that the Cowles group approach was unlikely to result in meaningful estimated parameters. Little confidence was held out for future developments: 'Data as bad as economic data' was incapable of accurately discriminating between alternative models (Tukey, cited by Epstein, 1987: 100). The attempt to derive an exact model of the capitalist system was derided by Schumpeter; Irving Fischer concluded that he had seen 'a lot of people burn their fingers over discoveries of cycles. The discoverer "sees things" almost as bizarre as drunkards' (cited by Epstein, 1987: 103). The most persistent critic was Milton Friedman who presented to the 1947 Econometrics Society meeting a manifesto entitled 'A Monetary and Fiscal Framework for Economic Stability' (1948a), which offered an alternative to the short-run stabilization perspective of the Cowles workers. Koopmans asked 'can we meet the Friedman critique: that Christ's experiments

have shown that the information contained in the data so far processed have been insufficient for good forecasting' (cited by Epstein, 1987: 111). Marschak retreated from his previous position with respect to the NBER survey research method. The Friedman critique, plus reviews by Arrow, Orcutt, Solow, Samuelson, Leontieff, Wold and others, plus disappointing empirical results and an increasing awareness of the paucity of reliable data, effected a 'retreat from structure' from 1947: 'The empirical work was an exhausting disappointment both for the tedium of computation and the lack of professional acceptance' (Epstein, 1987: 110); 'The econometric approach of the Cowles Commission seems to be petering out rapidly or not getting anywhere beyond extensive methodological discussions' (Haberler, 1949: 84).

14. The Cowles econometricians were perceived to be seeking a 'social analogue for Newtonian mechanics... Tycho and Kepler are becoming fairly regular attenders of economic discussions these days' (Vining, 1949: 80, 77). This analogy was also prevalent among the LSE econometricians. In September 1608, a trader at the annual Frankfurt Fair offered for sale a telescope which could magnify seven times. In March 1610, Galileo published his first booklet, a short but dramatic work called *Sidereus Nuncius*, or *Messenger from the Stars*. The universe would never appear to be the same again. The walled-in Aristotelian universe, with its immutable social order, would be destroyed by a seventeenth-century retreat to the heliocentric perceptions of Aristarchus (Koestler, 1959: 43–65; Butterfield, 1957: 55–76). Exactly three and a half centuries later, Phillips (November 1958) and Lipsey (February 1960) turned the newly refined econometric telescope onto the problem of the behaviour of money wages during the course of the business cycle. With pioneering optimism the M^{2}T economists sought to use this telescope to turn economics into a fully empirical science. There was also an Aristotelian authority to be vanquished. In the first edition of his textbook, Lipsey cited Robbins on empirical analysis:

    > But is it not desirable to transcend such limitations? Ought we not to be in a position to give numerical values to the scales of valuation, to establish qualitative laws of supply and demand?... No doubt such knowledge would be useful. But a moment's reflection should make it plain that we are here entering into a field of investigation *where there is no reason to suppose that uniformities are to be discovered*... Is it possibly reasonable to suppose that coefficients derived from the observations of a particular herring market at a particular time and place have any *permanent* significance – save as Economic History [emphasis in text].

    Lipsey (1966: 219, 218, n. 1) bemoaned that these views were 'still held by economists'. In a seminar on 'Refutation and Comparison', Kurt Klappholz also mentioned Robbins. Chris Archibald retorted: 'Robbins Aristotelian, not relevant' (M^{2}T Seminar notes, 7 March 1958). Further evidence of the importance of this historical analogy is provided by the opening extract from Beveridge, and the final sentence, in Lipsey's (1966: xi–xii, 860–1) best-selling textbook. In seeking to rigorously scrutinize economic data they were aspiring to the highest standards of science. They hoped to resolve conflicts over perceptions and policies, and to effect a Newtonian-style revolution in economics.

15. Econometric agnosticism, or at least reservations about policy relevance, remained a minority taste in the 1960s, with potentially explosive critiques such as Phillips's (1968) being almost entirely ignored. The exchange between Basmann and Klein and associates (in Brunner, 1972) reflected the determination of practitioners to press on almost regardless. Unorthodox and problematic ideas tended to be ignored because they 'would have inconveniently impeded the progress of econometrics at the time of its most rapid growth' (Desai, 1981: 116–17, 120). Applied econometrics in the age of the computer, and in the presence of an increasing demand for financially lucrative expert consultancy from government agencies, acquired an *ad hoc* character which was often cut adrift from professional disquiet. The statistical economists believed that potential regularities and relationships could be revealed by an interaction with the data. Econometricians believed that the data would 'speak' when a model had been imposed upon it. Tinbergen was also very knowledgable about his data and was concerned about its quality. Post-pioneering econometrics gradually entered a less creative, more mechanical phase, where concerns about the quality of the data were less prominent. Frisch and his co-workers were aware of the possibilities of deriving 'fictitious' results from econometric analysis (Epstein, 1987: 91). Koopmans persistently, if vainly, emphasized the need to report all results, not just the preferred set. Coal-face enthusiasm for model estimation appeared to be largely oblivious to the scepticism and concern expressed by some about the lack of model evaluation.
16. Don Patinkin (1976: 1095) found it 'somewhat depressing to see how many of [Keynes's criticisms] are, in practice, still of relevance today.' Maurice Allais (1992: 35), a theoretical physicist, in addition to being the recipient of the 1988 Nobel Prize in economic science, bemoaned 'the crop of pseudo-theories based on the mechanical application, devoid of any real intelligence, of econometrics and statistical techniques . . . *pseudo-models*, accompanied by a mathematical-statistical panoply of *untamed*, totally unjustified economics which seem to the naive to be scientific theories, whereas they are generally just empty shells' [emphases in original].

3 The Chicago Counter-Revolution and the Sociology of Economic Knowledge

1. This paper was planned around 1990, after having read Neil De Marchi's account of Popper and the M^2T economists. Unfortunately, by the time I got round to writing it, George Stigler and Chris Archibald had passed away, and so I never benefited from their thoughts.
2. Together with W. Allen Wallis, they were the 'three musketeers' of the post-war Chicago School (Leube, 1986: xiii).
3. Chamberlin (1957: 93, 148) wrote that 'It is possible that the economy should be made "more competitive"; it is also quite possible that it should be made "more monopolistic"'. He also referred to the 'fallacious ideal of perfect competition.'

4. In 1982, after winning the Nobel prize, Stigler (1988a: 137) held an impromptu press conference at the White House and was 'removed from the platform in a manner reminiscent of vaudeville days' after mentioning the word 'depression'. The unemployment associated with the monetary disinflation of the early Reagan years had rendered this word 'obscene'. Despite Stigler's lack of tact or discretion, Robert Barro's (1991) concluded that he acquired an influence which 'exceeded that of any economist who has spent much time in Washington.'
5. Stigler (1961a: 330) noted that 'the study of how economic theory influences views on policy by non-economists is still an essentially unstudied subject.'
6. Melvin Reder (correspondence, 1 June 1997) is doubtful that this presentation would have been successful: 'I doubt that he would have owned up to it, even if he had been made aware of it. George was very sceptical of "big think" in all its forms and very likely would have tried hard to puncture such a theory had it been presented to him.'
7. Chamberlin (1957: 300) juxtaposed two quotes from Stigler and Friedman (emphasizing the repetitive use of the word 'meaninglessness') and concluded that 'The idea is virtually the same, and I am unfortunately unable to identify its origins as between the two writers cited.'
8. Johnson arrived at Chicago in 1959, shortly after Stigler's return. According to Shils (1977: 87), Johnson found the atmosphere uncongenial and considered leaving shortly after arriving. One of the first articles he published at Chicago was entitled 'The Consumer and Madison Avenue', but the title 'epitomizes the pervasive and subtly corrupting influence of the hucksters on the American way of life' and had been chosen for him by 'a senior professor of economics who is presumably more expert than I in the mass marketing of economic wares' (1960: 3).
9. McCloskey (correspondence, 26 September 1997) also reflected that 'I was nearly the last student of Chamberlin at Harvard. It was a strange experience to go from an environment in which one sneered at Stigler to one in which one sneered at Chamberlin.'
10. There is evidence in Stigler's writings to support these concerns. Stigler (1967d), for example, in criticizing Galbraith's framework as a 'poor vehicle to carry us to an understanding of our times' also stated that he was guilty of making a 'nightime leap over the ocean of motive.'
11. 'Here was a Chicago theory that didn't even annoy socialists!' (Stigler, 1986 [1982]: 144).
12. Stigler (1987a: 52) reflected that 'a great nation can survive and prosper no matter how misinformed its political leaders.'
13. While advising Presidential candidate Barry Goldwater, Friedman noted (on leave at Columbia) a chink in the Old Keynesian armour:

    > I was appalled at what I found. There was an unbelievable degree of intellectual homogeneity, of acceptance of a standard set of views complete with cliche answers to every objection, of smug self-satisfaction at belonging to an ingroup. The closest similar experience I have ever had was at Cambridge, England, and even that was a distant second. The homogeneity and provincialism of the New York intellectual community made them pushovers in discussions about Goldwater's views. They had

> cliche answers but only to their self-created straw men. To exaggerate only slightly, they had never talked to anyone who really believed, and had thought deeply about, views drastically different from their own. As a result, when they heard real arguments they had no answers, only amazement...
>
> (1974: 16; 1967; see also Stigler, 1973a)

14. Rose Friedman (1976a: 30; 1976b: 23) described Stigler as 'one of our dearest friends'. It was Stigler who persuaded the Friedmans to come to the University of Minnesota in 1945.
15. Friedman was President of the Society during its twenty-fifth anniversary and believed that it should disband having accomplished its major purpose (Rose Friedman, 1976 (9): 26).
16. 'George was and is a delight and a treasure as a friend and as an intellectual influence... Few economists have germinated so many new ideas and so profoundly influenced the course of economic research' (Friedman, 1986: 84).
17. Friedman (1976: 235) wrote:

    > Let there be an unanticipated decline in aggregate demand, so that employers are willing to hire fewer workers at each real wage rate as perceived by them. Workers searching for jobs will find fewer offers that, on the basis of their unchanged anticipations, are attractive enough to compensate them for giving up the search. The average time between jobs will lengthen, and so will recorded unemployment. As the less attractive employment situation becomes more widely known, job-seekers will revise their anticipation about opportunities, become less choosy, and recorded unemployment will decline towards its natural level.

    Stigler's (1962a: 94, 104) 'Information in the Labor Market' is concerned, in large part, with the problem of how job seekers 'acquire information on the wage rate... a highly rewarding area for future research.'
18. Rosen (1993: 813–14) concluded that Stigler's unrelenting opposition to monopolistic competition hindered the development of the economics of product differentiation.
19. Keynes did not utilize an imperfect competition framework in the *General Theory* for tactical reasons: he apparently informed Gardiner Means that he 'wanted to beat the buggers at their own game' (cited by Marris, 1992: 1241, n. 13).
20. At least one (recently arrived) Chicago economist concluded that economists were no longer 'concerned with matters of vital importance to the affluence society', and had turned away 'from intellectual interest into professional competence' as expressed in mathematical and econometric techniques (Johnson, 1960: 119–120).
21. Stigler (1970: 426; 1957a: 159; 1982a: vii, 86) cautioned that 'biography distorts rather than illuminates the understanding of scientific work', although he also thought that Rogin's history of economic theory intentionally added little, but unintentionally shed 'an illuminating light' on a species of American late-New Deal radical thought.

22. Sherwin Rosen (correspondence, 23 April 1997) recalled that the question of influence came up in conversations with Stigler 'rather often, but in a rather oblique casual way and not particularly in a formal way'. Deirdre McCloskey (correspondence, 2 June 1997) recalled that 'they were self-conscious counter-revolutionaries. They talked about it all the time.'
23. Empirical workers 'do not give [their] generalisations the abstract and systematic formulation that characterises conventional economic theory. As a result, the generalisations seem closely bound to the specific empirical researches on which they are based, and they lend themselves much less to cumulative refinement and elaboration and to widening areas of application.'
24. He argued that 'received theory deserves more respect and quantitative materials less respect than are commonly accorded them.'
25. 'Unless an author explicitly sets out to refute a theory, one should characterise his attitude towards that theory as favourable, or at worst neutral, if he actually refers to the theory. For he is reviving its currency and advertising its existence' (1978: 196).
26. 'The theorist is a dangerous person to let loose on economic reform' (1980: 349).
27. He stated that 'two thirds *at a minimum* made no positive contribution to received knowledge on oligopoly behaviour: they contain neither a new fact nor a new idea [emphasis in text]'. Likewise, papers that were critical of Reaganomics contained 94 per cent malice and about 2 per cent knowledge (1988d: 91).
28. The 'scientific content of a man's work is the content as interpreted by his contemporaries' (1990b: 765).
29. Stigler (1949a: 95) also noted that: 'Tactically this is perhaps Lord Keynes's greatest contribution: his contributions need not be itemised.'
30. On 12 February 1992, Samuelson wrote to Patinkin (just after Stigler's death): 'Often I would write a paper really with George Stigler in mind. Almost never would he vouchsafe a reaction. Still we shall miss him.' Patinkin replied (6 March 1992): 'I'm glad that we had the same experience with George Stigler. In my case it was even worse . . . ' (Patinkin Papers, Duke University).
31. Whatever Stigler's motives, he succeeded in provoking his audience; Robert Solow thought that the contents of his Harvard lecture were 'untrue' (1970: 98; see also Coats, 1960 and Rothbard, 1960). Robert Solow (correspondence, 23 April 1997) points out that his friendship with Stigler transcended any disagreements they had over economics; Stigler was 'never an ideologue' (Solow, cited by Passell, 1991).
32. For example, Stigler (1989: 659–60) declined to deal in detail with a 'discursive and imprecise' *History of Political Economy* review of his essay on Smith and public choice.
33. 'The strong hostility of most intellectuals towards Madison Avenue is possibly due to the rivalry between the two groups. Could the failure of Madison Avenue to reciprocate this overt dislike be an instance of the professional's indifference to the amateur?' (1975: 317).
34. Stigler (1988a: 108–9; 1962b: 1; 1964b: 20; 1964c: 83) was only 'provoked to attack' Means's theory of price determination – after it became integral to macroeconomic fox hunts of controversy via the Kefauver Committee on

administered pricing and inflation, and when it seemed there may be 'No End to Means'. The few remaining economists with an interest in administered prices were left '[without] a subject.'

35. 'The fact, however, is indisputable that economists generally abandoned a traditional doctrine [the quantity theory of money] in important part because of a question of fact which they decided by casual observation . . . A single contrary observation causes consternation, for the whole edifice may tumble – indeed it will tumble if a few prominent economists capitulate.'
36. He also reflected that 'a formal position' was easier to overcome than an opposition that was 'inarticulate and unrationalised' (1966b: 278).
37. Knight had a functional, almost tactics-driven approach to economic theory and its history: 'to contribute to the understanding of how by consensus based upon rational discussion we can fashion liberal society in which individual freedom is preserved and a satisfactory economic performance achieved' (Stigler, 1987b: 57–8). In an unpublished lecture, Knight stated that 'truth in society is like strychnine in the individual body, medicinal in special conditions and minute doses; otherwise and in general a deadly poison . . .' (cited by Stigler, 1987b: 59).
38. Knight advised his students that 'You can be with the majority or you can be in the right' (Patinkin, 1973: 798). Rose Friedman (1976: 30) who was Knight's research assistant (1934–6) recalled that Knight's scepticism 'unfortunately discouraged some of his students from making the contribution that they might otherwise have made.'
39. Stigler (1962d: 71) thought the title invited a 'slovenly stereotype'; it was also geographically inaccurate in that Friedman, he rather provocatively claimed, was the leader of the 'Berkeley–Cambridge axis.'
40. Stigler has been accused of misinterpreting the Coase Theorem; Coase stated this in conversation, and hinted at it in his writing (correspondence from McCloskey 3 June 1997; McCloskey 1997). Stigler (1966a: 113) wrote that 'the Coase theorem thus asserts that under perfect competition private and social costs will be equal . . . this procedure obviously leads to the correct social results'; it was a 'remarkable proposition to us older economists who have believed the opposite for a generation.' Coase (1988: 14; 1993: 239–40, 249) migrated to the Unites States in 1951, in part because of his admiration for Stigler and Knight. He distinguished between the 'Coase Theorem' (with inverted commas) as 'formalised by Stigler . . . It would not seem worthwhile to spend much time investigating the properties of such a world', and the Coase Theorem (without inverted commas), a 'preliminary to the development of an analytical system capable of tackling the problems posed by the real world of transactions costs.'
41. This agenda (law and economics, the economics of the state, regulation, etc.) increasingly dominated research at Chicago and 'George was as much product of this atmosphere as producer' (correspondence from Reder, 1 June 1997).
42. 'The traditional approach has tended to obscure the nature of the choice that has to be made . . . the suggested courses of action are inappropriate' (Coase, 1960: 1–2).
43. Referring to 'focus', Telser continued: 'I believe this is the main lesson I learned from Friedman' (correspondence, 29 April 1997).

44. Bhagwati's obituary of Johnson was not well received at Chicago; it was perceived to be self-serving and inaccurate (correspondence from McCloskey 2 June 1997). Friedman (correspondence, 5 February 1995) took great exception to aspects of it. He also recalled that:

> So far as I know, the seminars were never testing imperfect competition yet there is an element of truth in what Bhagwati said. That is that most of the empirical work that was going on was undertaken to see whether the simple assumption of competitive hypotheses for apparently imperfectly competitive industries led to results that were contradicted or not contradicted by the available evidence. However, that did not arise from any attempt to test imperfect competition but, much more fundamentally, to see how much you could explain by the competitive approach and how much was left that would have to be explained by monopoly. There were also quite a number of articles during that period which offered explanations relying on monopolistic competition positions for many observed phenomena such as retail price fixing, tie-in arrangements, and the like.

Lester Telser (correspondence, 28 April 1997) also informed me of the empirical work on issues raised by monopolistic competition by members of the industrial organization group at Chicago (e.g. Telser, 1962a, 1962b and 1971; Demsetz, 1962). Telser also points out that Stigler's *Theory of Price* (1966: 32, n. 18) refers to one of these articles (Telser, 1962b).

45. 'Chamberlin pointed the way to a revolutionary change in price theory ...The major defence of Chamberlin's principal contribution rests on the methodologically sound proposition that an economic theory can only be as good as its assumptions... [the Chicago] stand is transparently ludicrous' (Bain, 1967: 150–3); Chamberlin provided an 'inspiring vision of realistic economics' (Kuenne, 1967: v); 'it has to be recognised that a general abandonment of the assumption of perfect competition, a universal adoption of the assumption of monopoly, must have very destructive consequences for economic theory' (Hicks, 1946: 83). Bronfenbrenner (1950: 82–3) offered a 'compromise' by attempting to integrate monopolistic competition into economic theory 'without disturbing the fundamentals of neoclassical economic thought.'
46. Edward Mason, Gardiner Means and others at Harvard pioneered 'The Market Concentration Doctrine' (Demsetz, 1973) which is associated with the development of industrial organization as a subdivision of economics (Phillips and Stevenson, 1974).
47. There is some homogeneity behind these disagreements: only 3 per cent of graduate students believed that a successful economist required a thorough knowledge of the economy ('very important'), and 68 per cent thought it to be unimportant.
48. First-year graduate students at Columbia would find no reference to Chamberlin or Robinson in Gary Becker's (1971) price theory course, outside the reading list (which contains twenty references to Friedman and Stigler). In the recommended reading list for his Economics 300 A and B (September 1948), Friedman included Robinson (1933, chapter 2) and Chamberlin (1933, chapter 3, sections 1, 4, 5 and 6 and chapter 5).

49. One reviewer claimed that he had 'unduly idealised' limited competition, just as the older generation had previously done with perfect competition (Nichol, 1934: 337).
50. Chamberlin (1962: 5, n. 4, 226, n. 1) was sensitive about timing with respect to the reconstruction of value theory. Sraffa's famous essay was published in 1926; but Chamberlin stated that his thesis (submitted on 1 April 1927) was at the time of Sraffa's article 'virtually complete'. Likewise, Hotelling's 'Stability in Competition' appeared in March 1929, several months before Chamberlin's essay on duopoly (November 1929), and Chamberlin felt obliged to explain why he had not referred to it.
51. Stigler was 'deeply impressed by the fact that if any one person had dictated the lines of research [in economics] fifty years ago, we would be much behind where we are today. It is worse than that. If I had this power twenty years ago, our discipline would have suffered grievously.'
52. His *Theory of Competitive Price* (1942: v) was written with the intention of including this material at a later date.
53. Stigler (1940: 364) complained about monographs which paid no attention to market forms 'other than perfect competition and simple monopoly.'
54. 'George and I carried on an intensive correspondence while he was exiled to Brown and Columbia. On perusing the surviving records recently, I was struck by his contribution to my methodology article, in the course of exchanges between us about an article that he was writing on imperfect competition' (Friedman, 1993: 770).
55. The Friedman–Stigler correspondence shows a concern about the struggle for influence: 'I keep feeling that you arouse skepticism and opposition by stopping where you do... [elaboration] will create sympathy for and receptiveness to your thesis and make the paper much more influential' (letters from Stigler to Friedman, cited by Hammond, 1991b: 12, 23). Friedman's methodology was constructed in opposition to the desire for descriptive 'realism' and the 'assumption questioning' tendency of both monopolistic competition and Keynesian macroeconomics. One rhetorical device employed by Friedman (1953: 3) was to invoke the authority of Keynes (John Neville, *The Scope and Method of Political Economy*) in the opening sentence of his famous methodological essay. Ten years earlier, Stigler (1943: 358, n. 7) noted the potential potency of this rhetorical device: 'I did not realise how neglected this excellent book had become in America until, when I recently referred to it, several friends expressed surprise that I did not know Keynes' middle name was Maynard!'
56. 'A good deal of support for this theory stems from the mistaken demand for correspondence between "reality" and premises.' Chamberlin, a 'true revolutionary', and his disciples had assigned a 'fundamentally mistaken role... to general theory'. The Walrasian theory of general equilibrium had 'proven to be relatively uninformative'; formalism, in its mathematical guise, 'should not be made a puppet of a scientific oligarchy'. This had been the 'period of the clever gadget and the plausible surmise... the triumph of statistics over history as the source of empirical knowledge', when hasty statistical studies falsely concluded that the consumption function was more stable than the velocity of money.

57. 'My appraisal of the theory in 1947 was stimulated more by a growing interest in the empirical testing of theories than by the intrinsic interest of the kinked demand curve . . . The main task of the article was a test of the empirical fruitfulness of the theory.'
58. In 1995, Milton Friedman very kindly invited me to visit him at the Hoover Institution, but the day before I arrived he fell sick and he was only able to spend an afternoon with me. While he was in hospital I spoke to a number of his colleagues. One Senior Fellow expressed his admiration for both Friedman and Stigler but was surprised when they both walked out of a seminar given by a newly recruited junior economist who had expressed support for some aspects of Galbraith's work. The junior economist was promptly removed from the Hoover Institution. Likewise, Galbraith (1978: 150–1) did not forget his adversaries. The Hoover Institution economists who advocated the 'romance' of deregulation were 'trying to recapture the world of Herbert Hoover – it's a very worthy ideal, intellectual archaeology as it were. Once ageing and righteous scholars of conservative mood dreamt of going to Heaven. Now it's to the American Enterprise Institute.' Galbraith (1981: 31) was told that Friedman opposed his nomination as AEA President: 'He offered as his clinching evidence that Veblen had never been president.' Mark Perlman (correspondence, 6 June 1997) was present when Friedman was chairman of the nomination committee: 'Friedman can be a perfect gentleman, and he presented [Galbraith's] nomination in good grace. All present knew what pain it cost him, but we all admired his composure.'
59. 'With the decline of independent marker behaviour – or perhaps more accurately its decay as a plausible assumption – a gap has been left in our explanation of the operative mechanics by which the economy is governed.'
60. Stigler (1943: 357) attributed responsibility for the decline in the prestige of economists to Galbraith's Office of Price Administration, where he had briefly been employed (Telser, 1996: 2). Later, he attributed the 'weakened . . . status' of economists to their high-profile involvement in the government apparatus (1967c: 360). Later still, Stigler (1987a: 56) referred to Galbraith's 'impressive record for error.'
61. Senator Kefauver (1965 [1963]: 211–12, 180–1), the Chairman of the Senate Subcommittee on Antitrust and Monopoly, suggested that 'to give us a new focus for our thinking' a 'new term' was required, replacing 'private enterprise' with 'collective enterprises' or 'private socialism' or 'private economic government'. Kefauver also noted the availability of a 'plethora' of government statistics with which to pursue these investigations: 'There has been something of a tendency to gather statistics which *might* be valuable in the examination of a 'controversial' topic [emphasis in text]'.
62. Stigler (1943: 529) thought that the 'chief policy applications' of national income figures were made to monetary analyses.
63. Friedman (1965: 51) stated that 'there is no general theory of the second best. There is the proposition that there may exist a theory of the second best.'
64. Friedman and John Savage (1948: 282) in their 'Utility Analysis of Choices Involving Risk' proposed 'a crude empirical test by bringing together a few broad observations', but Archibald (1959b: 437) proposed 'a crucial test' which Friedman and Savage had 'apparently overlooked.'

65. This was comment 20 in Stigler's (1977: 442) Conference Handbook: 'What empirical findings would contradict your theory?'
66. '[S]ignificant implications cannot be obtained without more information than is usually assumed or readily available... When we turn to Chamberlin's defence we again fail to find any statement of predictions.'
67. Sowell was specifically referring to Stigler's ex-Columbia colleague, J.M. Clark's concept of workable competition, which Stigler (1964b: 20) regarded as an academic employment-creating research agenda.
68. Lester Telser (1964: 562, n. 20, 558) found Archibald's challenge 'interesting' but deficient with respect to the identification problem; he found little empirical support for an inverse association between advertising and competition, 'despite some plausible theorising to the contrary.'
69. Rosenberg (1993: 837) concluded that 'no previous scholar had ever examined the development of the discipline with anything like the same insistence that intellectual progress had to be measured in terms of its ability to generate empirically refutable implications.'
70. Stigler (1988a: 116) wrote: 'The computer has made it easy to fish for results. If the statistical analysis doesn't come out "right" the first or the twentieth time, one can drop a year from the data, add a new variable to explain contradictions, take the logarithm of another variable, and so on until, lo, the desired answer appears – all in just a few minutes.' Econometricians were the 'most quarrelsome class of economists' (1988c: 12).
71. Stigler contributed to this development: in 1972, he successfully proposed that the history of thought requirement be dropped at Chicago. Most other economics departments later followed suit (Rosen, 1993: 811). At the same meeting Stigler unsuccessfully proposed that the economic history requirement also be dropped (correspondence from McCloskey, 2 June 1997).
72. '[W]e would be shocked if two teams called off the event.'
73. Archibald and Rosenbluth (1975: 588) outlined some of 'the implications of an analytically tractable definition of a monopolistically competitive group.'
74. In another context, Stigler (1943: 357) deplored the constraint that some approaches to economics imposed: 'The familiar admonition not to argue over differences in taste leads not only to dull conversation but also to bad sociology.' With respect to 'the economics of scholarly advice... I have always thought that revealed preference is the only reliable guide to what a scholar believes to be fruitful research problems: If he doesn't work on them, he provides no reason for us to do so' (Stigler, 1981: 76).
75. According to the Director of the Hoover Institution (Campbell, 1986: x), this renewed faith in competition and deregulation was due to Stigler's Copernican-like role.
76. As Reder put it: 'Why should Friedman or Stigler have entered into a controversy which could, at best, only serve to highlight a possible deficiency of laissez-faire and (in their view) exaggerate its importance' (correspondence, 1 June 1997).
77. Rosenberg (1993: 841) described some of Stigler's questions as 'whether there were laws or regularities shaping the growth of knowledge itself... How does the research agenda of any science get to be determined?... How do scientists persuade one another? To put it in its boldest possible form: What are the underlying laws governing the evolution of a science?'

78. Stigler (1986 [1981]: 333) referred to 'my friend, the competitive economy'. Deviations from neoclassical perspectives produced, in James Meade's work, 'bastard demand curves' (Stigler, 1966c: 479). During the war, he passionately objected to (finding it 'especially hard to excuse') a book that remained silent about political questions: 'Is the purpose of the study of economics the production of impartial pages? Has the democratic citizen no moral responsibility to state and strive for that order of things which he believes is best?' (Stigler, 1943c: 78).
79. 'Not only do we not know how to teach students how to invent theories, but much of the advice is surely wrong. The admonition to keep one's mind open and sceptical, for example, is fatal. Every useful hypothesis will soon encounter facts that are at least superficially adverse, and one must love one's own creations and cling stubbornly to them until the contradictory evidence is overwhelming. On the whole economists fully meet this recommendation.'
80. Some of his critics found his testing procedures to be defective: 'a triumph of ideology over scholarship' (Friend and Herman, 1964: 382).

4 The Rise of the Natural-Rate of Unemployment Model

1. Following the shock of the Tet offensive, Johnson concluded his 31 March television address on the Vietnam war with an unprecedented announcement: 'I shall not seek and I will not accept the nomination of my party for another term as your President' (cited by Alpert, 1981: 97).
2. Steven Resnick, in correspondence to the author, concluded:

   > What Friedman and others accomplished was the transformation of their idea about reality into *the* reality. That is an accomplishment worthy of economic priests . . . an intellectual war had to be waged against collective support for higher wages. Friedman became the Luther of an individualism that helped to win the war. The struggle over Phillips' work is but one important battle in that war.

3. Ironically, Robert Solow's (1978b: 207) instincts were predictively more successful in this context: 'Nobody believes the deflationary half of the [Natural-Rate] proposition. I don't know anybody who would lie out in the sun, let alone be burned at the stake, for the belief that if the unemployment rate is U* [the Natural-Rate] plus epsilon and we wait long enough, there would be accelerating deflation. That part nobody believes.'
4. *Time Retrospective: Economics 1923–1989*, 58.
5. Pratson does not disclose a source for this statement.
6. They concluded that 'the available evidence seems to suggest that the Guideposts did make a notable though modest contribution to stability in 1962–65' (cited by Okun, 1972: 198).
7. On 12 August 1966, Gardner Ackley, Chairman of the CEA, admitted that this period of restraint had ended: the 'guideposts had recently suffered some stunning defeats . . . this problem must be solved if we are to maintain full employment' (*Time Retrospective: Economics 1923–1989*, 62).
8. *Time* concluded on 12 August 1966 that 'more inflationary effects may be expected to set in soon' (*Time Retrospective: Economics 1923–1989*, 58).

9. Richard Crossman (1978: 208, 341) confided to his *Diary* that 'we have just given huge concessions to the doctors, the judges and the higher civil servants. It is an ironical interpretation of a socialist incomes policy.' Callaghan's 1967 Budget was a reflection of 'his new doctrine that we should abandon an artificial prices and incomes policy and revert to a higher rate of unemployment'.
10. Alternatively, a younger and more energetic labour supply might increase productivity and therefore restrain inflation. I am grateful to A.J. Brown for this suggestion.
11. Miernyk (1966: vii) concluded that 'By the end of 1965 it should have been evident to even the most casual observer that the demand stimulus [of the 1965 tax cuts] was not enough and that further application of the same medicine could have at least mildly inflationary consequences'. (Unemployment had reached 4 per cent by December 1965.)
12. Demsetz (1961: 84–5, n. 2) concluded that the CEA report contained a 'serious logical error... the discriminating powers of the Council's test are practically nil... the Council's test... leaves much to be desired'.
13. In 1964 the US Secretary of Labor stated that 'The confluence of surging population and driving technology [is creating] a human slag-heap... a separate nation of the poor, the unskilled, the jobless' (cited by Theobald, 1968 [1964]: 64).
14. It may be anachronistic to refer to these activities by the term 'search', which perhaps only entered the vocabulary of economists in the late 1960s.
15. These points were also emphasized by the CEA's 1961 Statement and 1962 Report (Tobin and Weidenbaum, 1988).

5 Does the Expectations Trap Render the Natural-Rate Model Invalid in the Disinflationary Zone?

1. 'Phillips translated this analysis into an observable relation by plotting the level of unemployment on one axis and the rate of change of wages over time on the other as in Fig. 12.3' (Friedman, 1976: 218).
2. One of the purposes of Phillips's (1958: 283) empirical investigation was to quantify the observation that 'workers are reluctant to offer their service at less than the prevailing rates when the demand for labour is low and unemployment is high so that wage rates fall only very slowly.' Richard Lipsey (1981: 558), in his Presidential address to the Canadian Economics Association, recalled that 'neither Phillips nor myself, nor any one else whom I know of in the early Phillips curve tradition, ever drew an empirical Phillips curve which did not display the asymmetry that wages could rise fast in the face of excess demand, and would fall only very slowly in the face of excess supply. Phillips, for example, calculated the asymptotic rate of decrease in U.K. money wages as unemployment went to 100 per cent. as 1 per cent. per annum.' A. J. Brown also discovered a wage change floor (1955: 199; see also Haberler, 1961: 7). The dominant pre-Keynesian view at the University of Chicago was that wages were highly resistant to downward pressure (Davies, 1971: 24–9).
3. Friedman (1976: 218) states that he is 'very ready [to go] from rates of wage change to rates of price change'.

4. I am grateful to James Dean for suggesting this phrase to me. Friedman (1968a: 8–9) believed that Phillips's curve was 'reasonably stable and well defined' for the hundred years that Phillips examined, because inflationary expectations had been 'unshaken and immutable' at a zero value.
5. 'The weakest and least satisfactory part of current economic theory seems to me to be in the field of monetary dynamics, which is concerned with the process of adaptation of the economy as a whole to changes in conditions and so with short-period fluctuations in aggregate activity' (Friedman, 1953: 42). At the start of the monetarist decade, he wrote 'I believe we have a reasonably good dynamic theory [... we now have a more secure grasp on the quantitative magnitudes involved] – what we lack for policy purposes is not the theory but the political capacity to use the theory effectively' (1975a: 176, 178).

6 Language and Inflation

1. Sometimes economists are sloppy with their language – the *term* Non-Accelerating Inflation Rate of Unemployment (NAIRU) has slipped a derivative – it is the price *level* which is supposedly non-accelerating, while inflation is merely non-increasing (Nickell, 1990: 427, n. 27). It is surprising, in the formalist era, that such a confusion between a first and a second derivative should persist.
2. George Stigler – a perceptive Chicago sociologist of economic knowledge and the author of *The Economist as Preacher* – noted that 'The attention to monopoly grew between the wars ... the word changed its meaning' (1988a: 92–4); he also made insinuations about the kinked demand curve – referring to it as 'The Kinky Oligopoly Demand Curve' (1947a).
3. It wasn't just 'Nutters' who were influenced by this 'peculiar Chicago madness' (Desai, 1981: 2), but Warren Nutter (who had been Friedman's first dissertation student) en route to a seminar at Rochester changed the title of his paper from 'The Fallacy of the Coase Theorem' to 'A New Proof of the Coase Theorem', solely because of the persuasiveness of the arguments presented by his travelling companion, Milton Friedman (Stigler, 1983c: 227).
4. This was the 'day of the rationally designed econometric studies' (Solow, 1957: 312), and later, mark-two monetarists would add *rational* expectations, inviting their opponents to embrace irrationality. There is also appeal in a *real* theory of the business cycle and a *real* Phillips curve.
5. Stigler (1962d: 71) objected to the term 'Chicago School', preferring instead to describe Friedman as 'the leader of the Berkeley–Cambridge axis'.
6. Hansen was ranked 20th, and Slichter 39th, in the list of most frequently cited economists, 1925–69 (Stigler and Friedland, 1979: 12).
7. Just before his death, Johnson was working on 'The Role of Networks of Economists in International Monetary Reform' (Kindleberger, 1978: 26). In a letter to the editor of *Minerva* accompanying what may have been his final paper, 'The Shadow of Keynes', he wrote that he was 'getting into something deep – the causes of the decline of academic departments' (1977: 202); 'I am really after something complex – what causes the decay of academic excellence' (Shils, 1977: 85).

8. Schumpeter made similar 'Kuhnian' observations in 1935–7 (Samuelson, 1996: 163).
9. With a 17 year gap between 1948 and 1965.
10. This perception is grossly unfair to Keynes, and somewhat unfair to the Old Keynesians.
11. Cairncross (1996: 87) recalled that Keynes had 'a resonant and melodious voice'.
12. McCann and Perlman (1993: 994) described Stigler's powerful wit as 'mordant'. According to Shils (1977: 87), Harry Johnson considered leaving Chicago, in part because he found Stigler's jocularity not to his liking (he then settled down into the most creative and productive part of his career). Anyone who has spoken to Milton Friedman rapidly becomes aware of his delightful and mischievous humour.

7 Friedman and the Walrasian Equations of the Natural-Rate Counter-Revolution

1. Stigler (1962d: 71) thought the title invited a 'slovenly stereotype'; it was also geographically inaccurate in that Friedman, he rather provocatively claimed, was the leader of the 'Berkeley-Cambridge axis'.
2. Certainly, Leijonhuvud (1965) made a favourable impression on Friedman (1974b: 16, n. 7).
3. Rose Friedman felt she had been the victim of 'sex discrimination' at Koopmans' hands when he had her removed from their joint office shortly after being appointed to the War Shipping Board: 'It colored my opinion of Tjalling then and later when, for some years, he was a colleague of Milton's at the University of Chicago' (Friedman and Friedman, 1998: 109–10).
4. Chicago economists continued to despair of the theory of expectations: 'the promised land to some economists and a mirage to others. The reviewer must admit that he leans towards the latter view: much of the literature on expectations consists of obvious and uninformative generalisations of static analysis.' With respect to 'the revision of anticipations... progress depends much more on the accumulation of data (of a type almost impossible to collect!) than on an increase in the versatility of our technical apparatus' (Stigler, 1941: 358–9; see also Schultz, 1949; Woking, 1949; Boulding, 1949; Norton, 1949). Phillips solved the problem of the measurement of adaptive inflationary expectations for Friedman in 1952; Friedman was so impressed that twice, in 1955 and 1960, he attempted to recruit Phillips to the University of Chicago (Hammond, 1996, 123, n. 15).
5. Schumpeter formed this judgement about the seminal importance of Walras's work in 1908, if not before (Hutchison, 1953: 191–3). Also, in the 1930s, von Neumann and Wald published proofs of the existence of general equilibrium (Weintraub, 1983; Debreu, 1987).
6. In an earlier attempt to provide a guide to 'long-run objectives', Friedman (1953 [1948]: 133, 144) stated that 'Under existing circumstances, when many prices are moderately rigid, at least against declines, the monetary and fiscal framework described above cannot be expected to lead to reasonably full employment of resources... The brute fact is that a rational

economic program . . . must have flexibility of prices (including wages) as one of its cornerstones.'

7. Paul Samuelson (1967a: 113) was a leading proponent of these three General Theory revolutions. In his essay in honour of Edward Chamberlin, Samuelson (just prior to Friedman's Presidential Address), stated that 'a proper understanding of general equilibrium [is necessary] . . . to attain . . . an understanding of partial equilibrium'.
8. According to Edmund Phelps (1996), the co-author of the natural rate model, the natural rate is a weak, not a strong, attractor; the system is perceived to be path-dependent.
9. Referring to the economic analysis of political institutions, Stigler commented that had Friedman 'been what he likes to call a Walrasian instead of a Marshallian, the intellectual atmosphere would have been very inhospitable and uncordial to this kind of development.' Stigler (1939: 471) also concluded that 'the general equilibrium method is not fertile: we sacrifice content to formal generality until we achieve the state of the perfect dilettante, and know nothing about everything.'
10. The disinflation component of the natural rate model could be described as theory without adequate measurement.
11. Friedman (1976: 25–6) was discussing demand curves: the Walrasian demand curve was derived by 'mathematical economists' who were 'unwilling to put anything' into the 'everything else in the world' category.

Bibliography

Ackley, G. (1961) *Macroeconomic Theory*. New York: Collier Macmillan.

Akerlof, G. A. (1982) 'A Personal Tribute and a Few Reflections', in Feiwel (ed.) (1982).

Allais, M. (1992) 'The Passion for Research', in Szenberg (ed.) (1992).

Alpert, J. (1981). *Growing Up Underground*. New York: William Morrow.

American Enterprise Institute (1988) *Ideas, Their Origins and Their Consequences: Lectures to Commemorate the Life of G. Warren Nutter*. Washington: American Enterprise Institute.

Ando, A. and Modigliani, F. (1965) 'Velocity and the Investment Multipliers', *American Economic Review*, September: 693–728.

Andvig, J. C. (1985) *Ragnar Frisch and the Great Depression*. Oslo: Norsk Utenrikspolitisk.

Archibald, C. G. (1959a) 'The State of Economic Science', *British Journal of the Philosophy of Science*, 10: 58–69.

——(1959b) 'Utility, Risk and Linearity', *Journal of Political Economy*, LXVII(5): 437–50.

——(1960) 'Testing Marginal Productivity Theory', *Review of Economic Studies*, 27: 210–13.

——(1961) 'Chamberlin versus Chicago', *Review of Economics and Statistics*, October: 2–28.

——(1963) 'Reply to Chicago', *Review of Economics and Statistics*, 30: 68–71.

Archibald, G. C. and Rosenbluth, G. (1975) 'The "New" Theory of Consumer Demand and Monopolistic Competition', *Quarterly Journal of Economics*, LXXXIX: 569–90.

Arrow, K. J. (1960) 'The Work of Ragnar Frisch, Econometrician', *Econometrica*, 28.(2): 173–92.

——(1978) 'Jacob Marschak's Contributions to the Economics of Decision and Information', *American Economic Association Papers and Proceedings*, May: xiii–xiv.

——(1990) 'Harold Hotelling', in Eatwell, Milgate and Newman (eds) (1990).

——and Debreu, G. (1954) 'Existence of an Equilibrium for a Competitive Economy', *Econometrica*, 22(3): 265–90.

Backhouse, R. (ed.) (1994) *New Directions in Economic Methodology*. London: Routledge.

Bain, J. (1948) 'Price and Production Policies', in Ellis (ed.) (1948).

——(1964) 'The Impact on Industrial Organization', *American Economic Association Papers and Proceedings*, May: 28–32.

——(1967) 'Chamberlin's Impact on Microeconomic Theory', in Kuenne (ed.) (1967).

Ball, R. J. and Burns, T. (1977) 'Macroeconomic Models and Policy in Britain', in Intriligator (ed.) (1977).

Basmann, R. L. (1972) 'The Brookings Quarterly Econometric Models: Science or Number Mysticism? ', In Brunner (ed.) (1972).

Bateman, B. W. (1990) 'Keynes, Induction and Econometrics', *History of Political Economy* 22(2): 359–79.
Baumol, W. J. (1964) 'Monopolistic Competition and Welfare Economics', *American Economic Association Papers and Proceedings*, May: 44–52.
Becker, G. (1971) *Economic Theory*. Alfred Knopf: New York.
——(1991) 'Milton Friedman', in Shils (ed.) (1991).
——(1993) 'George Joseph Stigler: January 17, 1911–December 1, 1991', *Journal of Political Economy*, 101(5): 761–7.
Beckman, M. J. (1991) 'Tjalling C. Koopmans', in Shils (ed.) (1991).
Bender, T. (1987) *New York Intellect: A History of Intellectual Life in New York City from 1750 to the Beginning of Our Own Time*. New York: Alfred Knopf.
Bergstrom, A. R., Catt, A. J. L., Peston, M. H. and Silverston, B. D. J. (eds) (1978) *Stability and Inflation: A Volume of Essays to Honour the Memory of A. W. H. Phillips*. New York: John Wiley & Sons.
Berle, A. A. Jr (1953) 'American Capitalism', *Review of Economics and Statistics*, February: 81–4.
Bhagwati, J. N. (1977) 'Harry G. Johnson', *Journal of International Economics*, 7: 221–9.
Bishop, R. L. (1964) 'The Theory of Imperfect Competition After Thirty Years: The Impact on General Theory', *American Economic Review*, 54: 33–43.
Bjerkholt, O. (1995) 'Ragnar Frisch, Editor of Econometrica 1933–1954', *Econometrica*, 65(4): 755–65.
Blaug, M. (1980) *The Methodology of Economics or How Economists Explain*. Cambridge: Cambridge University Press.
——(1985) *Great Economists Since Keynes*. Cheltenham: Harvester.
Blinder, A. (1979) *Economic Policy and the Great Stagflation*. New York: Academic Press.
——(1986) 'Keynes After Lucas', *Eastern Economic Journal* XII(3): 209–16.
Bodkin, R. G., Klein, L. R. and Marwah, K. (1988) 'Keynes and the Origins of Macroeconometric Modelling', in Hamouda and Smithin (eds) (1988).
Bordo, M. (ed.) (1989) *Essays in Honour of Anna J. Schwartz*. Chicago: University of Chicago Press.
Boulding, K. E. (1949) 'Discussion', *American Economic Review* XXXIX, (3) 167–8.
——(1957) 'A New Look at Institutionalism', *American Economic Review*, XLVII(2): 1–12.
Boylan, T. A. and O'Gorman, P. F. (1995) *Beyond Rhetoric and Realism in Economics*. Routledge: London.
Bradley, P. D. (ed.) (1959) *The Public Stake in Union Power*. Charlottesville: University of Virginia Press.
Brainard, W. C. and Cooper, R. N. (1975) Empirical Monetary Economics: What Have We Learned in the Last 25 Years?', *American Economic Association Papers and Proceedings*, LXV(2): 167–75.
Breit, W. and Ransom, R. (1971) *The Academic Scribblers*. New York: CBS Publishers.
Breit, W. and Spencer, R. G. (eds) (1986) *Lives of the Laureates*. Cambridge, MA: MIT Press (reprinted 1988).
——(eds) (1995) *Lives of the Laureates*, 3rd edn. Cambridge, MA: MIT Press.
Brittan, S. (1975) *Second Thoughts on Full Employment Policy*. London: Centre for Policy Studies.

Bronfenbrenner, M. (1950) 'Imperfect Competition on a Long-Run Basis', *Journal of Business of the University of Chicago*, April: 81–93.

Brown, A. J. (1955) *The Great Inflation, 1939–1951*. London: Oxford University Press.

Brown, E. C. and Solow, R. (eds) (1983) *Paul Samuelson and Economic Theory*. New York: McGraw-Hill.

Brunner, K. (ed.) (1972) *Problems and Issues in Current Econometric Practice*. Columbia: Ohio State University.

——and Meltzer A. H. (eds) (1976) *The Phillips Curve and Labor Markets*, Vol. 1. Amsterdam: North Holland.

——(eds) (1977) *Stabilisation of the Domestic and International Economy*. Carnegie-Rochester Conference Series on Public Policy.

Buchanan, J. M. (1987) 'Keynesian Follies', in Reese (ed.) (1987).

——(1991) 'Frank H. Knight', in Shils (ed.) (1991).

Burns, A. (1972) 'The Basis for Lasting Prosperity', in Okun (ed.) (1972).

Butterfield, H. (1957) *The Origins of Modern Science, 1300–1800*. London: G. Bell.

Cagan P. (1989) 'Money–Income Causality – a Critical Review of the Literature since the *Monetary History*', in Bordo (ed.) (1989).

——(1979) *Persistent Inflation: Historical and Policy Essays*. New York: Columbia University Press.

Cairncross, A. (1996) 'Keynes the Man', *The Economist*, 20 April: 87–8.

Caldwell, B. J. (1982) *Beyond Positivism: Economic Methodology in the Twentieth Century*. London: George Allen & Unwin.

Campbell, W. G. (1986) 'Foreword', in Stigler (1986).

Carabelli, A. M. (1988) *On Keynes's Method*. London: Macmillan.

Chamberlin, E. H. (1933) *The Theory of Monopolistic Competition*. Cambridge, MA: Harvard University Press.

——(1946) 'Discussion', *American Economic Association Papers and Proceedings*, May: 139–42.

——(1947) 'Review of Stigler's *Theory of Price*', *American Economic Review*, June: 414–18.

——(1954a) 'Measuring the Degree of Monopoly and Competition', in Chamberlin (ed.) (1954b).

——(ed.) (1954b) *Monopoly and Competition and Their Regulation*. London: Macmillan.

——(1957) *Towards a More General Theory of Value*. New York: OUP.

Christ, C. (1952) 'History of the Cowles Commission, 1932–52', in *Econometric Theory and Evidence. A Twenty Year Research Report*. University of Chicago: Cowles Commission.

——(1960) 'Simultaneous Equations Estimations: Any Verdict Yet?', *Econometrica*, 28: 835–45.

——(1967), 'Econometrics in Economics: Some Achievements and Challenges', *Australian Economic Papers*, 6(9): 155–70.

——(1985) 'Early Progress in Estimating Quantitative Economic Relationships in America', *American Economic Review*, 75: 39–52.

Clark, R. W. (1984) *Einstein: The Life and Times*. New York: Avon.

Clarke, P. (1988) *The Keynesian Revolution in the Making, 1924–1936*. Oxford: Clarendon.

Clower, R. W. (1964) 'Monetary History and Positive Economics', *Journal of Economic History* 24: 364–80.
——(1965) 'The Keynesian Counter Revolution: A Theoretical Reappraisal', in Hahn and Brechling (eds) (1965).
Coase, R. (1960) 'The Problem of Social Cost', *Journal of Law and Economics*, 15(2): 1–44.
——(1988) *The Firm, the Market and the Law.* Chicago: University of Chicago Press.
——(1993) 'Law and Economics at Chicago', *Journal of Law and Economics*, XXXVI: 239–54.
——(1995) 'Ronald H. Coase', in Breit and Spencer (eds) (1995).
Coats, A. W. (1960) 'The Politics of Political Economists: Comment', *Quarterly Journal of Economics*, November: 666–9.
——(1993) *British and American Economic Essays*. Routledge: London.
Cochrane, J. L. (1975) 'The Johnson Administration: Moral Suasion Goes to War', in Goodwin (ed.) (1975).
Colander, D. (1989) 'The Invisible Hand of Truth', in Colander and Coats (eds) (1989).
——and Coats, A. W. (eds) (1989) *The Spread of Economic Ideas*. Cambridge: Cambridge University Press.
——and Klamer, A. (1987) 'The Making of an Economist', *Journal of Economic Perspectives*, 1(2): 95–111.
——and Landreth, H. (eds) (1996) *The Coming of Keynesianism to America*. Cheltenham: Edward Elgar.
Cole, K., Cameron, J. and Edward, C. (1983) *Why Economists Disagree*. London: Longman.
Committee for Economic Development (1958) *Problems of United States Economic Development*. New York: CED.
Conant, J. B. (1970) *My Several Lives*. New York: Harper & Row.
Congdon, T. (1989) 'British and American Monetarism Compared', in Hill (ed.) (1989).
Connolly, C. (1983) *Enemies of Promise*. New York: Persea.
Cooley, T. F. and LeRoy, F. (1981) 'Identification and Estimation of Money Demand', *American Economic Review*, September: 825–44.
Cooper, S. and Johnston, D. (1965) 'Labor Force Projections', *Monthly Labor Review*, February: 129–40.
Cowles, A. (1960) 'Ragnar Frisch and the Founding of the Econometric Society', *Econometrica*, 28(2): 172–3.
Court, R. (1999) 'The Lucas Critique: Did Phillips make a Comparable Contribution', in Leeson (ed.) (1999).
Craver, E. and Leijonhufvud, A. (1987) 'Economists in America: The Continental Influence', *History of Political Economy*, 19(2): 173–82.
Croome, D. R. and Johnson, H. G. (eds) (1970) *Money in Britain*. London: OUP.
Cross, R. (ed.) (1996) *The Natural Rate of Unemployment: Reflections on 25 Years of the Hypothesis*. Cambridge: Cambridge University Press.
Crossman, R. (1978) *The Crossman Diaries: Condensed Version*. London: Magnum Books.
Darnell, A. C. and Evans J. L. (1990) *The Limits of Econometrics*. Cheltenham: Edward Elgar.
Davidson. P. (1989) 'Keynes and Money', in Hill (ed.) (1989).

Davies, J. R. (1971) *The Old Economists and the New Economics*. Ames, IA: University of Iowa Press.

Davis, T. E. (1952) 'The Consumption Function as a Tool for Prediction', *Review of Economics and Statistics*, 34: 270–7.

Debreu, G. (1984) 'Economics in a Mathematical Mode', *American Economic Review*, 74: 267–78.

——(1987) 'Existence of General Equilibrium', in Eatwell et al. (eds) (1987).

de Marchi, N. (1975) 'The First Nixon Administration: Prelude to Controls', in Goodwin (ed.) (1975).

——(ed.) (1988) *The Popperian Legacy in Economics*. Cambridge: Cambridge University Press.

Demsetz, H. (1961) 'Structural Unemployment: A Reconsideration of the Evidence and the Theory', *Journal of Law and Economics*, October: 80–90.

——(1962) 'The Effect of Consumer Experience on Brand Loyalty and the Structure of Market Demand', *Econometrica*, 30(1): 22–33.

——(1973) *The Market Concentration Doctrine*. Washington: AEI-Hoover Policy Studies.

——(1993) 'George J. Stigler: Midcentury Neoclassicalist with a Passion to Quantify', *Journal of Political Economy*, 101(5): 793–808.

de Prano, M. and Mayer, T. (1965) 'Autonomous Expenditures and Money', *American Economic Review*, September: 729–52.

Desai, M. (1981) *Testing Monetarism*. London: Frances Pinter.

Dharmapala, D. (1993) 'On the History and Methodology of Econometrics', *Journal of Economic Surveys*, 7: 85–103.

Dornbusch, R. and Fischer, S. (1978) *Macroeconomics*. New York: McGraw-Hill.

Dow, C. (1967) *The Management of The British Economy*. Cambridge: Cambridge University Press.

Dreze, J. H. (1991) *Unemployment Equilibria: Essays in Theory, Econometrics and Policy*. Cambridge: Cambridge University Press.

Dunlop, J. (ed.) (1961) *Potentials of the American Economy: Selected Essays of Sumner H. Slichter*. Cambridge, MA: Harvard University Press.

Dyson, F. (1979) *Disturbing the Universe*. New York: Harper & Row.

Eady, W. (1951) 'Maynard Keynes at the Treasury', *The Listener*, 7 June: 903, 920.

Eatwell, J., Milgate, M. and Newman, P. (eds) (1987) *The New Palgrave Dictionary of Economics*. London: Macmillan.

Eatwell, J., Milgate, M. and Newman, P. (eds) (1990) *Time Series and Statistics – the New Palgrave*. London: W.W. Norton.

Eisner, R. (1958a.) 'The Permanent Income Hypothesis – Comment', *American Economic Review*, 48: 972–90.

——(1958b). 'On Growth Models and the Neoclassical Resurgence', *Economic Journal* December, LXVII(272): 707–21.

Ellis, H. S. (ed.) (1948) *A Survey of Contemporary Economics*, Vol. 1. Homewood, IL: AEA Richard D. Irwin.

Eltis, W. A., Scott, M. Fg. and Wolfe, J. N. (eds) (1970) *Induction, Growth and Trade: Essays in Honour of Sir Roy Harrod*. Oxford: Clarendon.

Epstein, R. (1987) *A History of Econometrics*. Amsterdam: North Holland.

Eshag, E. (1963) *From Marshall to Keynes: An Essay on the Monetary Theory of the Cambridge School*. Oxford: Basil Blackwell.

Farrell, M. J. (1959) 'The New Theories of the Consumption Function', *Economic Journal*, LXIX(276): 678–96.

Feiwel, G. R. (ed.) (1982) *Samuelson and Neoclassical Economics*. Boston: Kluwer.

——(ed.) (1989) *The Economics of Imperfect Competition and Employment: Joan Robinson and Beyond*. London: Macmillan.

Fellner, W. (1959) 'Demand Inflation, Cost Inflation and Collective Bargaining', in Bradley (ed.) (1959).

——(1967) 'The Adaptability and Lasting Contribution of the Chamberlin Contribution', in Kuenne (ed.) (1967).

——, Machlup, F. and Triffin, R. (eds) (1966) *Maintaining and Restoring Balance in International Payments*. Princeton, NJ: Princeton University Press.

Fetter, F. W. (1977) 'Lenin, Keynes and Inflation', *Economica*, XLIV: 77–80.

Feyerabend, P. (1975) *Against Method*. London: New Left Books.

Foster, J. I. (1973) 'The Behaviour of Unemployment and Unfilled Vacancies: Great Britain 1958–1971: A Comment', *Economic Journal*, 83(329): 192–201.

Frazer, W. (1988) *Power and Ideas: Milton Friedman and the Big U-Turn*. Gainsville, FL: Gulf/Atlantis.

Freedman, C. (1995) 'The Economist as Mythmaker – Stigler's Kinky Transformation', *Journal of Economic Issues*, XXIX(1): 175–209.

Friedland, C. (1993) 'On Stigler and Stiglerisms', *Journal of Political Economy*, 101(5): 780–83.

Friedman, M. (1940) 'Review of *Business Cycles in the United States*', *American Economic Review*, 30(4): 657–60.

——(1941) 'Review of Triffin's *Monopolistic Competition and General Equilibrium Theory*', *Journal of Farm Economics*, 23: 389–90.

——(1943) 'Methods of Predicting the Onset of Inflation', in Shoup, Friedman and Mack (1943).

——(1948a) 'A Monetary and Fiscal Framework for Economic Stability', *American Economic Review*, XXXVIII: 245–64.

——(1948b) 'Review of *Cycles: The Science of Prediction*', *Journal of American Statistical Association*: 139–41.

——(1949) 'Rejoinder', *American Economic Review*, XXXIX: 949–55.

——(1950) 'Wesley Mitchell as an Economic Theorist', *Journal of Political Economy*, LVIII (168): 465–93.

——(1951) 'Comment on "A Test of an Econometric Model for the United States 1921–47" by Carl Christ', in *Conference on Business Cycles*. New York: National Bureau of Economic Research: 107–14.

——(1952) 'Comment', in Haley (ed.) (1952).

——(1953) *Essays in Positive Economics*. Chicago: University of Chicago Press.

——(1955a) 'Leon Walras and His Economic System', *American Economic Review*, XLV(1): 900–9.

——(1955b) 'Comment', *Review of Economics and Statistics*: 401–6.

——(ed.) (1956) *Studies in the Quantity Theory of Money*. Chicago: University of Chicago Press.

——(1957) *A Theory of the Consumption Function*. Princeton, NJ: Princeton University Press.

——(1958a) 'The Permanent Income Hypothesis: A Comment', *American Economic Review*, 48: 990–1.

——(1958b) 'The Supply of Money and Changes in Prices and Output', in Lehman (ed.) (1958).
——(1958c) 'Minimising Government Control to Strengthen Competitive Private Enterprise', in *Problems of United States Economic Development*. New York: Committee for Economic Development.
——(1962a) *Price Theory: A Provisional Text*. Chicago: Aldine.
——(1962b) *Capitalism and Freedom*. Chicago: University of Chicago Press.
——(1963a) 'The Present State of Monetary Theory', *Economic Studies Quarterly*, XIV(1): 1–15.
——(1963b) 'More on Archibald versus Chicago', *Review of Economics and Statistics*, 30: 65–7.
——(1965) 'Discussion', in Ketchum and Strunk (eds) (1965).
——(1966a) 'What Price Guideposts? and Comments', in Shultz and Aliber (eds) (1966).
——(1966b) 'Inflationary Recession', *Newsweek*, 17 October: 92.
——(1967a) 'Value Judgements in Economics', in Hook (ed.)
——(1967b) 'Must We Choose Between Inflation and Unemployment?', *1967 Stanford Business Conference Bulletin*, pp. 10–42.
——(1968a) 'The Role of Monetary Policy', *American Economic Review*, 58: 1–17.
——(1968b) *Dollars and Deficits*. Englewood Cliffs, NJ: Prentice Hall.
——(1969) *The Optimum Quantity of Money*. Chicago: Aldine.
——(1970) 'A Theoretical Framework for Monetary Analysis', *Journal of Political Economy*, 78, 193–238.
——(1974a) 'Schools at Chicago', *University of Chicago Magazine*: 11–16.
——(1974b) 'A Theoretical Framework for Monetary Analysis and Comments on the Critics', in Gordon (ed.) (1974).
——(1975a) 'Discussion', *American Economic Association Papers and Proceeding*, 65: 176–9.
——(1975b) *Unemployment versus Inflation: An Evaluation of the Phillips Curve*. London: Institute of Economic Affairs.
——(1975c) *There's No Such Thing as a Free Lunch*. Open Court, IL: LaSalle.
——(1976) *Price Theory*. Chicago Aldine.
——(1977) 'Nobel Lecture: Inflation and Unemployment', *Journal of Political Economy*, 85(3): 451–72.
——(1980) 'Evidence', *The House of Commons Treasury and Civil Service Committee: Memoranda on Monetary Policy*. London: HMSO.
——(1981) *Taxation, Inflation, and the Role of Government*. Sydney: Centre for Independent Studies.
——(1988a) in Breit and Spencer (eds) (1986, reprinted 1988).
——(1988b) 'Money and the Stock Market', *Journal of Political Economy*, 96(2): 222–45.
——(1991) 'Old Wine in New Bottles', *Economic Journal*, 101(404): 33–40.
——(1992) *Money Mischief: Episodes in Monetary History*. San Diego, CA: Harcourt Brace & Co.
——(1993) 'George Stigler: A Personal Reminiscence', *Journal of Political Economy*, 101(5): 768–73.
——(1994) 'Milton Friedman', in Snowden et al. (1994).
——(1996a) 'Review of Groenewegen's *A Soaring Eagle: Alfred Marshall 1842–1924*', *Journal of Economic Literature*, December: 1989–91.

——(1996b) 'Fed and the Natural Rate', *Wall Street Journal*, 25 September.
——(1998) 'A Comment on CSWEP', *Journal of Economic Perspectives*, 12(4): 197–9.
——and Becker, G. (1957) 'A Statistical Illusion in Judging Keynesian Models', *Journal of Political Economy*: 64–75.
——and Friedman, R. (1982) *Capitalism and Freedom*. Chicago: University of Chicago Press.
——(1998) *Two Lucky People*. Chicago: University of Chicago Press.
——and Heller, W. (1969) *Monetary vs Fiscal Policy*. New York: W.W. Norton.
——and Kuznets, S. (1945) *Income from Independent Professional Practice*. New York: National Bureau of Economic Research.
——and Meiselman, D. (1963) 'The Relative Stability of Monetary Velocity and the Investment Multiplier in the United States, 1897–1958', in *Stabilization Policies*. NJ: Commission on Money and Credit. Englewood Cliffs, NJ Prentice Hall.
——(1965) 'Reply to Ando and Modigliani and to De Prano and Mayer', *American Economic Review*, LV(4): 753–85.
——and Savage, J. L. (1948) 'The Utility Analysis of Choices Involving Risk', *Journal of Political Economy*, LVII: 270–304.
——and Schwartz, A. (1963) *Monetary History of the United States*. New York: NBER.
——(1970) *Monetary Statistics of the United States: Estimates, Sources and Methods*. New York: NBER.
——(1982) *Monetary Trends in the United States and the United Kingdom*. Chicago: University of Chicago Press.
——(1991) 'Alternative Approaches to Analysing Economic Data', *American Economic Review*, 81(1): 39–50.
Friedman, R. (1976) 'Milton Friedman – Husband and Colleague (3)', *The Oriental Economist* July: 17–23.
——(1977) 'Milton Friedman – Husband and Colleague (12)', *The Oriental Economist* August: 20–6.
Friend, I. and Herman, E. S. (1964) 'The S.E.C. Through a Glass Darkly', *Journal of Business*, 37: 382–405.
Frisch, R. (1970) 'Econometrics in the World of Today', in Eltis et al. (eds) (1970)
Fromm, G. (ed.) (1981) *Studies in Public Regulation*. Cambridge, MA: MIT Press.
Galbraith, J. K. (1948) 'Monopoly and the Concentration of Economic Power', In Ellis (ed.) (1948).
——(1952) *Theory of Price Control*. Cambridge, MA: Harvard University Press.
——(1955) *Economics and the Art of Controversy*. New York: Vintage.
——(1971) *Economics, Peace and Laughter*. Harmondsworth: Penguin.
——(1972) *The New Industrial State*, 2nd edn. Harmondsworth: Penguin.
——(1973) 'Power and the Useful Economist', *American Economic Review*, 63(1): 1–11.
——(1975) *Money Whence It Came and Where It Went*. London: Penguin.
——(1978) in Galbraith and Salinger (1978).
——(1981) *A Life in Our Times: Memoirs*. Boston: Houghton Mifflin.
——(1987) *A History of Economics: The Past as the Present*. London: Hamish Hamilton.
——and Salinger, N. (1978) *Almost Everyone's Guide to Economics*. New York: Bantum.
Garraty, J. (1978) *Unemployment in History*. New York: Harper.

Garvy, G. (1943) 'Kondratieff's Theory of Long Cycles', *Review of Economic Statistics* XXV(4): 203–20.
Gayer, A. (ed.) (1937) *Lessons of Monetary Experience: Essays in Honour of I. Fischer.* New York: Rinehart.
Gifford, J. K. (1962) 'Wicked Words and Wicked Ideas', *Economic Record,* 38: 63–73.
Gilbert, C. L. (1991) 'Richard Stone, Demand Theory and the Emergence of Modern Econometrics', *Economic Journal,* 101(405): 288–302.
Gill, R. T. (ed.) (1976) *Great Debates in Economics.* Pacific Palisades, CA: Goodyear.
Gilpatrick, E. (1966) *Structural Unemployment and Aggregate Demand: A Study of Employment and Unemployment in the United States 1948–1964.* Baltimore, MD: Johns Hopkins University Press.
Goldsmith, R. W. (1955) *A Study of Savings in the United States, I.* Princeton, NJ: Princeton University Press.
Goodhart, C. (1982) 'Monetary Trends in the United States and the United Kingdom: A Critical Review', *Journal of Economic Literature,* XX: 1540–51.
Goodwin, C. D. (ed.) (1975) *Exhortation and Controls: The Search for a Wage Price Policy 1945–71.* Washington, DC: Brookings Institution.
Gordon, H. S. (1975) 'The Eisenhower Administration: The Decline of Shared Responsibility', in Goodwin (ed.) (1975).
Gordon, L. (1949) 'Libertarians at Bay', *American Economic Review,* XXXIX(1): 976–8.
Gordon, R. A. (1949) 'Business Cycles in the Inter-War Period: The "Quantitative-Historical" Approach', *American Economic Association Papers and Proceedings,* XXX.X.3,: 47–72.
Gordon, R. J. (1978) *Macroeconomics,* 1st edn. Boston: Little, Brown.
Gordon, R. J. (ed.) (1974) *Milton Friedman's Monetary Framework: A Debate with His Critics.* Chicago: University of Chicago Press.
Gort, M. (1962) *Diversification and Integration in American Industry.* Princeton, NJ: Princeton University Press.
Granger, C. and Newbold, P. (1974) 'Spurious Regression in Econometrics', *Journal of Econometrics,* 2: 111–20.
Granger, C. W. J. (1981) in Kmenta and Ramsey (eds) (1981).
Gujarati, D. (1972a) 'The Behaviour of Unemployment and Unfilled Vacancies: Great Britain 1958–1971', *Economic Journal,* 82(325): 195–203.
——(1972b) 'A Reply to Mr. Taylor', *Economic Journal,* 82(328): 1365–8.
——(1973) 'A Reply to Mr. Foster , *Economic Journal,* 83(329): 201–3.
Haavelmo, T. (1944) 'The Probability Approach to Econometrics', *Econometrica,* 12, Supplement.
Haber, W. (1964) 'Unemployment: Inadequate Demand or Structural Imbalance', *Michigan Business Review,* November: 10–15.
Haberler, G. (1939) *Prosperity and Depression: A Theoretical Analysis of Cyclical Movements.* Geneva: League of Nations.
——(1949) 'Current Issues in Business Cycles – Discussion', *American Economic Review*: 84–8.
——(1958) 'Creeping Inflation Resulting from Wage Increases in Excess of Productivity', in Committee for Economic Development (1958).
——(1961) *Inflation: Its Causes and Cures.* Washington, DC: American Enterprise Association.

——(1966) 'Adjustment, Employment and Growth', in Fellner, Machlup and Triffin (eds) (1966).
Hahn, F. and Brechling, F. (eds). *The Theory of Interest Rates*. London: Macmillan (1965).
Halberstam, D. (1972) *The Best and The Brightest*. New York: Random House.
Haley, B. F. (ed.) (1952) *A Survey of Contemporary Economics*. Vol. 1. Homewood, IL: Irwin.
Hall, R. E. and Taylor, J. B. (1986) *Macroeconomics: Theory Performance and Policy*. London: W.W. Norton.
Hammond, J. D. (1990) 'McCloskey's Modernism and Friedman's Methodology: A Case Study With New Evidence', *Review of Social Economy*, 48: 158–71.
——(1991a) 'Frank Knight's Antipositivism', *History of Political Economy* 23(3): 359–81.
——(1991b) *Early Drafts of Friedman's Methodological Essay*. Mimeo.
——(1996) *Theory and Measurement: Causality Issues in Milton Friedman's Monetary History*. Cambridge: Cambridge University Press.
Hamouda, O. F. and Smithin, J. N. (eds) (1988) *Keynes and Public Policy after Fifty Years: Volume 2: Theories and Methods*. Cheltenham: Edward Elgar.
Hands, D. W. (1994) 'The Sociology of Scientific Knowledge: Some Thoughts on the Possibilities', in Backhouse (ed.) (1994).
Hansen, A. (1953) *A Guide to Keynes*. New York: McGraw-Hill.
——(1958) 'The Sweeping Rise of Urbanisation', in *Problems of United States Economic Development*. New York: Committee for Economic Development.
——(1960) *Economic Issues For The 1960s*. New York: McGraw-Hill.
——(1964) *Business Cycles and National Income*. New York. W.W. Norton.
Harberger, A. (1954) 'Monopoly and Resource Allocation', *American Economic Association Papers and Proceedings*, 44(2): 77–87.
Hargreaves Heap, S. (1980) 'Choosing the Wrong Natural Rate: Accelerating Inflation or Decelerating Employment and Growth?', *Economic Journal*, 90: 611–20.
Harris, S. E. (ed.) (1947) *The New Economics*. New York: Dobson.
Harrod, R. (1934) 'Doctrines of Imperfect Competition', *Quarterly Journal of Economics*: vol. 58(3) 442–70.
——(1949) 'Wesley C. Mitchell in Oxford', *Economic Journal* 50: 459–60.
——(1951) *The Life of John Maynard Keynes*. London: Macmillan.
Hayek, F. (1958) 'Inflation Resulting from Downward Inflexibility of Wages', in Committee for Economic Development.
——(1972) *A Tiger by the Tail*. London: IEA.
Hawtrey, R. (1928) *Trade and Credit*. London: Longman.
Heller, W. (1966) *New Directions in Political Economy*. Cambridge, MA: Harvard University Press.
——(1969) 'Is Monetary Policy Being Oversold?', in Friedman and Heller, (1969).
——(1972) 'The Fiscal Route to Full Employment', in Okun (ed.) (1972).
Henderson, W. (1995) *Economics as Literature*. London: Routledge.
Hendry, D. (1980) 'Econometrics: Alchemy or Science?', *Economica*, November: 388–406.
——and Ericsson, N. R. (1991) 'An Econometric Analysis of U.K. Money Demand', *American Economic Review*, 81(1): 8–38.

——and Wallis, K. (eds) (1984) *Econometrics and Quantitative Economics*. Oxford: Basil Blackwell.

Hester, D. (1964) 'Keynes and the Quantity Theory: Comment on Friedman and Meiselman CMC Paper', *Review of Economics and Statistics*, November: 364–8.

Hicks, J. R. (1934) 'Leon Walras', *Econometrica*, 2: 338–48.

——(1937) 'Mr. Keynes and the "Classics": A Suggested Interpretation', *Econometrica*, 5: 147–59.

——(1939) *Value and Capital*. Oxford: Clarendon.

——(1946) *Value and Capital: An Inquiry into Some Fundamental Principles of Economic Theory*. Oxford: Clarendon.

——and Weber, W. (eds) (1973). *Carl Menger and the Austrian School of Economics*. Oxford: OUP.

Hildreth, C. (1986) *The Cowles Commission in Chicago, 1939–55*. Berlin: Springer-Verlag.

Hill, R. (ed). (1989) *Keynes, Money and Monetarism*. London: Macmillan.

Hook, S. S. (ed.) (1967) *Human Values and Economic Policy*. New York: New York University Press.

Houthakker, H. S. (1958a) 'The Permanent Income Hypothesis: A Review Article', *American Economic Review*, 48: 396–404.

——(1958b) 'The Permanent Income Hypothesis: Reply', *American Economic Review*, 48: 991–2.

Howey, R. S. (1989) *The Rise of the Marginal Utility School*. Albany, NY: Columbia University Press.

Hutchison, T. W. (1953) *A Review of Economic Doctrines, 1870–1929*. Oxford: Clarendon.

Intriligator, M. D. (1977) *Frontiers of Quantitative Economics*, Vol. B. Amsterdam: North Holland.

Jacoby, N. (1958) 'Full Employment, Economic Freedom and Stable Prices', in *Problems of United States Economic Development*. New York: Committee for Economic Development.

Jaffe, W. (1934) 'Imperfect Competition', *American Economic Review*, March: 27–30.

——(1935) 'Unpublished Papers and Letters of Leon Walras', *Journal of Political Economy*, 43: 187–207.

Jay, D. (1986) *Sterling*. Oxford: OUP.

Johnson, E. S. (1977) 'Keynes as a Literary Craftsman', in Patinkin and Leith (eds) (1977).

——and Johnson, H. G. (1978) *The Shadow of Keynes*. Oxford: Basil Blackwell.

Johnson, H. G. (1960) 'The Consumer and Madison Avenue', *Current Economic Comment*, August: 3–10.

——(1969) *Essays in Monetary Economics*, 2nd edn. London: George Allen & Unwin.

——(1970) 'Recent Developments in Monetary Theory – A Commentary', in Croome and Johnson (eds) (1970).

——(1971) 'The Keynesian Revolution and the Monetarist Counter-Revolution', *American Economic Review*, 61(2): 91–106.

——(1975) *On Economics and Society*. Chicago: University of Chicago Press.

——(1976a) 'The American Tradition in Economics', *Journal of Economics and Business*, 16: 17–26.

——(1976b) 'The Nobel Milton', *The Economist*, 23 October: 95.
——(1977) 'The Shadow of Keynes' *Minerva*: 201–13.
——(1978) 'Comment on Mayer on Monetarism', in Mayer (1978).
Johnson, P. (1989) *Intellectuals*. London: Weidenfeld & Nicolson.
Kahn, R. (1933) 'Public Works and Inflation', *Journal of the American Statistical Association*, Supplement: 168–73.
Kaldor, N. (1972) 'The Irrelevance of Equilibrium Economics', *Economic Journal*, 82(325): 1237–55.
Kavanagh, D. (1990) *Thatcherism and British Politics: The End of Consensus*. Oxford: OUP.
Kefauver, E. (1965) *In A Few Hands: Monopoly Power in America*. Harmondsworth: Penguin.
Kern, W. S. (1987) 'Frank Knight's Three Commandments', *History of Political Economy* 19(4): 639–46.
Ketchum, M. D. and Bartell, H. R. (eds) (1966) *Conference on Savings and Residential Financing*. Chicago: US Savings and Loan League.
Ketchum, M. D. and Kendall, L. T. (eds) (1965) *Readings in Financial Institutions*. Boston: Houghton Mifflin.
Ketchum, M. D. and Strunk, N. (eds) (1965) *Conference on Savings and Residential Financing*. Chicago: US Savings and Loan League.
Keuzenkamp, H. A. (1991) 'A Precursor to Muth: Tinbergen's 1932 Model of Rational Expectations', *Economic Journal*, 101: 1245–53.
Keynes, J. M. (1924) 'Alfred Marshall 1842–1924', *Economic Journal*, XXXIV (135): 311–72.
——(1930) *A Treatise on Money*, Vol. II. London: Macmillan.
——(1936a) *The General Theory of Employment Interest and Money*. London: Macmillan.
——(1936b) 'W.S. Jevons 1835–82: A Centenary Allocution on His Life and Work as an Economist and Statistician', *Journal of the Royal Statistical Society*, 99: 516–55.
——(1937) 'The Theory of the Rate of Interest', in Gayer (ed.) (1937).
——(1938a). 'Obituary – George Broomhall 1857–1938', *Economic Journal*, September: 576–8.
——(1938b) 'Review of *The Development of the Graphical Representation of Statistical Data* by Gray Funkhouser', *Economic Journal*, June: 281–3.
——(1939) Professor Tinbergen's Method', *Economic Journal*, 49: 558–68.
——(1940) 'Comment', *Economic Journal*, 50: 154–6.
——(1943) 'The Objective of International Price Stability', *Economic Journal*, June–September: 185–7.
——(1946) 'The Balance of Payments of the United States', *Economic Journal*, June: 172–87.
——(1972–89) *Collected Writings*, ed. D. Moggridge. London: Macmillan.
Kilmister, C. (1971) *The Nature of the Universe*. London: Thames & Hudson.
Kindleberger, C. (1978) *Manias, Panics and Collapses*. London: Macmillan.
Kitch, E. W. (ed.) (1983) 'The Fire of Truth: A Remembrance of Law and Economics at Chicago, 1932–1970', *Journal of Economics and Law*, XXVI: 163–234.
Klamer, A., McCloskey D. and Solow R. (eds) (1988) *The Consequences of Economic Rhetoric*. Cambridge: Cambridge University Press.
Klant, J. (1985) 'The Slippery Transition', in Lawson and Pesaran (eds) (1985).

Klappholz, K. and Agassi, J. (1959) Methodological Prescriptions in Economics. *Economica* February 60–74.

Klein, L. (1946) 'A Post Mortem on Transitional Predictions of National Product', *Journal of Political Economy*, 54: 289–308.

——(1947) 'The Use of Econometric Models as a Guide to Economic Policy', *Econometrica*, 15: 111–51.

——(1951) 'The Life of J. M. Keynes', *Journal of Political Economy*, LIX: 443–51.

——(1971a) 'Whither Econometrics?', *Journal of The American Statistical Association*, 66: 415–21.

—— (1971b) *An Essay on the Theory of Economic Prediction*. Chicago: University of Chicago Press.

——(1978) 'Jacob Marschak 1898–1977', *International Statistical Review*, 46: 326.

——(1985) *Economic Theory and Econometrics*, ed. J. Marquez. Oxford: Basil Blackwell

——(1988) in Breit and Spencer (eds).

——(1992. 'My Professional Life Philosophy', in Szenberg (ed.) (1992).

——and Goldberger, A. (1955) *An Econometric Model of the United States: 1929–52*. Amsterdam: North Holland.

Kline, M. (1990) *Mathematics in Western Culture*. London: Penguin.

Kmenta, J. and Ramsey, J. (eds) (1981) *Large-Scale Macroeconometric Models*. Amsterdam: North Holland.

Knight, F. (1960) *Intelligence and Democratic Action*. Cambridge, MA: Harvard University Press.

Knoester, A. and Wellink, A. H. E. M. (eds) (1993) *Tinbergen Lectures on Economic Policy*. Amsterdam: North Holland.

Knowles, J. W. and Kalacheck, E. D. (1961) *Higher Unemployment Rates, 1957–60: Structural Transformation and Inadequate Demand*. Washington, DC: US Government Printing Office for the Joint Economic Committee, Congress of the US.

Koestler, A. (1959) *The Sleepwalkers: A History of Man's Changing Vision of the Universe*. England: Penguin.

Kol, J. and de Wolff, F. (1993) 'Tinbergen's Work: Change and Continuity', in Knoester and Wellink (eds) (1993).

Koopmans, T. C. (1947) 'Measurement without Theory', *Review of Economics and Statistics* August: 161–72.

——(1949) 'The Econometric Approach to Business Fluctuations', *American Economic Review* May: 64–72.

——(1957) *Three Essays on the State of Economic Science*. New York: McGraw-Hill.

——(1978) 'Jacob Marschak, 1939–1977', *American Economic Association Papers and Proceedings*, May: xi–xii.

Kostelanetz, R. (ed.) (1968) *Beyond Left and Right*. New York: William Morrow.

Kuenne, R. E. (ed.) (1967) *Monopolistic Competition Theory: Studies in Impact: Essays in Honour of E. H. Chamberlin*. New York: John Wiley.

——(1987) 'Edward Hastings Chamberlin', in Eatwell et al. (eds) (1987).

Kuhn, T. (1970) *The Structure of Scientific Revolutions*, 2nd edn. Chicago: University of Chicago Press.

Kuznets, S. (1942) *Uses of National Income in Peace and War*. National Bureau of Economic Research, Occasional Paper No. 6.

Laidler, D. (1975) 'The End of Demand Management: How to Reduce Unemployment in the Late 1970s', in Friedman (1975b).

——(1976) 'Expectations and the Phillips Curve Trade-Off', *Scottish Journal of Political Economy* XXIII(I): 55–72.
——(1977) *The Demand for Money: Theories and Evidence*, 2nd edn. New York: Harper & Row.
——1981. 'Monetarism: An Interpretation and An Assessment', *Economic Journal*, 91(361): 1–28.
——(1985) 'Monetary Policy in Britain: Successes and Shortcomings', *Oxford Economic Papers*, 1(1): 35–43.
——(1993) 'Hawtrey, Harvard and the Origins of the Chicago Tradition', *Journal of Political Economy* 101: 1068–103.
——(1998a) 'More on Hawtrey, Harvard and Chicago', *Journal of Economic Studies*, 25(1): 4–16.
——(1998b) 'Hawtrey, Harvard and Chicago: A Final Comment', *Journal of Economic Studies*, 25(1): 22–3.
Lange, O. (1944) *Price Flexibility and Employment*, Cowles Commission Monograph No. 8. Bloomington, IN: Principia Press.
Lawson, N. (1992) *The View From Number 11: Memoirs of a Tory Radical*. London: Bantum.
Lawson, T. and Pesaran H. (ed.) (1985) *Keynes' Economics: Methodological Issues*. Sydney: Croom Helm.
Leamer, E. E. (1983) 'Let's Take The Con Out of Econometrics', *American Economic Review*, 73: 31–43.
Leeson, R. (1997a) 'The Political Economy of the Inflation-Unemployment Trade-off', *History of Political Economy*, 29(1): 117–56.
——(1997b) 'The Eclipse of the Goal of Zero Inflation', *History of Political Economy*, 29(3): 445–96.
——(1997c) 'The Trade-Off Interpretation of Phillips' Dynamic Stabilisation Exercise', *Economica*, 64(253): 155–73.
——(1998) 'The Early Patinkin–Friedman Correspondence', *Journal of the History of Economic Thought*, 20(4): 433–48.
——(ed.) (1999a) *A.W.H. Phillips: Collected Works in Contemporary Perspective*. Cambridge: Cambridge University Press.
——(1999b) 'Keynes and the Keynesian Phillips Curve', *History of Political Economy*, 31(3): 71–87.
——(2000) 'Patinkin, Johnson and "The Shadow of Friedman"', *History of Political Economy*.
Lehman, J. (ed.) (1958) *The Relationship of Prices to Economic Stability and Growth*. Papers Submitted before the Joint Economic Committee. Washington, DC: USGPO.
Leijonhufvud, A. (1967) 'Keynes and the Keynesians: A Suggested Interpretation', *American Economic Review*, 57(2): 401–10.
Lekachman, R. (ed.) (1964a) *Keynes' General Theory: Report of Three Decades*. London: Macmillan.
——(ed.) (1964b) *Keynes and the Classics*. Boston: Heath.
——(1966) *The Age of Keynes*. London: Penguin.
——(1973) *Inflation: The Permanent Problem of Boom and Bust*. New York: Random House.
Leontief, W. (1971) 'Theoretical Assumptions and Non Observable Facts', *American Economic Review*, 612: 1–7.

Lerner, A. P. (1958) 'Inflationary Depression and the Regulation of Administered Prices', in Lehman (ed.) (1958).

——(1967) 'Employment Theory and Employment Policy', *American Economic Review*, LVII(2): 1–18.

Leube, K. R. (1986). 'George J. Stigler: A Biographical Introduction', in Stigler (1986).

Lewis, J. P. (1959) 'The Problem of Price Stabilization: A Progress Report', *American Economic Review*, May: 309–20.

Lipsey, R. G. (1960) 'The Relation Between Unemployment and the Rate of Change of Money Wage Rates in the United Kingdom 1862–1957: A Further Analysis', *Economica*, 27: 1–31.

——(1966) *An Introduction to Positive Economics*, 2nd edn. London: Weidenfeld & Nicolson.

——(1978) 'The Place of the Phillips Curve in Macroeconomic Models', in Bergstrom et al. (eds) (1978).

——(1981) 'The Understanding and Control of Inflation: Is There a Crisis in Macro-economics?', *Canadian Journal of Economics*, XIV(4): 545–76.

Little, I. (1982) *Economic Development: Theory Policy and International Relations*. New York: Basic Books.

Lucas, R. (1976) 'Econometric Policy Evaluation: A Critique', in Brunner and Meltzer (eds) (1976).

——(1977) 'Understanding Business Cycles', in Brunner and Meltzer (eds) (1977).

——(1994) 'Robert Lucas', in Snowden et al (1994).

——and Sargent, T. (1978) 'After Keynesian Macroeconomics', in *After the Phillips Curve: The Persistence of High Inflation and Unemployment*. Federal Reserve Bank of Boston, Conference Series No. 19.

McCann, C. R. and Perlman, M. (1993) 'On Thinking about George Stigler', *Economic Journal*, 103(419): 994–1014.

McCloskey, D. N. (1986) *The Rhetoric of Economics*. Brighton: Wheatsheaf.

——(1994) *Knowledge and Persuasion in Economics*. Cambridge: CUP.

McCord Wright, D. (1954) 'Discussion', *American Economic Association Papers and Proceedings*, May: 26–30.

Machlup, F. (1939) 'Evaluation of the Practical Significance of the Theory of Monopolistic Competition', *American Economic Review*, XXIX(2): 227–36.

McIvor, R. C. (1983) 'A Note on the University of Chicago's Academic Scribblers', *Journal of Political Economy*, 91(5): 888–93.

Magnus, J. R. and Morgan, M. (1987. The ET Interview: Professor J. Tinbergen. *Econometric Theory*: 117–42.

Maler, K. (ed.) (1992) *Nobel Lectures: Economic Science*. London: World Science.

Malinvaud, E. (1988) 'Econometric Methodology at the Cowles Commission: Rise and Maturity', *Econometric Theory*: 187–209.

——(1991) 'Review of *The History of Econometric Ideas* by Mary Morgan', *Economic Journal* 101(406)4: 634–6.

Mankiw, G. (1990) 'A Quick Refresher Course in Macroeconomics', *Journal of Economic Literature* XXVIII: 1645–60.

Markham, J. (1964) 'Discussion', *American Economic Association Papers and Proceedings*, May: 53–5.

Markowitz, H. (1992) 'The Foundations of Portfolio Theory', in Maler (ed.) (1992).

Marshall, A. (1920) *Principles of Economics*. London: Macmillan.

Mayer, T. (1978) *The Structure of Monetarism*. New York: W.W. Norton.
Meier, G. M. and Seers, D. (eds) (1984) *Pioneers in Development*. Oxford: Oxford University Press.
Menger, K. (1973) 'Austrian Marginalism and Mathematical Economics', in Hicks and Weber (eds) (1973).
Miernyk, W. H. (1966) 'Forward', in Gilpatrick (1966).
Millikan, M. F. (ed.) (1953) *Income Stabilization for a Developing Democracy*. New Haven, CT: Yale University Press.
Minford, P. (1994) 'Patrick Minford', in Snowden et al. (1994).
Mini, P. V. (1991) *Keynes, Bloomsbury and the General Theory*. London: Macmillan.
Mirowsky, P. (1989) 'The Probabilistic Counter-Revolution, or How Stochastic Concepts Came to Neoclassical Economic Theory', *Oxford Economic Papers*, 41(1), 217–35.
Mitchell, W., Hand, J. and Walter, I. (eds) (1974) *Readings in Macroeconomics*. New York: McGraw-Hill.
Modigliani, F. (1977) 'The Monetarist Controversy or Should We Forsake Stabilisation Policies?', *American Economic Review*, 67(2): 1–19.
——(1989) 'An Interview', in Feiwel (ed.) (1989).
Morgan, M. S. (1990) *The History of Econometric Ideas*. Cambridge: Cambridge University Press.
Morrison, L. A. (1934) 'Imperfect competition', *American Economic Review* March: 30.
Moss, S. (1984) 'The History of the Theory of the Firm from Marshall to Robinson and Chamberlin: The Source of Positivism in Economics', *Economica*, 51: 307–18.
Musgrave, R. A. (1996) in Colander and Landreth (eds) (1996).
National Planning Association (1961) *The Rise of Chronic Unemployment*. Planning Pamphlet No. 113. Washington, DC: NPA.
Navasky, V. S. (1967) 'Galbraith on Galbraith', *New York Times*, 25 June: 2–39.
Neff, P. (1949a) 'Professor Friedman's Proposal: A Comment', *American Economic Review*, XXXIX: 946–9.
——(1949b) 'Final Comment', *American Economic Review*, XXXIX: 955–6.
Nelson, R. L. (1959) *Merger Movements in American Industry 1895–1956*. Princeton, NJ: Princeton University Press.
Nichol, A. J. (1934) 'Professor Chamberlin's Theory of Limited Competition', *Quarterly Journal of Economics*: 317–37.
Nickell, S. (1990) 'Unemployment: A Survey', *Economic Journal*, 100(401): 391–439.
Norton, L. J. (1949) 'Discussion', *American Economic Review*, XXXIX(3): 168–170.
Nove, A. (1992) 'Kondratieff's Final Work', *Royal Economic Society Newsletter*, 77: 2–3.
O'Connor, J. (1973) *The Fiscal Crisis of the State*. New York: St. Martin's Press.
O'Donnell, R. (1992) *New Light on Keynes' Views of Mathematics, Economics and Econometrics*. Mimeo.
Okun, A. (1972) 'The Fiscal Fiasco of the Vietnam Period', in Okun (ed.) (1972).
——(ed.) (1972) *The Battle Against Unemployment*. New York: W.W. Norton.
——(1975) 'Inflation: Its Mechanics and Welfare Costs', *Brookings Papers on Economic Activity*, 2: 351–90.
Ormerod, P. (1994) *The Death of Economics*. London: Faber & Faber.

Pagan, A. (1984) 'Model Evaluation by Variable Addition', in Hendry and Wallis (eds) (1984).
——(1987) 'Three Econometrics Methodologies: A Critical Appraisal', *Journal of Economic Surveys*, 1(1): 3–24.
Parkin, M. (1986) '*Essays On and In The Chicago Tradition*: A Review Essay', *Journal of Money Credit and Banking*, 18(1): 104–16.
Parsons, W. (1989) *The Power of the Financial Press*. Cheltenham: Edward Elgar.
Patinkin, D. (1947) 'Multiple-Plant Firms, Cartels, and Imperfect Competition', *Quarterly Journal of Economics*, February: 173–205.
——(1969) 'The Chicago Tradition, the Quantity Theory and Friedman', *Journal of Money Credit and Banking*, 1: 46–70.
——(1972) 'Friedman on the Quantity Theory and Keynesian Economics', *Journal of Political Economy*, 80, Sept–Oct, 883–905.
——(1973) 'Frank Knight as Teacher', *American Economic Review*, 63(5): 787–810.
——(1974) 'Friedman on the Quantity Theory and Keynesian Economics', in Gordon (ed.) (1974)
——(1976) 'Keynes and Econometrics: On the Interaction between the Macroeconomic Revolutions of Inter-War Period', *Econometrica*, 44(6): 1091–123.
——(1986) 'A Reply', *Journal of Money Credit and Banking*, 18(1): 116–21.
——and Leith, J. C. (eds) (1977) *Keynes, Cambridge and The General Theory*. London: Macmillan.
Perry, G. L. (1967) 'Wages and the Guideposts', *American Economic Review*, LVII(4): 897–904.
Pesaran, H. and Smith R. (1985) 'Keynes on Econometrics', in Lawson and Pesaran (eds) (1985).
Phelp, J. (1985) 'Are Popperian Criticisms of Keynes Justified?', in Lawson and Pesaran (eds) (1985).
Phelps, E. (1967) 'Phillips Curves, Expectations of Inflation, and Optimal Unemployment over Time', *Economica*, 34: 254–81.
——(1968) 'Money Wage Dynamics and Labour Market Equilibrium', *Journal of Political Economy*, 76: 638–711.
——(1996) 'The Origins and Further Development of the Natural Rate of Unemployment', in Cross (ed.) (1996).
Phelps Brown, H. (1972) 'The Underdevelopment of Economics', *Economic Journal*, 82(325): 1–10.
Phillips, A. W. H. (1953) *Dynamic Models in Economics*. PhD Thesis, University of London.
——(1954) 'Stabilisation Policy in a Closed Economy', *Economic Journal*, June: 290–323.
——(1958) 'The Relation Between Unemployment and the Rate of Change of Money Wage Rates in the United Kingdom, 1861–1957', *Economica*, 25: 283–99.
——(1962) 'Employment, Inflation and Growth', *Economica*, 29: 1–16.
——(1968) 'Models for the Control of Economic Fluctuations', in *Scientific Growth Systems, Mathematical Model Building in Economics and Industry*. London: Griffin: 159–65.
Phillips, A. and Stevenson, R. E. (1974) 'The Historical Development of Industrial Organization', *History of Political Economy*, Fall: 324–42.
Phillips, P. (1999) in Leeson (ed.) (1999a).
Plosser, C. (1994) 'Charles Plosser', in Snowden et al. (1994).

Plumptre, A. (1947) 'Keynes in Cambridge', *Canadian Journal of Economics*, XIII: 366–71.
Poole, W. and Kornblith, E. B. F. (1973) 'The Friedman-Meiselman CMC Paper: New Evidence on an Old Controversy', *American Economic Review*, 63(5): 908–17.
Potvin, G. (1969) *Hearings Before the House of Representatives Select Committee on Small Business*, Vol. 1. Washington, DC: US Government Printing Office.
Pratson, F. J. (1978) *Perspective on Galbraith: Conversations and Opinions*. Boston: CBI Publishing.
Randall, C. (1958) 'Wage Inflation', in *Problems of United States Economic Development*. New York: Committee for Economic Development.
Reder, M. W. (1982) 'Chicago Economics: Permanence and Change', *Journal of Economic Literature* XX: 1–38.
——(1987) 'The Chicago School', in Eatwell et al. (1987).
Rees, A. (1970) 'The Phillips Curve as a Menu of Policy Choice', *Economica*, XXXVII (May), 227–38.
Reese, D. A. (ed.) (1987) *The Legacy of Keynes*. San Francisco: Harper & Row.
Rima, I. H. (1988) 'Keynes' Vision and Econometric Analysis', in Hamouda and Smithin (eds) (1988).
Rivlin, A. M. (1987) 'Economics and the Political Process', *American Economic Review*, 77(1): 1–10.
Robinson, E. A. G. (1947) 'John Maynard Keynes, 1883–1946', *Economic Journal*, March: 1–68.
——(1972) 'John Maynard Keynes, Economist, Author, Statesman', *Economic Journal*, 82(326): 531–46.
——(1992) 'My Apprenticeship as an Economist', in Szenberg (ed.) (1992).
Robinson, J. (1933) *The Economics of Imperfect Competition*. London: Macmillan.
——(1952) 'Review of Galbraith's *American Capitalism*', *Economic Journal*, LXII, Dec, 925–8.
——(1962) *Economic Philosophy*. London: Penguin.
Rogerson, R. (1996) 'Theory Ahead of Language in the Economics of Unemployment', *Journal of Economic Perspectives*' 11(1): 73–92.
Roos, C. F. (1955) 'Survey of Economic Forecasting Techniques', *Econometrica* 23(4): 363–95.
Rosen, S. (1969) 'Keynes without Gadflies', in Roszac (ed.) (1969).
——(1993) 'George J. Stigler and the Industrial Organisation of Economic Thought', *Journal of Political Economy*, 101(5): 809–17.
Rosenberg, N. (1993) 'George Stigler: Adam Smith's Best Friend', *Journal of Political Economy*, 101(5): 833–48.
Roszac, T. (ed.) (1969) *The Dissenting Academy*. London: Chatto & Windus.
Rothbard, M. N. (1960) 'The Politics of Political Economists: Comment', *Quarterly Journal of Economics*, November: 659–65.
Rottenberg, S. (ed.) (1980) *Occupational Licensure and Regulation*. Washington, DC: American Enterprise Institute for Public Policy.
Rousseas, S. W. (ed.) (1968) *Inflation: Its Causes, Consequences and Control*. Wilton, CT: Calvin K. Kazanjian Economics Foundation.
Rowley, J. C. R. (1988) 'The Keynes–Tinbergen Exchange in Retrospect', in Hamouda and Smithin (eds) (1988).
——and Wilton, D. A. (1973) 'Quarterly Models of Wage Determination: New Efficient Estimates', *American Economic Review*, 68(3): 380–9.

Salant, W. (1977) 'Keynes as Seen by his Students in the 1930s', in Patinkin and Leith (eds) (1977).
Samuelson, P. A. (1944a) 'Unemployment Ahead 1: A Warning to the Washington Experts', *The New Republic*, 11 September: 297.
——(1944b) 'Unemployment Ahead 2: The Coming Economic Crisis', *New Republic* 18 September: 333–5.
——(1946) 'Lord Keynes and the General Theory', *Econometrica*, 14(3): 187–200.
——(1947) *Foundations of Economic Analysis*. Cambridge, MA: Harvard University Press.
——(1953) 'Full Employment versus Progress and Other Economic Goals', in Millikan (ed.) (1953).
——(1958a) 'The Threat of Inflation', in *Problems of United States Economic Development*. New York: Committee for Economic Development.
——(1958b) *Economics: An Introductory Analysis*, 4th edn. New York: McGraw-Hill.
——(1962a) *Problems of the American Economy*. London: Athlone.
——(1962b) 'Economists and the History of Ideas', *American Economic Review*, LII(1): 1–18.
——(1964) 'The General Theory'. in Lekachman (ed.) (1964a).
——(1967a) 'The Monopolistic Competition Revolution', in Kuenne (ed.) (1967).
——(1967b) 'Second Lecture', in Burns, A. F. and Samuelson, P. A. *Full Employment, Guideposts and Economic Stability*. Washington, DC: American Enterprise Institute.
——(1972) 'Liberalism at Bay' *Social Research*, Spring: 16–31.
——(1973) 'Monetarism Objectively Evaluated', in Gill (ed.) (1976).
——(1974) 'The President's New Economic Program: Domestic Wage and Price Controls', in Mitchell et al. (eds) (1974).
——(1975a) 'Alvin H. Hansen', *Newsweek*, 16 June: 43.
——(1975b) 'In Search of the Elusive Elite', *New York Times* 26 June.
——(1976a) 'Alvin Hansen as a Creative Theorist', *Quarterly Journal of Economics*, XL(1): 24–31.
——(1976b) *Economics*, 10th edn. New York: McGraw-Hill.
——(1977) 'Discussion', in Patinkin and Leith (eds) (1977).
——(1983a) 'Economics in a Golden Age', in Brown and Solow (eds) (1983).
——(1983b) 'Comments', in Worswick and Trevithick (eds) (1983).
——(1988) 'Paul Samuelson', in Breit and Spencer (eds) (1986, reprinted 1988).
——(1992) 'My Life Philosophy: Policy Credos and Working Ways', in Szenberg (ed.) (1992).
——(1996) in Colander and Landreth (eds) (1996).
——(1998) 'How *Foundations* Came to Be', *Journal of Economic Literature*, XXXVI(3): 1375–86.
——and Solow, R. (1960) 'Analytical Aspects of Anti Inflation Policy', *American Economic Review*, 50: 177–94.
Saulnier, R. J. (1963) *The Strategy of Economic Policy*. New York: Fordham University Press.
Scherer, F. M. (1970) *Industrial Market Structure and Economic Performance*. Chicago: Rand McNally.
Schlesinger, A. M. Jr (1965) *A Thousand Days: John F. Kennedy in the White House*. London: Mayflower-Dell.

Schneider, E. (1967) 'Milestones on the Way to the Theory of Monopolistic Competition', in Kuenne (ed.) (1967).
Schultz, T. W. (1949) 'Spot and Future Prices as Production Guides', *American Economic Review,* XXXIX(3): 135–149.
Schultze, C. (1959) *Recent Inflation in the United States.* Study Paper No. 1. Joint Economic Committee, Washington, US Government Printing Office.
Schumpeter, J. A. (1933) 'The Common Sense of Econometrics', *Econometrica,* 1: 5–12.
——(1946) 'Keynes and Statistics', *The Review of Economic Statistics,* 28: 194–6.
——(1954) *History of Economic Analysis.* Cambridge, MA: Harvard University Press.
Schweitzer, A. (1975) 'Frank Knight's Social Economics', *History of Political Economy,* 7(3): 279–92.
Selden, R. (ed.) (1975) *Capitalism and Freedom: Problems and Prospects.* Charlottesville: University Press of Virginia.
Shaw, G. K. (ed.) (1991) *Economics, Culture and Education: Essays in Honour of Mark Blaug.* Cheltenham: Edward Elgar.
Sherrard, A. (1951) 'Advertising, Product Differentiation, and the Limits of Economics', *Journal of Political Economy,* 59 126–42.
Shils, E. (1977) 'Harry Johnson', *Encounter,* November: 85–9.
——(1981) 'Some Academics, Mainly in Chicago', *American Scholar*: 179–96.
——(ed.) (1991) *Remembering the University of Chicago: Teachers, Scientists and Scholars.* Chicago: University of Chicago Press.
Shoup, C., Friedman, M. and Mack, R. (1943) *Taxing To Prevent Inflation.* New York: Columbia University Press.
Shultz, G. P. and Aliber, R. Z. (eds) (1966) *Guidelines: Informal Controls and the Market Place.* Chicago: University of Chicago Press.
Sills, D. L. (ed.) (1968) *International Encyclopaedia of the Social Sciences.* New York: Free Press.
Skidelsky, R. (1977) *The End of The Keynesian Era.* London: Macmillan.
——(1983) *John Maynard Keynes: Hopes Betrayed 1883–1920.* London: Macmillan.
——(1992) *John Maynard Keynes: The Economist as Saviour 1920–1937.* London: Macmillan.
Slichter, S. (1958) 'Use of Growth to Narrow Inflationary Gap', in *Problems of United States Economic Development.* New York: Committee for Economic Development.
Smith, D. (1987) *The Rise and Fall of Monetarism.* Harmondsworth: Penguin.
Snowden, B., Vane, H. and Wynarczyk, P. (1994) *A Modern Guide to Macroeconomics.* Cheltenham: Edward Elgar.
Solow, R. (1954) 'The Survival of Mathematical Economics', *Review of Economics and Statistics,* November: 372–4.
——(1957) 'Technical Change and the Aggregate Production Function', *Review of Economics and Statistics,* 39: 312–20.
——(1964a) 'Friedman on America's Money', *Banker,* November: 710–17.
——(1964b) *The Nature and Sources of Unemployment in the United States.* Stockholm: Wicksell Lectures, Almqvist & Wicksell.
——(1965) 'Economic Growth and Residential Housing', in Ketchum and Kendall (eds) (1965).

——(1966) 'The Case Against the Case Against the Guideposts', in Shultz and Aliber (eds) (1966).
——(1967) 'A Rejoinder', *Public Interest*, 9: 118–19.
——(1968) 'Discussion', in Rousseas (ed.) (1968).
——(1970) 'Science and Ideology in Economics', *Public Interest*, 21: 94–107.
——(1975) 'The Intelligent Citizen's Guide to Inflation', *Public Interest*, 26, 30–66.
——(1978a) 'Summary and Evaluation', in *After the Phillips Curve: Persistence of High Inflation and Unemployment*. Boston: Federal Reserve Bank of Boston.
——(1978b) 'Down the Phillips Curve with Gun and Camera', in Teigen (ed.) (1978).
——(1987) 'The Conservative Revolution: a Roundtable Discussion', *Economic Policy*, October: 181–5.
——(1990) 'Robert Solow', in Breit and Spencer (eds).
Solzehenitsyn, A. (1973) *The Gulag Archipelago: 1918–56*. Australia: Collins/Fontana.
Sowell, T. (1993) 'A Student's Eye View of George Stigler', *Journal of Political Economy*, 101(5): 785–92.
Stein, H. (1986) 'The Washington Economics Industry', *American Economic Review*, 16(2): 1–9.
Stein, J. L. (1982) *Monetarists, Keynesians and New Classical Economics*. Oxford: Basil Blackwell.
Steindl, F. (1990) 'The "Oral Tradition" at Chicago in the 1930s', *Journal of Political Economy*, 96(2): 430–2.
Steiner, P. (1964) 'Discussion', *American Economic Association Papers and Proceedings*, May: 55–7.
Stigler, G. (1937) 'A Generalisation of the Theory of Imperfect Competition', *Journal of Farm Economics*, August: 707–17.
——(1939) 'The Limitations of Statistical Demand Curves', *Journal of the American Statistical Association*, 34(207): 469–81.
——(1940) 'Review of Carlson's *A Study on the Pure Theory of Production*', *American Economic Review*, June: 364–5.
——(1941) 'Review of Hart's *Anticipations, Uncertainty and Dynamic Planning*', *American Economic Review*, June: 358–9.
——(1942) *The Theory of Competitive Price*. London: Macmillan.
——(1943a) 'The New Welfare Economics', *American Economic Review*, June: 355–9.
——(1943b) 'Review of Kuznets' National Income and Its Composition, 1919–1938', *Journal of Farm Economics*, May: 528–33.
——(1943c) 'Review of *Fiscal Planning for Total War* by Crum *et al.*', *Journal of Political Economy*, 51: 77–8.
——(1944) 'Review of Saxton's *The Economics of Price Determination*', *Journal of Political Economy*, 52: 81–2.
——(1946) *The Theory of Price*, 1st edn. London: Macmillan.
——(1947a) 'The Kinky Oligopoly Demand Curve and Rigid Prices', *Journal of Political Economy*, LX: 342–9.
——(1947b) 'Notes on the History of the Giffen Paradox', *Journal of Political Economy* 55, April 152–6.
——(1947c) *Domestic Servants in the United States*. New York: NBER.
——(1947d) *Trends in Output and Employment*. New York: NBER.

——(1948) 'Review of Bain's *Pricing, Distribution and Employment – Economics of an Enterprise System*', *American Economic Review*, 38: 915–16.
——(1949a) 'A Survey of Contemporary Economics', *Journal of Political Economy*, LVII(2): 93–105.
——(1949b) *Five Lectures on Economic Problems*. London: Longman and LSE.
——(1950a) 'Monopoly and Oligopoly by Merger', *American Economic Association Papers and Proceedings*, XL(2): 23–34.
——(1950b) *Employment and Compensation in Education*. New York: NBER.
——(1951) 'Discussion: Economic Theory, Statistics and Economic Practice', *American Economic Association Papers and Proceedings*, May: 126–8.
——(1952) *The Theory of Price*, 2nd edn. New York: Macmillan.
——(1954a) 'The Economist Plays with Blocs', *American Economic Association Papers and Proceedings*, May: 7–14.
——(1954b) 'The Early History of Empirical Studies of Consumer Behaviour', *Journal of Political Economy* LXII(2): 95–113.
——(1955a) 'Mathematics in Economics: Further Comments', *Review of Economics and Statistics*, 37: 299–300.
——(1955b) 'The Nature and Role of Originality in Scientific Progress', *Economica*, November: 293–302.
——(1955c) 'Introduction', in *Business Concentration and Pricing Policy*. Princeton, NJ: Princeton University Press (for NBER).
——(1956a) 'Industrial Organisation and Economic Progress', in White (ed.) (1956).
——(1956b) 'The Statistics of Monopoly and Merger', *Journal of Political Economy*, 64, Feb: 33–40.
——(1957a) 'Review of Rogin's The Meaning and Validity of Economic Theories', *American Economic Review*, 47, March: 159–64.
——(1957b) 'Perfect Competition, Historically Contemplated', *Journal of Political Economy*, LXV(1): 1–17.
——(1959a) 'The Politics of Political Economists', *Quarterly Journal of Economics*, 73: 522–32.
——(1959b) 'Foreword', in Nelson (1959).
——(1961a) 'Review of Grampp's *The Manchester School of Economics*', *Economica*, August: 329–330.
——(1961b) 'The Economics of Information', *Journal of Political Economy*, LXIX(3): 213–25.
——(1962a) 'Henry L. Moore and Statistical Economics', *Econometrica*, 30(1): 1–21.
——(1962b) 'Information in the Labour Market', *Journal of Political Economy*, 70(1): 94–105.
——(1962c) 'Administered Prices and Oligopolistic Inflation', *Journal of Business*, 35(1): 1–13.
——(1962d) 'Comment on the Chicago School', *Journal of Political Economy*, 70: 70–1.
——(1962e) 'Foreword', in Gort (1962).
——(1963a) 'Archibald versus Chicago', *Review of Economics and Statistics*, 30: 63–4.
——(1963b) *The Intellectual and the Market Place*. London: Free Press.
——(1963c) 'Policies for Growth', in *Proceedings of a Symposium on Economic Growth*. Washington, DC: American Bankers Association.

——(1964a) 'Comment', *Journal of Business*, 37: 414–22.

——(1964b) 'Competition and Concentration: Interview', *Challenge*, January: 18–21.

——(1964c) 'Comment', *Journal of Business*, 37: 414–22.

——(1965a) 'The Economist and the State', *American Economic Review*, 55: 1–18.

——(1965b) *Essays in the History of Economics*. Chicago: University of Chicago.

——(1965c) 'The Problem of the Negro', *New Guard*, December: 11–12.

——(1965d) 'The Formation of Economic Policy', in *Current Problems in Political Economy*. Paul L. Morrison Lectures in Political Economy. Greencastle, In: Depauw University.

——(1966a) *The Theory of Price*, 3rd edn. London: Macmillan.

——(1966b) 'Report', in Shultz and Aliber (eds) (1966b).

——(1966c) 'Review of Meade's *The Stationary Economy*', *Economica*, November: 479.

——(1967a) 'The Foundations and Economics', in Weaver (ed.) (1967).

——(1967b) 'Alice in Fundland', *Barron's*, 27: 8–9, 12.

——(1967c) 'The Changing Problem of Oligopoly', *Il Politico*, 32: 355–61.

——(1967d) 'Galbraith's New Book: A Few Problems', *Wall Street Journal*, 26 June.

——(1968a) *The Organisation of Industry*. Homewood, IL: Irwin.

——(1968b) 'Competition', in Sills (ed.) (1968).

——(1969a) *Hearings Before the House of Representatives Select Committee on Small Business*, Vol. 1. Washington, DC: US Government Printing Office.

——(1969b) Text of Report of Nixon Task Force on Productivity and Competition. Antitrust and Trade Regulation Report No. 413. Washington, DC.

——(1969c) 'Does Economics Have a Useful Past?', *History of Political Economy*, 1, Fall: 217–230.

——(1970) 'Review of Robbins' *The Evolution of Modern Economic Theory*', *Economica*, November: 425–6.

——(1971) 'The Theory of Economic Regulation', *Bell Journal of Economics and Management Sciences*, 1: 3–21.

——(1972a) 'Economic Competition and Political Competition', *Public Choice* 8, Fall: 91–106.

——(1972b) 'The Law and Economics of Public Policy: A Plea to the Scholars', *Journal of Legal Studies*, VI: 1–12.

——(1973a) 'Professors Suppressing Freedom?', *Compact*, December: 15–17.

——(1973b) 'Frank Knight as Teacher', *Journal of Political Economy*, 81: 518–20

——(1974) 'Free Riders and Collective Action: an Appendix to Theories of Economic Regulation', *Bell Journal of Economics and Management Sciences*, 5: 359–65.

——(1975) 'The Intellectual and his Society', in Selden (ed.) (1975).

——(1976a) 'Do Economists Matter?', *Southern Economic Journal*, 42(3): 347–54.

——(1976b) 'The Size of Legislatures', *Journal of Legal Studies*, 5: 17–34.

——(1977) 'The Conference Handbook', *Journal of Political Economy*, 85(2): 441–3.

——(1978) 'The Literature of Economics: The Case of the Kinked Oligopoly Demand Curve', *Economic Inquiry*, 16(2): 185–204.

——(1980) 'Occupational Licensure for Economists?', in Rottenberg (ed.) (1980).

——(1981) 'Comment', in Fromm (ed.) (1981).

——(1981) 'A Historical Note on the Short Run: Marshall and Friedman', *History of Economics Society Bulletin*, 3: 13–14.

——(1982a) *The Economist as Preacher.* Chicago: University of Chicago Press.

——(1982b) 'Review of Reid's *The Kinked Demand Curve Analysis of Oligopoly*', *Economic Journal*, 92(365): 203–4.

——(1982c) *The Pleasures and Pains of Modern Capitalism.* London: IEA.

——(1982d) 'The Economist and the Problem of Monopoly', *American Economic Association Papers and Proceedings*, 72(2) May: 1–11.

——(1983a) 'Nobel Lecture: The Process and Progress of Economics', *Journal of Political Economy* 91(4): 529–45.

——(1983b) 'Review of *Papers and Correspondence of William Stanley Jevons*', *Economic Journal* 93(370): 415–17.

——(1983c) in Kitch (ed.) (1983).

——(1984) 'Economics – The Imperial Science', *Scandinavian Journal of Economics*, 86(3): 303–13.

——(1985) 'The Origins of the Sherman Act', *Journal of Legal Studies*, XIV: 1–12.

——(1986) *The Essence of Stigler.* eds Kurt Leube and Thomas Gale Moore. Stanford, CA: Hoover Institution Press.

——(1987a) 'Are We Hissing the Wrong Guys?', *Forbes*, 13 July: 52–6.

——(1987b) 'Frank Hyneman Knight', in Eatwell et al. (eds) (1987).

——(1988a) *Memoirs of an Unregulated Economist.* New York: Basic Books.

——(1988b) in Breit and Spencer (eds) (1986, reprinted 1988).

——(1988c) 'The Effect of Government on Economic Efficiency', *Business Economics*, January: 7–13.

——(1988d) 'Economists and Public Policy', in American Enterprise Institute.

——(1989) 'Adam Smith and Public Choice: A Reply to Anderson', *History of Political Economy*, 21(4): 659–60.

——(1990a) 'The Place of Marshall's *Principles* in the Development of Economics', in Whitaker (ed.) (1990).

——(1990b) 'Ricardo or Hollander?', *Oxford Economic Papers*, 42: 765–8.

——(1991) 'The Direction of Economic Research', in Shaw (ed.) (1991).

——(1992) 'Law or Economics?', *Journal of Law and Economics*, XXXV: 455–68.

——and Friedland, C. (1962) 'What Can Regulators Regulate?', *Journal of Law and Economics*, V: 1–16.

——(1975) 'The Citation Practices of Doctorates in Economics', *Journal of Political Economy*, 83(3): 477–507.

——(1979) 'The Pattern of Citation Practices in Economics', *History of Political Economy*, 11(1): 1–20.

——(1983) 'The Literature of Economics: The Case of Berle and Means', *Journal of Law and Economics*, XXVI: 237–68.

——and Kindahl, J. K. (1973) 'Industrial Prices, as Administered by Dr. Means', *American Economic Review*, 63(4): 717–21.

——and Sherwin, R. A. (1985) 'The Extent of the Market', *Journal of Law and Economics*, XXVIII: 555–85.

Stigler, S. (1994) 'Some Correspondence on Methodology Between Friedman and Wilson, November–December 1946', *Journal of Economic Literature*, XXXII: 1197–203.

Stone, R. (1978) 'Keynes, Political Arithmetic and Econometrics', *Proceedings of the British Academy*, 64: 55–92.

——(1980) 'Political Economy, Economics and Beyond', *Economic Journal* 90: 719–36.

Sutton, J. (1989) 'Is Imperfect Competition Empirically Empty', in Feiwel (ed.) (1989).
Szenberg, M. (ed.) (1992) *Eminent Economists: Their Life Philosophies*. Cambridge: Cambridge University Press.
Tarshis, L. (1977) 'Discussion', in Patinkin and Leith (eds) (1977).
——(1996) in Colander and Landreth (eds) (1996).
Tavlas, G. (1997) 'Chicago, Harvard and the Doctrinal Foundations of Monetary Economics', *Journal of Political Economy*, 105: 153–77.
——(1998a) 'More on the Chicago Tradition', *Journal of Economic Studies*, 25(1): 17–21.
——(1998b) 'Was the Monetarist Tradition Invented?', *Journal of Economic Perspectives*, 12(4): 211–22.
Taylor, J. (1972) 'The Behaviour of Unemployment and Unfilled Vacancies: Great Britain 1958–1971: An Alternative View', *Economic Journal*, 82(328): 1352–65.
——(1979) 'Staggered Wage Setting in a Macro Model', *American Economic Review*, 69: 108–13.
Teigen, R. L., (ed.) (1978) *Readings in Money, National Income, and Stabilization Policy*. Homewood, IL: R. D. Irwin.
Telser, L. G. (1962a) 'Advertising and Cigarettes', *Journal of Political Economy*, 70: 470–99.
——(1962b) 'The Demand for Branded Goods as Estimated from Consumer Panel Data', *Review of Economics and Statistics*, August: 300–24.
——(1964) 'Advertising and Competition', *Journal of Political Economy*, LXXII(6): 537–62.
——(1971) *Competition, Collusion and Game Theory*. London: Macmillan.
——(1996) *Stigler, George Joseph (1911–1991)*. Mimeo.
Theobald, R. (1968) 'Cybernation and Human Rights', in Kostelanetz (ed.) (1968).
Tinbergen, J. (1937) *An Econometric Approach to Business Cycle Problems*. Paris: Hermann & Cie.
——(1947) 'Keynes' Theories from an Econometric Point of View', in Harris (ed.) (1947).
——(1956) *Economic Policy: Principles and Design*. Amsterdam: North Holland.
——(1967) 'Quantitative Economics, Macroeconomics and Monopolistic Competition', in Kuenne (ed.) (1967).
——(1969) 'The Use of Models: Experience and Prospects. Lecture to the Memory of Alfred Nobel', *Economic Sciences 1969–1980*, ed. A. Lindbeck. London: World Scientific.
——(1979) 'Recollections of Professional Experience', *Banca Nazionale del Lavorno Quarterly Review*, December: 331–60.
——(1984) 'Development Cooperation as a Learning Process', in Meier and Seers (eds) (1984).
——(1992) 'Solving the Most Urgent Problems First', in Szenberg (ed.) (1992).
Tobin, J. (1964) 'Barry's Economic Crusade', *New Republic*, 24 October: 13–16.
——(1966) *National Economic Policy*. New Haven, CT: Yale University Press.
——(1968) 'Discussion', in Rousseas (ed.) (1968).
——(1970) 'Money and Income: Post Hoc Ergo Propter Hoc?', *Quarterly Journal of Economics*, 84: 301–17.
——(1972) 'Cambridge (U.K.) versus Cambridge (Mass)', *Public Interest*, 23: 102–9.
——(1976) 'Hansen and Public Policy', *Quarterly Journal of Economics*, XC(1): 32–7.

——(1977) 'Macroeconomic Models and Policy', in Intriligator (ed.) (1977).
——(1987) 'Keynesian Economics and its Renaissance', in Reese (ed.) (1987).
——and Weidenbaum, M. L. (eds) (1988) *Two Revolutions in Economic Policy.* Cambridge, MA: MIT Press.
Triffin, R. (1940) *Monopolistic Competition and General Equilibrium Theory.* Cambridge, MA: Harvard University Press.
Valdes, J. G. (1995) *Pinochet's Economists: the Chicago School in Chile.* Cambridge: Cambridge University Press.
Viner, J. (1964) 'Comment on My 1936 Review of Keynes' *General Theory*', in Lekachman (ed.) (1964a).
Vining, R. (1949) 'Koopmans on the Choice of Variables to be Studied and of Methods of Measurement', *Review of Economics and Statistics*, 31: 77–86.
——(1959) '*The Affluent Society*: A Review Article', *American Economic Review*, 39(2) March: 112–19.
von Mises, L. (1974) *Planning for Freedom.* South Holland, IL: Libertarian Press.
Wallich, H. C. (1966) 'Monetary versus Fiscal Policy', in Ketchum and Bartell (eds) (1966).
Wallis, W. A. (1949) 'Review of Lever's *Advertising and Economic Theory*', *American Economic Review*, XXXIX(2) March: 558–9.
——(1980) 'The Statistical Research Group 1942–1945', *Journal of the American Statistical Association*, 75(370): 320–55.
——(1993) 'George J. Stigler: In Memorandum', *Journal of Political Economy*, 101(5): 774–89.
Walras, L. (1954) *Elements of Pure Economics*, ed. W. Jaffe. London: Allen & Unwin.
Walters, A. (1977) 'Comment', in Intriligator (ed.) (1977).
Warsh, D. (1988) '"Yellow Rain" and Supply Side Economics: Some Rhetoric that Failed', in Klamer, McCloskey and Solow (eds) (1988).
Weintraub, E. R. (1983) 'On the Existence of a Competitive Equilibrium: 1930–54', *Journal of Economic Literature*, XXI: 1–39.
——(1985) *General Equilibrium Analysis: Studies in Appraisal.* Cambridge: Cambridge University Press.
Weaver, W. (ed.) (1967) *US Philanthropic Foundations: Their History, Structure, Management and Record.* New York: Harper & Row.
Whitaker, J. K. (ed.) (1990) *Centenary Essays on Alfred Marshall.* Cambridge: Cambridge University Press.
White, L. D. (ed.) (1956) *The State of the Social Sciences.* Chicago: University of Chicago Press.
Whyte, W. H. (1952) *Is Anybody Listening?* New York: Simon & Schuster.
Woking, H. (1949) 'The Investigation of Economic Expectations', *American Economic Review*, XXXIX(3) May: 150–66.
Worswick, G. D. N. (1972) 'Is Progress in Science Possible?', *Economic Journal*, 82: 73–86.
Worswick, D. and Trevithick, J. (1983) Keynes and the Modern World. Proceedings of the Keynes Centenary Conference, King's College, Cambridge. Cambridge University Press.
Yordon, W. J. (1992) 'Stigler's Adaptable and Indivisible Plant and the Micro/Macro Schism', *History of Political Economy*, 24(2): 456–70.
Young, W. (1987) *Interpreting Mr. Keynes: The IS-LM Enigma.* New York: Reinhart.

——and Lee, F. (1993) *Oxford Economics and Oxford Economists*. London: Macmillan.

Yule, G. U. (1926) 'Why Do We Sometimes Get Nonsense Correlations Between Time Series – A Study in Sampling and the Nature of Time Series', *Journal of the Royal Statistical Society*, 84: 1–64.

Zarnowitz, V. (1968) 'Prediction and Forecasting', in *International Encyclopedia of the Social Sciences*. London: Macmillan and the Free Press.

——(ed.) (1972) *The Business Cycle Today*. New York: National Bureau of Economic Research.

——(1992) *Has Macro Forecasting Failed?* National Bureau of Economic Research Inc., Working Paper No. 3867.

Index

Names

Subjects